Helion & Company Limited
Unit 8 Amherst Business Centre
Budbrooke Road
Warwick
CV34 5WE
England
Tel. 01926 499 619
Email: info@helion.co.uk
Website: www.helion.co.uk
Twitter: @helionbooks
Visit our blog http://blog.helion.co.uk/

Published by Helion & Company 2023
Designed and typeset by Farr out
  Publications, Wokingham, Berkshire
Cover designed by Paul Hewitt, Battlefield
  Design (www.battlefield-design.co.uk)

Text © David François 2023
Illustrations © as individually credited
Colour artwork © David Bocquelet, Luca
  Canossa, Anderson Subtil 2023
Maps drawn by and © Tom Cooper,
  Anderson Subtil 2023

Every reasonable effort has been made to trace copyright holders and to obtain their permission for the use of copyright material. The author and publisher apologise for any errors or omissions in this work, and would be grateful if notified of any corrections that should be incorporated in future reprints or editions of this book.

ISBN 978-1-804512-18-0

British Library Cataloguing-in-Publication Data
A catalogue record for this book is available from the British Library

All rights reserved. No part of this publication may be reproduced, stored in a retrieval system, or transmitted, in any form, or by any means, electronic, mechanical, photocopying, recording or otherwise, without the express written consent of Helion & Company Limited.

We always welcome receiving book proposals from prospective authors.

CONTENTS

Abbreviations		2
Introduction:		3
1	The FAES makeover	3
2	The 1984 turning point	12
3	The Failure of Low Intensity Warfare, 1985–1986	21
4	The strategic balance 1987–1988.	32
5	1989 – the decisive year	40
6	The November 1989 offensive	46
7	The path to peace	59
Conclusion		72
Selected Bibliography		74
Notes		75
Acknowledgements		78
About the Author		80

ABBREVIATIONS

ARENA	Allianza Republicana Nacionalista (Nationalist Republican Alliance)
BCA	Carlos Arias Bataillon
BIAT	Bataillons de Infanteria Antiterroristas (Anti-terrorist Infantry Bataillons)
BIC	Batallon de Infanteria de Contrasubvercion (Countersubversion Infantry Battalion)
BIRI	Batallones de Infantería de Reacción Inmediata (Immediate Reaction infantry Battalions)
BRAC	Rafael Aguiñada Carranza Bataillon
BRAZ	Brígada Rafael Arce Zablah (Rafael Arce Zablah Brigade)
CEAT	Comando Especial Antiterrorista (Special Anti-terrorist Commando)
CEBRI	Centro de Entrenamiento de Batallones de Reaccion Inmediata (Immediate Reaction Battalion Training Center)
CEMFA	Centro de Entrenamiento Militar de la Fuerza Armada (Military Training Centre of the Armed Force)
CETIPOL	Centro Técnico de Instrucción Policial (CETIPOL), Technical Center of Police Instruction
CG	Comandancia General (General Command)
CIA	Central Intelligence Agency
CICFA	Centro de Instruccion de Comandos de la Fuerza Armada (Armed Forces Commando Training Centre)
CIIFA	Centre de Instruccion de Ingenieros de la Fuerza Armada (Training Centre of Engineers of the Armed Forces)
CITFA	Centro de Instruccion de Transmisiones de la Fuerza Armada (Armed Force Transmissions Instruction Centre)
COPARU	Compañía de Operaciones Antiterroristas para Áreas Rurales y Urbanas (Anti-Terrorist Operations Company for Rural and Urban Areas)
COPAZ	Comision Nacional para la Consolidacion de la Paz (National Commission for the Consolidation of Peace)
CPSU	Communist Party of Soviet Union
DM	Destacamento Militar (Military Detachment)
DMIFA	Destacamento Militar de Ingenieros de la Fuerza Armada (Military Detachment of Engineers of the Armed Forces)
DNI	Direccion Nacional de Inteligencia (National Intelligence Directorate)
EMCFA	Estado Mayor Conjunto de la Fuerza Armada (Joint Staff of the Armed Forces)
EPS	Ejercito Popular Sandinista (Sandinista People's Army)
ERP	Ejercito Revolucionario del Pueblo (People's Revolutionary Army)
FAL	Fuerzas Armadas de Liberacion (National Liberation Forces)
FAS	Fuerza Aerea Salvadoreña (Salvadoran Air Force)
FAES	Fuerzas Armadas de El Salvador (El Salvador Armed Forces)
FAPL	Fuerzas Armadas Populares de Liberacion (People's Armed Forces of Liberation)
FAPU	Frente de Acción Popular Unificada (Unified Popular Action Front)
FAR-LP	Fuerzas Armadas Revolucionarias de la Liberacion popular (Revolutionary Armed Forces of Popular Liberation)
FARN	Fuerzas Armadas de la Resistencia Nacional (Armed Forces of the National Resistance)
FDR	Frente Democrático Revolucionario (Revolutionary Democratic Front)
FENASTRAS	Federación Nacional Sindical de Trabajadores Salvadoreños (National Union Federation of Salvadoran Workers)
FES	Fuerzas Especiales Seleccionadas (Select Special Forces)
FMLN	Frente Farabundo Marti para la Liberacion Nacional (Farabundo Marti National Liberation Front)
FPL	Fuerzas Populares de Liberacion (Liberation People's Forces)
GN	Guardia Nacional (National Guard)
GOE	Grupo de Operaciones Especiales (Special Operations Group)
JRGs	Junta Revolucionaria de Gobierno (Revolutionary Government Junta)
KGB	Komitet gossoudarstvennoï bezopasnosti (Committee for State Security)
MANPADS	Man-portable air-defence system
MEA	Municipios en Acción (Municipalities in Action) programme
MTT	Mobile Training Team
NSA	National Security Agency
OAS	Organisation of American States
ONUSAL	United Nations Observer Group in El Salvador
OPATT	Operations, Plans and Training Teams
ORDEN	Organizacion Democratica Nacionalista (National Democratic Organization)
PCS	Partido Comunista Salvadoreño (Salvadoran Communist Party)
PN	Policia Nacional (National Police)
PNC	Policia Nacional Civil (National Civil Police)
PAR	Partido de Acción Renovadora (Renewal Action Party)
PCN	Partido de Conciliacion Nacional (National Conciliation Party)
PDC	Partido Democrata Cristiano (Democratic Christian Party)
PH	Policia de Hacienda (Treasury Police)
PRAL	Patrullas de Reconocimiento de Alcance Largo, (Long Range Reconnaissance Patrols)
PRTC	Partido Revolucionario de los Trabajadores Centroamericanos (Revolutionary Party of Central America Workers)
RN	Resistencia Nacional (National Resistance)
SI	Socialist International
UCA	Universidad Centroamericana (Central American University)
UNTS	Union Nacional de Trabajadores Salvadoreños (National Union of Salvadoran Workers)
US$	United States Dollar

INTRODUCTION:

At the beginning of 1984, the civil war in El Salvador had been happening for three years. The conflict had its source in the turbulent history of this country, economically dominated since the end of the nineteenth century by an oligarchy of large landowners who grow coffee and politically, since the 1930s by the military who maintained power through Coups or rigged elections. At the start of the 1970s, when part of the population was living in misery and the democratic opposition was reduced to impotence, various Left-wing groups emerged, determined to use armed struggle to seize power and establish a socialist regime. They were stimulated in their effort by the spectacle of the victory of the Sandinista revolutionaries in neighbouring Nicaragua.

The year 1979 marked a turning point in the Salvadoran crisis. President Romero, a military man elected in fraudulent elections, was ousted from power by reformist military backed by the United States. Their desire to resolve the crisis affecting El Salvador nevertheless came up against the reality of a deeply divided country. While the revolutionary groups intensified their actions and set up rural guerrillas in the eastern and northern regions of the country, the extreme Right, supported by part of the military, formed Death Squads which spread terror, not hesitating to assassinate the popular Archbishop of San Salvador. The coming to power of Napoleon Duarte, the leader of the Christian Democratic Party and historical opponent of the military regime, did not change the situation, which continued to worsen.

Under the aegis of Cuba and with the support of the Sandinistas, the Left forces gathered during the year 1980 and ended up uniting within the Frente Farabundo Marti para la Liberacion Nacional (Farabundo Marti National Liberation Front or FMLN). For his part, Duarte, under pressure from the Fuerzas Armadas de El Salvador (El Salvador Armed Forces or FAES) could not prevent the increase in repression against Left-wing opponents before opting for a military solution to the conflict.

If from 1980, the FAES became more and more involved in the fight against the FMLN guerrillas, the situation changed radically on 10 January 1981 when the latter launched a strategic offensive that affected almost the entire country. The offensive was a failure but demonstrated both the operational capabilities of the guerrillas and the weaknesses of the FAES. It also led to a more massive intervention by Washington in the conflict. The new President Reagan wanted to halt the revolutionary progress in Central America and thus inflicted a defeat on Cuba and, more broadly, on the socialist camp.

After the failure of its January 1981 offensive, the FMLN favoured the military aspect of the conflict in the hope of inflicting a series of military defeats on the FAES and driving the Salvadoran regime to collapse. For this, it patiently built an armed force capable of competing with the military and until 1984, it demonstrated its power by combining conventional and unconventional strategies. While occasionally fighting in large-scale formations, FMLN forces used guerrilla or rather revolutionary war strategies stirring together military actions and political organisation in the establishment of rearguards, the *retaguardias* which provided it with bases to organise itself and continue its fight against the government.

For their part, the FAES tried to reduce these *retaguardias* during large-scale operations mobilising large forces but which gave little result. The FMLN managed to inflict a series of defeats on the military and seriously destabilised the national economy. It took the strategic initiative and, at the end of 1983, won various victories that suggested an imminent defeat for the FAES. This situation could only worry American officials who feared a collapse in El Salvador.

However, the civil war in El Salvador still lasted several years and only ended at the beginning of the 1990s. No side seemed capable of winning definitively. A strategic balance was established where the modernisation of the FAES was matched by the strategic flexibility of the FMLN. TThis was without relying on the international insertion of the Salvadoran conflict. The Cuban and Nicaraguan support to the FMLN enabled it to launch the January 1981 offensive while that of the United States to the FAES save them from defeat. It was this external context that ultimately, brought about the outcome of the Salvadorian conflict.

1
THE FAES MAKEOVER

From 1981 to 1983, American military aid only seemed to slow down the victorious progress of the guerrillas. In reality, it laid the foundations for a recovery of the FAES which allowed a better application of the strategy of Low Intensity Warfare, advocated by the Reagan Administration since 1981. This American military support took different forms and led to a profound FAES transformation.

Decisive American aid

In November 1983, for the first time, the FMLN Comandancia General (General Command or CG) met on Salvadoran territory. There was Leonard Gonzalez for the Fuerzas Populares de Liberacion (Liberation People's Forces or FPL), Schafik Handal for the Partido Comunista Salvadoreño (Salvadoran Communist Party or PCS), Joaquin Villalobos for the Ejercito Revolucionario del Pueblo (People's Revolutionary Army or ERP) and Roberto Roca for the Partido Revolucionario de los Trabajadores Centroamericanos (Revolutionary Party of Central America Workers or PRTC). Only Fermán Cienfuegos of the Resistencia Nacional (National Resistance or RN) was missing. FMLN leaders could therefore, be optimistic and even consider that final victory was near.

The guerrillas controlled approximately 5,000km² of Salvadoran territory and received the support of approximately 100,000 people.[1] Its military forces reached their peak with 10,000 to 12,000 fighters. According to the CIA, the FPL had between 2,800 and 3,500 men, the ERP between 3,000 and 3,500, the PRTC between 300 and 850, the FAL between 1,100 and 1,375, the RN between 1,000 and 1,500.[2]

This optimism was not only based on the successes of the guerrillas but on the weaknesses of the FAES. The latter were unable

An American military adviser explained the handling of the M16 rifle to a Salvadoran soldier. (Albert Grandolini Collection)

Components of the FMLN		
Political Party	Military Organisation	Primary Military Forces
Partido Revolucionario Salvadoreño (Salvadoran Revolutionary Party or PRS)	Ejercito Revolucionario del Pueblo (People's Revolutionary Army or ERP)	Rafael Arce Zablah Brigade (BRAZ)
Partido Comunista Salvadoreño (Salvadoran Communist Party or PCS)	Fuerzas Armades de Liberacion (Liberation Armed Forces or FAL)	Rafael Aguiñada Carranza Bataillon
Fuerzas Populares de Liberacion (Liberation People's Forces or FPL)	Fuerzas Armades Populares de Liberacion (Liberation People's Armed Forces or FAPL)	Felipe Pena Mendoza Bataillon Group
Resistencia Nacional (National Resistance or RN)	Fuerzas Armadas de la Resistencia Nacional (National Resistance Armed Forces or FARN)	Sergio Hernandoz and Carlos Arias Bataillon
Partido Revolucionario de los Trabajadores Centroamericanos (Revolutionary Party of Central America Workers or PRTC)	Fuerzas Armadas Revolucionarias de Liberacion Nacional (Revolutionary Armed Forces of National Liberation or FAR-LP)	Luis Adalberto Diaz Detachment

Officers from the Fuerzas Populares de Liberacion spoke to local and Western journalists (Albert Grandolini Collection)

to adopt an effective counter-insurgency strategy despite the advice of American military experts. This led them to retreat into areas they controlled, allowing the guerrillas to expand their *retaguardias*. The increase in the number of prisoners also illustrated the level of demoralisation of the FAES, while the mutiny of Lieutenant-Colonel Ochoa Pérez at the beginning of 1983, showed the contradictions were strong. The failure of the National Campaign Plan in the department of San Vicente,[3] along with the impossibility of the FAES to carry out the strategic plans designed by the Americans, reinforced the impression of near defeat for the military.

The FMLN was convinced it was enough to inflict on them new defeats to cause their total rout. In 1984, it wanted to provoke decisive battles which should allow, in the medium or long term, to lead to the final battle – the capture of San Salvador and the conquest of power over the whole country. For this, the guerrillas had to find a way to increase the scale of these operations, which they failed to do.

This assessment of the military situation carried out by the FMLN was shared by its adversaries. The highly publicised defeats suffered by the FAES during the attack on the El Paraiso barracks, the destruction of the Cuscatlán bridge and the annihilation of a Cazadores (Hunters) Battalion in El Cacahuatique, shook the confidence of the Salvadoran authorities. After these failures, a senior Salvadoran official lamented, 'We are losing the war … and the only way to salvage the situation is to give the troops something to fight for. Until that time, we cannot be saved, no matter how much military equipment arrives from the United States'.[4] This shared feeling caused deep fears in Washington. Secretary of State George Shultz had to admit that the military successes of the guerrillas were 'tough blows for the army and government'.[5]

On 11 January, the Kissinger Commission, formed at the request of President Ronald Reagan to define American policy in Central America and composed of Democratic and Republican representatives, presented a report which indicated that if the FAES had manpower much higher than those of the guerrillas, its forces still need to be reinforced rapidly to enable the success of Civic Action Plans and increase their mobility. It also recommended providing El Salvador with $8.4 billion between 1984 and 1990 under 'human development' programmes and making military aid

In early 1984, American leaders, notably Secretary of State George Shultz, were worried about the defeats suffered by the FAES. They formed the Kissinger Commission whose objective was to determine Washington's policy in Central America (Albert Grandolini Collection)

A partially disassembled UH-1H bound for El Salvador in Corpus Christi Air Base, Texas (Albert Grandolini Collection)

Military guards lined up in front of President José Napoleon Duarte's aircraft. (Albert Grandolini Collection)

conditional on an end to official killings and the punishment of perpetrators of human rights abuses.[6] At the same time, a campaign was launched by the Republican Party to accuse the democrats of endangering the security of the United States by supporting the revolutionary movements in Central America. Under this pressure, a bipartisan agreement was found in Congress to allow increased American aid to the Salvadoran regime.

The conclusions of the Kissinger Commission, which validated the strategy of the Reagan Administration in El Salvador, aimed to direct American aid towards the intensification of the strategy of Low Intensity Warfare. This was how Colonel John D. Waghelstein, the commander of the US Military Advisory Group (Milgroup), defined the conflict in El Salvador where the tactics of counter-insurgency warfare had to be applied.[7] It included a military component which consisted in transforming the FAES into an effective counter-insurgency force, capable if not of eliminating the guerrillas, of greatly reducing their activity. This modernisation also aimed to subject the military to the civilian power and to put an end to violations of human rights. More important was its political and social component, the objective of which was to rally the population, in particular through economic and social development programmes. At the political level, the Americans also wanted to replace the military regime with a civilian government supported by the citizens and recognised by the international community.[8]

Already, before the end of the work of the Kissinger Commission, the American vice president George Bush went to El Salvador in December 1983 to inform the FAES High Command that Washington no longer accepted the tolerance of the military towards the Death Squads. Bush therefore called for the arrest, exile or retirement of military officers suspected of complicity in the activities of these squads and the trial of the soldiers implicated in the murder of the American nuns murdered in December 1980. These were the essential conditions for a substantial increase in military assistance to the FAES. He also warned the military against a possible overthrow of the civilian government and threatened to end all assistance if the FAES interfered in future presidential elections or did not respect their results. These threats were taken seriously and some suspected Death Squad leaders were removed from their posts while their activities sharply declined.[9]

American leaders could count on General Carlos Eugenio Vides Casanova, Minister of Defence since the beginning of 1983, to reform the FAES and adapt them to the counter-insurgency doctrine advocated by Washington. During the last two months of 1983 and the first months of 1984, Vides reviewed the FAES command structure and made a general change. He appointed six Brigade Commanders and replaced 26 other senior officers. He wanted to break the loyalty system of the *tandas* to favour trained officers with leadership. It also initiated the decentralisation of command in order to give Brigade Commanders more latitude in deciding which counter-insurgency methods to use in their operational areas.[10]

Vides' initiatives were supported by American aid which, in 1984, reached 206.5 million dollars to responded to the demands of the Salvadoran General Staff, who wanted helicopters, radio communication equipment, vehicles and medicines. This aid also enabled the FAES to acquire a new National Training Centre, a National Command Complex, a modern Central Logistics Centre, a second military hospital complex in San Miguel and to modernise the Ilopango Air Base.[11]

A US Army Ranger provided Salvadoran military with counter-insurgency warfare training at Fort Benning (Albert Grandolini Collection)

| American Military Aid to El Salvador 1980–1989[12] ||
Years	Military Aid (millions of dollars)
1980	5
1981	40
1982	75
1983	80
1984	210
1985	140
1986	130
1987	120
1988	90
1988	90

American military aid was not only financial, it was also human. At the start of the war, the Reagan Administration negotiated with Congress, the presence in El Salvador of 55 military advisers, but in reality, there were many more. At the end of 1984, there were thus more than 100 American soldiers in the country. Three years later, there were more than 150. However, at the time, the number of soldiers operating in El Salvador did not exceed 300.[13]

Alongside the Milgroup, installed since November 1979, there was a Mobile Training Team (MTT) in charge of administrative, logistical and command tasks, a Naval Training Team to advise the Salvadoran Navy, training and helicopter maintenance personnel, as well as the three Small Unit Teams of five men for the training of the BIRI.[14] Above all, in order to increase the intensity of counter-insurgency operations and respect for human rights, Washington deployed, from 1984, Operations, Plans and Training Teams (OPATT) to work with the six FAES Infantry Brigades. The OPATTs were made up of a lieutenant-colonel who commanded the team, a captain in charge of troop training and a military intelligence officer. All were US Army officers, except for those stationed in the 6th Infantry Brigade in Usulutan, who were drawn from the United States Marine Corps. After 1985, these teams focused on improving the coordination of operations and intelligence activities with an emphasis on civil defence, civic affairs and psychological operations.[15]

Thus, from 1983, the American military advisers infiltrated all of the FAES, from the headquarters to the Brigades. They were also present at the Artillery Regiment barracks, the Logistics Centre and the National Training Centre. Their mission was to support their Salvadoran counterparts in the establishment of training programmes, as well as to assist in the military decision-making process on personnel and operational issues.[16]

Many military advisers came from the special forces, including the 3rd Battalion, 7th Special Forces Group, stationed in Panama, better known as the Green Berets. They were very active in the field, having carried out 46 missions with Salvadoran forces by mid-1982 in areas such as counter-guerrilla operations, small unit tactics, port and airfield security, communications training, dam safety, parachute training and the use of large calibre weapons.[17] In practice, relations with Salvadoran officers were not easy, firstly because of cultural differences, the language barrier, differences in ranks but also the refusal of some Salvadoran officers to adopt changes at the tactical level and to respect human rights.

While military advisers were prohibited from bearing arms, let alone taking part in armed action, the realities of the war in El Salvador had not always made it possible to comply with these prohibitions. In 1985, when the FMLN launched an attack on the

Despite the ban on direct participation in combat, US advisers were often armed to defend themselves against guerrilla attacks (Albert Grandolini Collection)

Centro de Entrenamiento Militar de la Fuerza Armada (Military Training Centre of the Armed Force or CEMFA), the barracks housed five Green Berets who took part in its defence and led a counter-attack. For this action, Captain Danny Egan was proposed to receive the Bronze Star.[18] In the end, many advisers took part in combat actions and were injured during the clashes, while 21 American soldiers were killed in El Salvador.

In the air domain, American forces based in Honduras were also involved in the Salvadoran conflict. OV-1 Mohawk reconnaissance aircraft stationed at Palmerola made regular reconnaissance flights over El Salvador to identify FMLN concentrations and installations.[19] American C-130s also flew at high altitude over this country for surveillance missions while Beechcraft King Air performed radio intercepts. In El Salvador, Air Force military advisers flew surveillance planes to determine targets. They thus actively participated in Operation Rosa which led to the capture of Nidia Diaz, a leader of the FMLN, in July 1985. In 1986, American crews were even at the controls of Salvadoran helicopters during combat operations.[20] This involvement of the American military in combat would be recognised later when the authorities in Washington would award combat badges to hundreds of former special forces advisers and the Purple Heart to five of them while the Marines awarded Stars Bronze and Air Force Air Medals.[21]

The Americans also provided intelligence assistance. The latter was often obtained through reconnaissance aircraft piloted by CIA agents and electronic surveillance equipment. Moreover, the main activity of the CIA and the NSA had been to collect intelligence on the operations of the guerrillas to provide it to the FAES.[22]

The conflict in El Salvador was also an opportunity for the Americans to use innovative technological weapons. This was the case of night vision devices that allowed FAES to operate at night. For reconnaissance operations, the Americans were experimenting with the use of R4E-40 Red Eye drones.[23]

Other countries provided military support to El Salvador. This was the case for Israel, which in 1981, granted it a credit of 21 million dollars to buy armaments. Tel-Aviv thus supplied trucks, rifles, ammunition, but also napalm, whilst a hundred Israeli military advisers were sent to El Salvador. Argentina offered military advisers from 1979, but in the fall of 1981, the Reagan Administration asked Buenos-Aires to increase its assistance. This translated into the supply of light and heavy weapons for 20 million dollars, in particular FMK-3 DM .9mm calibre for the police forces. The Argentine dictatorship also sent military advisers to the FAES and the Salvadoran security forces.[24] According to some testimonies, Italian and Canadian special forces instructors also trained the Salvadoran commandos.[25] At the end of 1982, it was Venezuelan advisers who organised and formed two Cazadores Battalions.[26]

FAES counter-insurgency units

By mid-1984, US aid began to change the nature of the conflict as the FAES became Central America's second largest military force behind Nicaragua's Ejercito Popular Sandinista (Sandinista People's Army or EPS). In May 1983, General Vides appointed Colonel Blandon as head of the

Learning first aid for the wounded was part of the teaching given by American advisers (Albert Grandolini Collection)

FAES General Staff;[27] an officer favourable to the counter-insurgency strategy and tactics advocated by American advisers. Under his direction, these became more methodical and fuller. The latter required an increase in FAES personnel, both to maintain offensive operations against the FMLN, whilst ensuring a static defence of sensitive areas, this mission taking up 2/3 of the Salvadoran forces.[28] The numbers of the FAES therefore increased from 12,000 soldiers in 1980 to 30,000 in 1982, 42,000 in 1984, 50,000 in 1986 and 60,000 by the end of the war.[29] The available artillery was also doubled whilst the workforce of the Navy exploded to bring together 15,000 men and 30 patrol craft.[30]

In parallel with the increase in these numbers, the FAES continued its transformation to equip itself with forces capable of waging a counter-insurgency war. They were helped on this point by American military advisers in El Salvador but also by the Regional Military Training Centre created by the Americans in Puerto Castilla, Honduras,which allowed the training of 3,500 FAES soldiers until June 1985.[31]

The six Infantry Brigades were restructured to become counter-insurgency forces whose companies were able to act independently and over a long period. In this system, the BIRIs always constituted the elite force. They theoretically had a regional distribution. The BIRIs Arce and Atonal covered the departments of Morazan, Usulutan, San Miguel and La Union, the BIRI Bracamonte the departments of Cabañas, San Vicente and La Paz and the BIRIs Atlacatl and Belloso the departments of San Salvador, La Libertad, Chalatenango, Cuscatlán, Santa Ana, Sonsonate and Ahuachapán. This distribution was not rigid and in the departments where there were no guerrilla forces, the BIRI were absent. Thus, the BIRI Atlacatl and Belloso continued to act on a national scale as did the Parachute Battalion used as a reaction force. The FAES also had Cazadores Battalions which became mobile special forces that could penetrate deep into disputed territories and into areas controlled by the FMLN. Between 1st June 1983 and 31 May 1984, 24 Cazadores Battalions were thus formed.[32]

Alongside these units, born at the start of the war, others were created. Lieutenant-Colonel José Domingo Monterrosa, commander of the 3rd Infantry Brigade, aware of the weakness of the Cazadores Battalions with their strength of 350 men (insufficient to face the FMLN brigades), created the Battalions of Infanteria Antiterroristas (Anti-terrorist Infantry Battalions or BIAT). They had 580 soldiers divided into three to four companies and grouped into detachments and brigades.[33]

The General Staff took over Monterrosa's innovation and BIATs were created in the six Infantry Brigades while the Cazadores Battalions, now called Batallon de Infanteria de Contrasubvercion (Countersubversion Infantry Battalion or BIC) were assigned to each of the seven Destacamento Militar (Military Detachment or DM). In the department of Chalatenango, the main strongholds of the FAPL, there were now four BIATs and three BICs. In Morazan, stronghold of the ERP, three BIATs supported by the four BIATs of the 3rd Infantry Brigade. With these

Lieutenant Colonel Domingo Monterrosa, centre, spoke with British television journalists during an interview in Joateca, Morazan department (Albert Grandolini Collection)

new troops, adding the five BIRIs and the Parachute Battalion, the FAES had about 6,000 men specialising in counter-insurgency.[34]

With regard to the creation of new tactical units, since 1984, efforts had been concentrated on the Guardia Nacional (National Guard or GN), in which BIATs were organised, formed by four infantry companies of 104 men each and a combat support company of 164 officers and men. The GN also set up BICs made up of 410 men divided into four infantry companies of 97 men with staff sections. The Policia Nacional (National Police or PN) and the Policia de Hacienda (Treasury Police or PH), also had structures similar to those of the BIATs.[35]

To improve its tactical capabilities, the FAES also created units capable of carrying out long-range actions, remaining in the field for several weeks and thus exerting persistent pressure on the FMLN, giving it no respite. These were the Patrullas de Reconocimiento de Alcance Largo, (Long Range Reconnaissance Patrols or PRAL), mobile forces, very similar to the US Rangers, which operated using 'irregular tactics' in the FMLN rearguard. Trained by the American Green Berets, with the help of the CIA, these aggressive units of six to 12 fighters had the main mission of tracking down and locating camps, guerrilla movements and radioing the exact location of these targets to be bombarded or attacked by airborne forces. They also sometimes struck directly at guerrilla command posts and troop concentrations.[36] The PRALs were particularly effective, as noted by

The GOE, trained by the US Special Forces, proved particularly effective against the guerrillas, forcing the FMLN to abandon large-scale military operations (Albert Grandolini Collection)

a former American adviser for whom these units, 'has (sic) proven that El Salvadoran troops, with the proper training and leadership can operate effectively in small groups and they have set a standard for valour for the rest of the FAES.[37]'

The PRAL quickly sowed terror among the guerrillas who feared at any time falling into an ambush. To fight them, the FMLN relied on its local militias and the population. The former were used to impede their movements, while the latter were used to alert the guerrillas to their presence in an area. These countermeasures did not, however, make it possible to put an end to their infiltrations and attacks.[38]

The FAES also created and developed special forces. The Grupo de Operaciones Especiales (Special Operations Group or GOE), comprising 100 soldiers trained at Fort Gulick, was created in July 1982 to carry out reconnaissance deep in areas controlled by the guerrillas. From December, the *Hachas* patrols were formed within it, assault units bringing together 40 men and whose mission was to strike targets reported by the PRAL.[39] At the end of 1983, the GOE, the *Hachas* and the PRAL were placed under the command of the FAS. Within each BIRI special forces called *Recondos* were developed and equipped with Motorola radio and MPK submachine gun, RPG-7 and RPG-2.[40] Among the special units formed by the American advisers, there were also the Naval Commandos, trained by the Navy Seals and divided into two companies named Barracuda and Piraña, gathering in 1987, approximately 450 soldiers.[41]

Within the security forces, in July 1985, a Comando Especial Antiterrorista (Special Anti-terrorist Commando or CEAT) was formed, whose members received training in anti-terrorist techniques provided by the Americans. They were thus able to manage hostage rescues, carry out counter-terrorism operations, employ snipers and crowd control. As a strategic unit, the CEAT was subordinate to the Joint Chiefs of Staff, but most of the unit's personnel came from the PH. In the same year, the Compañía de Operaciones Antiterroristas para Áreas Rurales y Urbanas (Anti-Terrorist Operations Company for Rural and Urban Areas or COPARU) was created to carry out anti-terrorist operations in the countryside and in the city.[42]

All these new units improved the tactical capacities of the FAES which became more mobile and able to move for a longer time with better security. However, they did not prevent the persistence of weakness within the FAES. Thus, a February 1986 CIA report indicated that the system of co-optation among senior officers was still based on personal ties rather than merit, that corruption and abuse of authority were still tolerated and that the military was still reluctant to submit to civil authorities.[43]

Strengthening the FAS

From the start of the war, American military advisers were concerned about the state of the FAS. For Washington, this air force suffered many weaknesses. Close air support suffered from a lack of aircraft capable of carrying an acceptable tonnage of bombs. Thus, the main fighter-bomber in service, the Ouragan, could barely lift two 500-pound bombs. Its capabilities were limited when conducting effective airmobile missions and it could only perform them by day. This explained why one-quarter of US aid was intended for the FAS, thus allowing it to double its size.[44]

Following the FMLN attack on Ilopango Air Base in February 1982, the Reagan Administration authorised the sending of a total of $55 million in military aid, including the supply of C-130 Hercules and Fairchild C-123K transport aircraft, UH-1H helicopters. From 1980 to December 1983, the Americans sent 33 Huey helicopters and in 1984, 20 more, along with AC-47 Spooky combat helicopters. They also supplied Hughes-500D helicopters, Cessna O-2A reconnaissance planes and Cessna A-37B Dragonfly Fighter Jets, aircraft designed for the American-led counter-insurgency war in Vietnam. Thus, the A-37Bs, with their 7.62mm minigun, could be used in front line missions, from convoy escort to immediate support and forward air control. Above all, these aircraft could be used in complementary ways to carry out counter-insurgency missions. The A-37-Bs made it possible to concentrate decisive firepower on one or more points in a very precise manner while the O-2s which remained in prolonged flight above the areas of operations provided information on the tactical situation for direct A-37 fire. These aircraft were generally equipped with a night vision system allowing night operations to be carried out. They were also equipped

The first six Cessna A-37B 'Dragonfly' arrived in El Salvador in June 1982. They quickly proved to be best-suited for fighting guerrillas. In 1988, five AC-37 were gathered in the 'Cuscatlán Squadron'. (Albert Grandolini Collection)

During the Salvadoran Civil War the Salvadoran Air Force received a total of 23 O-2As and two O-2Bs from the United States, the first arriving in 1981. The O-2s were employed to observe the movements of FMLN formations and direct air strikes against them, playing a major role in forcing the rebel movement to abandon large-scale operations. (Albert Grandolini Collection)

FAS Combat Air Groups		
Fighter and Bombardment Group	Helicopter Group	Transport Group
Fighter Squadron	Arce Acuña Squadron	Transport Squadron
Counter-insurgency Squadron	Cuellar Aguilar Squadron	Training squadron
Reconnaissance Squadron	Duarte Arevalo Squadron	

with a communication system, including UHF for communication between pilots, FM radio for communication with ground troops and VHF for communication between pilots, troops and the control tower. This allowed them to increase their efficiency.

UH-1H helicopters not only allowed the FAS to carry out more helicopter operations, to transport paratroopers and tactical units to any part of the country, but also to resupply units in combat zones, and to evacuate the wounded which reduced the number of killed in action.[45] Hughes 500Ds and transport planes also allowed for more possibilities to transport supplies to troops and to multiply medical interventions. AC-47 Spooky gunships, nicknamed 'Puff the Magic Dragon', armed with three .50 calibre machine guns, provided heavy fire support for ground operations.[46] They were used for the first time on 8 January 1985 when the Tehuacan Battalion of the 5th Infantry Brigade fell into an FAPL ambush 12km south of San Vicente. The soldiers had 15 killed and 43 wounded and had to receive help from the FAS which provided support with helicopters and AC-47Ds. These planes helped to avoid the complete annihilation of the battalion.[47]

At the same time, the number of pilots increased, many of them receiving training in counter-insurgency warfare in the United States. In 1984, 117 FAS personnel attended courses at the Inter-American Air Force Academy in Panama City, up from 98 the previous year. In 1986, three Salvadoran instructors took a course on missile evasion tactics in Panama, and upon their return, they trained the fighter-bomber group in these tactics.[48]

The FAS potential therefore continued to grow and ended up bringing together 25,000 soldiers and five squadrons while the flow of planes and helicopters from the United States did not cease. On 25 January 1985, the FAS received three new A-37Bs; in February, three UH-1H helicopters; in March, five Cessna O-2A/Bs, three UH-1Hs and a Douglas AC-47; in May, five armed Hughes-500Es and two AC-47s; in June, five Huey helicopters; in July, two armed AC-47s.[49]

In September 1985, 12 UH-1M helicopters arrived in El Salvador to quickly become a key element of airborne operations. They were equipped with rocket launchers that could fire 14 rockets from the M5 system with 40mm grenade launchers as well as the M134

Rocket launcher systems coupled with a machine gun were installed on FAS helicopters to enable them to provide fire support for ground troops. (Albert Grandolini Collection)

The Americans also provided technical assistance to the FAS by training the mechanics in charge of maintaining the aircraft supplied. (Albert Grandolini Collection)

The AC-47D gunship known as Puff the Magic Dragon or Spooky was produced for the USAF's 4th Air Commando squadron during the 1960s and was armed with three 7.62mm miniguns. The guns were angled so to fire at the same spot out of the door and two side windows, as the gunship circled. Between 1984–1985 five were delivered to El Salvador for use in its own counter-insurgency operations. (Albert Grandolini Collection)

FAES Equipment in 1988[55]		
Description	Country of Origin	Inventory
Tanks :		
AMS-13 (light)	United States	12
APC :		
M-3A1	United States	5
M-113	United States	20
AML 90	France	10
UR 416	West Germany	8
M-37B1	United States	66
Field Artillery :		
-105mm Howitzer	United States	50
-105mm M-101	United States	30
-105mm M-102	United States	6
M-56	Yugoslavia	14
155mm M-114	United States	6
Mortars :		
81mm	United States	300
120mm UB-M52	United States	60
Recoilless Rifles		
90mm M-67	United States	400
Anti-aircraft		
20mm M-55	United States	24

two others armed with rocket launchers.[50] It also forced it to expand its structures. Whilst in 1984 there was only one combat group consisting of three squadrons: a fighter and bomber squadron, a helicopter squadron and a transport squadron, between 1986 and 1987, the squadrons expanded and became Combat Air Groups, made up of specific squadrons.[51]

In 1987, the fighter squadron included eight Ouragan; the counter-insurgency squadron, 10 A-37B and two armed AC-47, the reconnaissance squadron, 11 O-2A, the transport squadron, five C-47, a DC-6, three Aravas and two C123-K, the training squadron, one T-41 and six CM-170 Magisters. The helicopter force had nine Hugues 500MD, 14 armed UH-1H, 38 UH-1H utility helicopters, three SA-315 Lamas and three SA-316 Alouette III, for a total of 67 helicopters.[52]

To increase the FAS firepower, many planes and helicopters, initially designed for transport, were transformed to be armed. Thus, two .50 calibre machine guns were placed on three C-47s and a 7.62mm machine gun on four Alouette IIIs. A system for dropping 100 and 250-pound bombs equipped four Lama helicopters. The Hughes-500D received a Gatlin weapon system while the UH-1H helicopters were equipped with a system of two LAU-3/A rocket launchers firing 19 rockets and two LAU-32A/A or LAU-68B/A with seven rockets or 52 70mm rockets.[53] The C-47 transport planes, which had a long-duration flight capacity, especially at night, were also modified and armed to provide fire support.

electric machine gun system with six 7.62mm cannons. In April 1986, the FAS received another two UH-1M helicopters, to which were added seven UH-1Hs in 1987 and nine others in 1988.

This increase in its air arsenal forced the FAS to organise three new Air Bases, one in Santa Ana in the west of the country, one in San Miguel in the east and the last, in La Union in the south-east. A base for helicopters was installed in Cabañas where squadrons were formed comprising one to two UH-1H transports and one or

Gradually, from 1984, the FAS began to regain the initiative on the battlefield. It repeatedly attacked contested areas, mainly in the north and east of the country. Certain regions, strongholds of the guerrillas, in the departments of Chalatenango, Morazan and in the volcano of Guazapa, were bombarded on numerous occasions. Between 1984 and 1985, Chalatenango department became a 'free fire' area for the FAS, which meant that all individuals in this area were considered guerrillas and therefore, legitimate targets. The inhabitants were subjected to repeated artillery barrages and air attacks. These bombings were often followed by major sweeps aimed at forcing them to flee and thus depriving the FMLN of its sources of supplies and intelligence.

The increased use of aerial firepower led to an increase in the displacement of civilians, forcing thousands of Salvadorans to flee to calmer areas or to exile, mainly to Honduras or the United States. In 1987, approximately 500,000 Salvadorans were displaced, or 10 percent of the population. Two years later, this figure had risen to 600,000 while 1.5 million people had fled El Salvador.[54]

With the support of Washington, the FAES modernised and reoriented its strategy towards the organisation of counter-insurgency operations which allowed it to regain the initiative and keep it. By mid-1984, if there was little confidence in the defeat of the FMLN, there was certainty that the FAES could no longer be defeated. This transformation put an end to the large-scale operations that characterised the beginning of the conflict in favour of a strategic balance that lasted from 1985 to 1989. During this period and whilst continuing their military operations, the FAES also had the mission to promote the democratisation process in order to deprive the FMLN of its international and domestic support.

2
THE 1984 TURNING POINT

1984 was a year of transition in the Salvadoran conflict. The FMLN continued its large-scale operations which had enabled it to achieve many successes since 1982, but now it came up against the counter-insurgency tactics adopted by the FAES. The guerrillas experienced a series of military setbacks that year as the presidential election marked a victory for the strategy inspired by the Americans.

Villa Dolores February 1984

On 15 January 1984, the guerrillas unsuccessfully attacked the DM-1 garrison in Chalatenango and tried again, in vain, to destroy the Colima bridge.[1] The Villa Dolores battle was the first test of the new FAES strategy. The ERP leadership, in its desire for decisive battles, decided to send its mobile forces of the Brígada Rafael Arce Zablah (Rafael Arce Zablah Brigade or BRAZ) outside the area where it usually acted, which was beyond the Rio Lempa, the natural limit between the west and the east of El Salvador.

The target was Villa Dolores, a small town at the southeastern end of the department of La Cabañas, 11km south of Sensuntepeque, capital of the department and 85km north-east of San Salvador. The city had no major strategic position, but the FMLN here inaugurated joint operations between the forces of the different groups that composed it. Thus, 300 BRAZ fighters from the ERP led by the experienced Raul Mijango, united with a hundred men from the FAR-LP, commanded by Luis Alberto Corvera Rivas alias Elsio Amaya, to attack the city. These FAR-LP forces came from the Cerros San Pedro and the Chichontepec volcano in the department of San Vicente where they had constantly fought the 5th Infantry Brigade.

After the departure of the FAR-LP leadership to the Morazan department, its leader, Roberto Roca, decided to approach the ERP, which Villalobos accepted, who wished to extend the field of operation of FMLN forces towards the west.

Villa Dolores was defended by 40 GN and 20 Defence Civil members at a time when the guerrillas blocked the town to the south to prevent the arrival of reinforcements from the 5th Infantry Brigade and to the north to prevent the arrival of DM-2 forces. The ERP troops moved at night from the east, crossed the Rio Lempa and established three axes of attack, one from the east, the second from the north and the last from the south. The western flank was left free to allow the escape of the garrison and destroy it in an ambush, this mission falling to the FAR-LP units.

The attack began on the morning 15 February 1984. Machine guns, rocket launchers and 60mm mortars went into action, but the casemates resisted and the defenders blocked the guerrilla advance. The FAS sent a UH-1H helicopter armed with an M-60D machine gun which attacked the FMLN positions south of the city. After fierce fighting, the BRAZ seized the first defences and by mid-morning, the GNs only held their garrison. It was at this point that reinforcements from the 5th Infantry Brigade arrived from the south but were pushed back towards San Ildefonso by guerrilla blocking troops. At the FAES General Staff, Colonel Onecifero Blandon decided on an airborne operation. The FAS mobilised 10 UH-1H helicopters, one armed Hughes-500D, two UH-1H armed with rocket launchers, three transport planes, four A-37B fighter-bombers, a Cessna O-2A reconnaissance plane and 230 paratroopers.

The first transport planes that arrived on the San Ildefonso runway were subjected to heavy fire and the helicopter gunners responded immediately. The paratroopers nevertheless managed to land thanks to the cover provided by the armed helicopters. Faced with this firepower, the guerrillas retreated north, pursued by the helicopters which inflicted significant losses on them. Then the latter attacked the ERP positions in Villa Dolores while the 1st parachute squadron landed south of the city. Commander Mijango nevertheless believed that his forces were still capable of taking the city while facing the paratroopers, in particular with the help of the FAR-LP column which had not yet fought. He gave the order for the column to attack towards the east while ERP troops had to attack from the north.

The paratroopers progressed north towards Villa Dolores. They violently confronted the ERP fighters and managed to enter the city. The FAR-LP forces also came into action. Faced with the firepower of paratroopers and helicopters, they nevertheless decided to withdraw but without warning their ERP comrades. The 3rd Parachute Squadron then landed under guerrilla mortar fire. To silence FMLN forces, an A-37B dropped two 500-pound bombs on them . Mijango finally decided to withdraw his forces, just as the GN garrison flew. The paratroopers were still advancing with difficulty in the face of the resistance of the rebels who were covering the escape of the bulk of the BRAZ. The last guerrilla forces left the city by truck at the end of the afternoon. They lost 20 fighters and two mortars were destroyed. On the other side, the GN had five wounded, the Civil Defence two wounded, the paratroopers six dead and six wounded. Three helicopters were damaged.

The BRAZ, still under Mijango leadership, withdrew to Nuevo Eden de San Juan before joining San Gerardo where the Brigade

Command Post, headed by Jorge Meléndez alias Jonas, was located. Analysing the failure of the Villa Dolores attack, the guerrilla leaders did not plan to give up using concentrations of mobile forces for large-scale operations. They only decided to equip themselves with a defence system against airborne landings. According to the guerrilla leaders, the increase in their firepower against the helicopters had to compensate for that of the FAS and allow the continuation of offensive operations.[2]

San Gerardo 19 February 1984

Following the Villa Dolores battle, BRAZ troops set up a defensive system around San Gerardo. The guerrillas held the northern part of the San Miguel department under their control, with the FAES controlling only the main towns. It was during this period that the new commander of the 3rd Infantry Brigade, Lieutenant Colonel Monterrosa, formed BIAT and BIC within his Brigade.

On February 18, a FAES informant announced that the next day, a meeting of the ERP leaders was to be held in San Gerardo. The FAES High Command decided to take advantage of this opportunity to organise an operation to decapitate the guerrillas' leadership. His plan was to turn the city into a trap with no escape.[3] It mobilised 14 UH-1H transport helicopters, two UH-1H armed helicopters, one Hughes-500 helicopter and also four A-37B, two MD.450 Ouragan fighters and one Cessna O-2A reconnaissance aircraft. In addition, there were 200 paratroopers from the Airborne Battalion and around 110 men from special forces, PRAL and *Hachas* units.

On the 19th, at 1 a.m., the special forces parachuted in at night and settled down, without being spotted, 150m east of San Gerardo. In the city were indeed the ERP main leaders, Jorge Meléndez, Julian Belloso, the head of the ERP intelligence services Ana Sonia Medina, Juan Ramon Medrano, Raul Mijango and Javier Negro. However, the ERP leader, Joaquin Villalobos was not present. In the sector were also 400 rebels and a little further still, 400 well-armed fighters, most survivors of the Villa Dolores battle.

The FAS Helicopter Squadron was divided into two groups. The first flew directly from Ilopango to San Gerardo where A-37s began bombing areas east of town where paratroopers would land. On landing, the latter were the target of ERP machine guns and rocket launchers. The armed helicopters went into action to destroy the guerrilla positions while the special forces opened fire on the fleeing rebels. A second paratrooper landing took place north-west of San Gerardo under intense anti-aircraft fire. The situation became desperate for the guerrillas who decided to flee while the PRAL and the *Hachas* advanced towards the south-east in the direction of the city.

An ERP group tried to escape by the west of San Gerardo in the direction of Nuevo Eden de San Juan. The order was then given to the second group of helicopters to land the troops in this sector to close the ring around the BRAZ. Whilst approaching the landing zone, the ERP's anti-aircraft fire hit a pilot who lost control of his helicopter and dragged down another aircraft. This accident killed 28 soldiers and injured three. The other helicopters disembarked the paratroopers who now had the mission of saving the survivors of the accident. Taking advantage of the confusion, the ERP forces managed to flee by the west and the north-west, before taking refuge in the north of the Morazan department.[4]

The San Gerardo operation was a half-success for the FAES who managed to surprise the guerrillas but nevertheless came up against the effectiveness of the FMLN's anti-aircraft defence, which was still quite basic.

Lieutenant-Colonel Monterrosa (right), former commander of the BIRI Atlacatl, was one of the best officers in the FAES and dealt severe blows to the guerrillas. (Albert Grandolini Collection)

Ciudad Barrios March – April 1984

At the beginning of 1984, the majority of the fighting was concentrated in the north of the San Vicente department, a FMLN strategic area since it linked its two *retaguardias* in the Chalatenango and Morazan departments. Already, by the end of 1983, the FAES had launched two offensives in the north of Morazan and San Miguel departments in an attempt to destroy the BRAZ northern group. These actions were part of a larger plan drawn up by the new commander of the 3rd Infantry Brigade, Lieutenant Colonel Monterrosa.

However, on 14 December, the BRAZ succeeded in destroying the Cazadores Battalion Tecana of the 2nd Infantry Brigade in the Cerro Cacahuatique. During the fighting, 60 soldiers were killed, 75 wounded and nine were taken prisoner while around 150 managed to flee. At the same time, other BRAZ units attacked and occupied Ciudad Barrios, north-west of Sesori, a small town 38km from San Miguel which controlled the access road between Morazan and Chalatenango departments.

The FAES decided to organise an operation in the Cacahuatique area to regain control and hit the guerrilla forces. About 160 paratroopers were given the mission to land north and south of Ciudad Barrios to confront the enemy. When they landed, the guerrillas withdrew from the town. Fighting nevertheless took place with the rebel rearguard, but the bulk of the ERP forces fled without incident.

On 21 December, the FAES concentrated on the north of the Morazan department to launch a new offensive against Azacualpa and Perquin with 2,000 soldiers and airborne troops who fought hard to capture these localities. After these attacks, the ERP decided to reinforce its fixed defences in the north of Morazan by building 17 firing posts, anti-aircraft defences and covered forts, particularly along the lines of communication.

A few months later, with the approach of the presidential elections in March 1984, Lieutenant-Colonel Jorge Adalberto Cruz, entrusted a search and destruction mission to the Lenca Battalion with the objective the town of Corinto which the soldiers reached without encountering resistance. At the beginning of May, Cruz launched a new operation, but this time he came up against BRAZ

FAS paratroopers form an elite unit widely employed in the fight against insurgency. (Albert Grandolini Collection)

killed 25 soldiers. In the San Vicente department, the FMLN occupied San Sebastian before withdrawing prior to the arrival of reinforcements and it also blocked portions of the Pan-American Highway. Above all, it continued to increase its pressure on the San Miguel department.[6] Thus, on 23 March, the ERP FES set up a mine on the small airstrip of Obrajuelo, near San Miguel, where the FAS regularly unloaded supplies for the military operating in the region. The next day, two C-123s approached Obrajuelo and one was destroyed when it triggered the mine as it landed.[7]

The main target of the FMLN was the garrison of the 3rd Infantry Brigade in San Miguel. It suffered a first, small-scale attack at the end of January, which was easily repelled. It would not be the same for the following; on 3 March, the guerrillas launched a larger operation, the main objective of which was not, however, the garrison. The FMLN blocked its access to prevent the arrival of reinforcements, took control of the Urbina bridge in San Miguel whilst the main assault force struck the Cazadores Bataillon Cuscatlán. The latter, dispersed and understaffed, was easily overwhelmed by 600 guerrillas. As the military began to panic and disband, Colonel Monterrosa had to intervene personally to regain control of the situation. He also received the support of an Airborne company which gave him time to reorganise his forces and launch a counter-attack. On 13 March, he attacked the BRAZ command post in Cerro Miracapa, north of Ciudad Barrios. After hard fighting, the guerrillas retreated to Carolina. Monterrosa then organised search and destroy operations with the support of the BIRI Atlacatl.[8]

forces near the small village of El Tabion. The fighting was violent but the guerrillas managed to withdraw.[5]

The various offensives in the Morazan department aimed to reduce the pressure exerted by the FMLN in the north of the San Miguel department where the BRAZ was still active. For its part, the guerrillas sought to divert the FAES from the Morazan department by launching attacks in the region of Suchitoto where an ambush

On 25 March, around 9:00 p.m., the occupants of a truck driving on the Pan-American Highway, fired on the main gate of the San Miguel garrison. Shortly after, mortar fire began. Hundreds of guerrillas rose almost simultaneously from the dark ground and stormed the barracks. Seven American special forces instructors who were present in San Miguel that day, actively participated in its defence. Around 11:00 p.m., a US AC-130 from Howard Air Force Base, Panama arrived to illuminate guerrilla locations with beams of infrared light. A home-made armoured vehicle then advanced towards where the main attack had begun. It stopped and fired with its .50 calibre machine gun. It was then caught under intense fire and had to retreat. The AC-130 spotted three trucks moving in convoy from San Miguel carrying heavy machine guns. They were greeted by intense fire. Finally, at dawn, two A-37s swept the sky in search of the retreating FMLN columns.[9]

Fighting continued the following days in the San Miguel region. Thus, on the morning of 2 April, while a FAES patrol was ambushed, the ERP mortars located to the west and north of Ciudad Barrios, began to fire on the Airborne Battalion defending the city. Its commander requested air support to repel a large-scale

Fairchild C-123 was a twin-engine tactical transport manufactured in the 1950s and 1960s. Mainly used by United States Air Force during the Vietnam War, it remained in service and began re-appearing in different corners of the world in the 1980s. Out of three C-123Ks supplied in 1982 to support the government in the Salvadoran civil war, only one survived. (Albert Grandolini Collection)

Soldiers from the Cuscatlán Brigade prepared to carry two of their men, wounded in a guerrilla ambush during an army sweep through a guerrilla-held area in Morazan. (Albert Grandolini Collection)

attack. A rebel force attacked from the east and the main assault was launched from the north. To the south, the ERP attack was weaker, the guerrillas believing that the area was well defended by the FAES.

During the morning, A-37Bs, each carrying six 500-pound bombs, attacked the rebel positions. Despite the strong pressure from the ERP, the paratroopers managed to hold their positions. Lieutenant Colonel Monterrosa then arrived in Ciudad Barrios and decided on a manoeuvrer to attack the rear of the guerrillas. To do this, he asked the General Staff to land the BIRI Arce by helicopter, north of the city. These reinforcements arrived at 6 p.m. and caused many losses in the ranks of the ERP. The guerrillas finally withdrew towards the south-west, but they fell into an ambush carried out by the Cuscatlán Battalion near Sesori, where a BRAZ column commander was killed.[10]

As the guerrillas retreated without taking control of Ciudad Barrios, the FAES turned the assault into a public relations disaster by lying about the number of wounded and killed, then getting caught up in the media.[11]

The 1984 presidential election

Alongside the military operations, the Salvadoran state and the United States were pursuing their plan to institutionalise democracy in El Salvador. The Constituent Assembly, elected in 1982, after having promulgated a new Constitution, decided to hold presidential elections in March and May 1984.

Unlike the 1982 elections, the FMLN and its political arm, the Frente Democrático Revolucionario (Revolutionary Democratic Front or FDR), did not intend to sabotage them. For the United States Embassy, this decision by the FMLN not to attack the electoral process was a sign of existing tensions on the question of the elections. A month later, FMLN leaders gave more specific instructions. In the areas it controlled, it did not authorise the voting but left voters free to go to the polling centres in the sectors controlled by the FAES. Despite these directives, in different regions local guerrilla forces confiscated the identity cards of citizens to prevent them from being able to vote.[12]

For its part, the Reagan Administration chose to support a Partido Democrata Cristiano (Democratic Christian Party or PDC) leader, Fidel Chavez Mena for these elections. Unfortunately, the latter did not obtain the PDC nomination against Duarte. Washington then turned to Francisco Guerrero of the Partido de Conciliacion Nacional (National Conciliation Party), the political party that led the country in the 1960s and 1970s but Guerrero only finally arrived in third place in the first round of voting and found

Government paratroopers returning from combat in El Salvador's north-eastern Cabañas department, March 1984 (Albert Grandolini Collection)

himself eliminated. For the second round, Duarte faced Roberto D'Aubuisson, candidate of the Allianza Republicana Nacionalista (Nationalist Republican Alliance or ARENA), a Right-wing party close to the Death Squads. Again the Americans backed Duarte and provided him with $10 million to pay his expenses and another $1.4 million for his election campaign.[13]

On the two election days, the guerrillas did not carry out attacks against the voting centres and the FAES fulfilled their role of guaranteeing the security of the elections. The high turnout of the population in the presidential elections, which saw Duarte win, was a further demonstration of the weakness of popular support for the FMLN. Above all, these elections made it possible to create a democratic facade in El Salvador.

In July, strengthened by this new legitimacy, Duarte went to Europe. From France and Germany, he launched several public appeals to the FMLN to seek political negotiation of the conflict. In October, during a speech at the UN, he again announced an offer of dialogue.[14]

The presidential elections were also a success for the Reagan Administration, facilitating the continuation of its policy in El Salvador. Although the US Congress still required it to certify aid to the country every six months, after the 1984 elections, the pressure from Congress waned as Reagan gave the impression that he was working to create a democratic government in El Salvador.[15] Thus, a few days after Duarte's electoral victory, the House of Representatives approved $229.4 million in military aid for fiscal year 1984 and $132.5 million for 1985.[16]

Duarte took office on 1 June 1984 and a few days later, faced the first major guerrilla attack since the beginning of the year.

Cerron Grande June 1984

It was in the Chalatenango department that the FMLN launched its major operation. It targeted the Cerron Grande power plant which produced 1/3 of El Salvador's electricity. This operation, which would weaken the economy and hamper the first steps of Duarte's presidency, also sought to consolidate the successful FMLN military

The airborne operations carried out by the FAES made it possible to put an end to the successes won by the guerrillas. This was the inside of the cabin of an UH-1H, with three airborne troops, and the helicopter's gunner at the pintle-mounted M60 machine gun. (Albert Grandolini Collection)

FPL guerrillas brought in their catch after fishing all night on Lake Suchitlan, near Cerron Grande. During the day, boats were sunk beneath weeds at the water's edge to avoid detection. (Albert Grandolini Collection)

campaign in Chalatenango, after the destruction of the 4th Infantry Brigade garrison in El Paraiso at the end of December 1983. For the FAPL, it was the way to demonstrate that the dispersal of forces into small units to evade the airborne operations of the FAES (now advocated by the ERP after the defeats of San Gerardo and Villa Dolores), was a mistake.

Cerron Grande was poorly protected by a single DM-1 infantry company. In the middle of 1983, the DM-1 started to form the Cazadores Battalions Suchitlan and Sumpul but it was severely weakened by the destruction of the 4th Brigade installations. In 1984, it had only three Battalions, one assigned to the defence of Cerron Grande, another to the surroundings of the Chalatenango city and the Troncal del Norte road, whilst the last was in operation in the north of the department.

In June, it was the Cazadores Battalion Suchitlan, under the command of Lieutenant Ricardo Alberto Chavez Carreño, which was responsible for defending Cerron Grande – although this battalion was incomplete. It was assisted in this mission by 45 members of the GN. The electrical installations were protected by two defensive rings, one external and 1km from the plant and one internal around the most vulnerable positions. The Cerron Grande power station could also rely on the protection, more distant however, of the 4th Infantry Brigade which had the Cazadorez Battalion El Sierpe, five rifle companies and a support company with three 120mm mortars.

For the attack, the FMLN gathered a large amount of forces and it was the Felipe Peña Mendoza Group which was responsible for ensuring the success of the operation. The X-21 Battalion was to attack Cerron Grande from the north-west and south while the K-93 Battalion was to storm Monte Redondo, north of the power station, to set up a defensive device against an airborne attack. These two battalions brought together 700 fighters. The SS-20 Battalion, with 300 men, had to cut the road coming from Sensuntepeque as well as that between Ilobasco and Cerron Grande. The Battalion Rafael Aguiñada Carranza (BRAC) of the FAL with 300 men, was in charge of blocking the road coming from San Rafael Cedros while the Detachment Luis Aberto Diaz Vicente of the FAR-LP with 300 men, had to do the same on the road coming from San Vicente. The operation against Cerron Grande therefore mobilised around 1,550 combatants while the FES teams were also used for reconnaissance against the enemy's defences. [17]

On 27 June, around 1 a.m., FES men infiltrated the power plant and attacked its command post located in the centre of the defensive perimeter, as well as the communication room and a position which dominated the entire defensive system at the south of the plant. At the same time, the X-21 Battalion went on the attack. In just 10 minutes, the FES eliminated or neutralised their objectives, but the X-21 Battalion had less success. This prevented the FES from seizing the bunker which protected the northern sector of the plant and the GN positions which defended the engine room. This forced the guerrilla command to order the destruction of the electricity pylons that left from the power station. North of this, the attack on Monte Redondo was a failure, the soldiers resisting the assaults of Battalion K-93.

Upon learning of the attack on Cerron Grande, the FAES General Staff organised a counter-attack with one company from DM-1, another from DM-2, the BIRI Belloso and the Airborne Battalion, i.e. from 800 to 900 soldiers. They were supported by a battery of four 105mm howitzers, two A-37 fighter-bombers, an O-2A reconnaissance aircraft, 16 UH-1H helicopters, an SA-315B Lama and two Hughes-500D. The paratroopers were divided into two groups which had to land north and south of Cerron Grande.

The FAES relief operation was experiencing difficulties. The DM-2 company fell into an ambush organised by the SS-20 Battalion south-west of Guacotecti, while the Sierpe Battalion, which came from Chalatenango, was blocked south-west of San Antonio Los Ranchos by regular units and FAPL militias. The BIRI Belloso was caught in an ambush by the FAL. It failed to advance and tried to reach Tejutepeque and Cinquera but encountered guerrilla forces who stopped it. The Luis Aberto Diaz Vicente Detachment halted the advance of the 5th Infantry Brigade troops coming from San Vicente. Thus, no relief force coming by road managed to reach Cerron Grande. [18]

In the power station, the GNs, entrenched in the engine room, were still resisting. The guerrillas then managed to get in touch with President Duarte and offered him a negotiation, otherwise they threatened to destroy the entire dam. For its part, the FAES High Command asked the president to give the order to send the paratroopers to Cerron Grande. Duarte hesitated and it was finally Colonel Bustillo, the FAS commander, who gave the order to take action.

At around 6 a.m., fighter-bombers dropped their bombs on guerrilla positions northeast and southeast of Cerron Grande while paratroopers were ready to land near Monte Redondo north of the plant. The installation of anti-aircraft positions by the K-93 Battalion in this sector finally forced them to choose another landing zone while the A-37Bs dropped 750-pound bombs on Monte Redondo. The paratroopers managed to land UH-1H helicopters near the guerrilla positions which they jostled before beginning to advance towards the power plant without encountering resistance. The bulk of the FMLN forces were concentrated elsewhere, notably in the west where the planned retreat route was.

The use of UH-1B (visible in this photograph) and UH-1H helicopters allowed the FAES to quickly transport reinforcements to support units under attack or to surprise concentrations of guerrillas. (Albert Grandolini Collection)

The second group of paratroopers landed south of Cerron Grande under intense fire from Battalion X-21. At this time, an artillery battery with 105mm howitzers, was in San Luis del Carmen nine kilometres west of the plant. It received the order to fire on the hamlets of Los Padillas and El Plan de las Mesas to the southwest, through which the guerrilla forces had to escape. A-37Bs also bombarded rebels fleeing encirclement by paratroopers advancing from the north and south. Nevertheless, the columns of the X-21 Battalion managed to withdraw by the south in the direction of Cinquera. North of Cerron Grande, the K-93 Battalion withdrew towards La Laguna in the centre of the Chalatenango department. At 9:30 a.m., the paratroopers took control of Cerron Grande which they secured before the arrival of President Duarte and the High Command at noon.[19]

The losses of the guerrillas amounted to 65 dead, whose bodies were buried in four mass graves. On the side of the paratroopers there were no deaths, while the defenders of Cerron Grande counted 100 killed. According to the American ambassador in El Salvador, if the attack was a success for the guerrillas in terms of its planning, it ended in failure. In the end, the FMLN destroyed only one transformer and did not cause major damage to the infrastructure.[20] Above all, the guerrillas were surprised at the very moment of their attacks and, by landing considerable forces, the FAES succeeded in reversing the tactical situation. All that remained was for the latter to go on the offensive with all the firepower available to strike the rebel concentrations as they approached.

During the rescue of Cerron Grande, the FAES demonstrated the advance of their air power and the importance of the helicopter gunships whose deployment defeated the FMLN.[21] They thus regained the strategic initiative and could now seek to strike the enemy as hard as possible.

Buena Vista battles July 1984

On 24 July 1984, an FAPL deserter informed the military that a force of about 200 rebels had been granted permission to visit their families for eight days before being dispersed into small units. For the FAES, the opportunity to strike a guerrilla concentration could not be overlooked. On 27th July, the guerrillas had to come back from their leave and gather at Cerro Buena Vista, in order to receive their equipment and their weapons. For this operation, the FAES mobilised 12 UH-1H helicopters, 120 paratroopers, a *Hachas* patrol and one of the PRALs. The latter had to guide the *Hachas* to Cerro Buena Vista to set up an ambush on the most likely route for a guerrilla retreat.

On 28 July, four A-37B fighter-bombers dropped four to eight 500-pound bombs on the area where the paratroopers were to land, then machine-gunned the guerrillas present in the sector. When paratroopers landed, they benefited from a considerable surprise

An Huey helicopter (nicknamed 'Death From Above') as seen while armed with double, pintle-mounted M60s in cabin doors. Shown while landing in a village in central El Salvador of September 1984. (Albert Grandolini Collection)

effect. The rebels, in the greatest confusion, fled to the northwest. They then fell into the ambush of the PRAL but managed to overcome the obstacle.

The paratroopers secured the Cerro Buena Vista and consolidated their positions before launching, , patrols in the surroundings during the following days. On 30 July, the *Hachas* and the PRAL joined the paratroopers to evacuate the area. The column of soldiers then became a target for the guerrillas who had regrouped. It ambushed them so violently that the FAES column was cut in two, the rear part which included the special forces was the hardest hit. The firing of 105mm howitzers and the 500-pound bombs launched by fighter-bombers, nevertheless allowed the soldiers to escape, regroup and entrench themselves to face enemy attacks. They were joined by the rearguard of the column and then by airborne reinforcements. All the fighting between 28 and 31 July left around 30 dead in the ranks of the guerrillas while the paratroopers had three dead and 22 wounded, the special forces three dead and 20 wounded.[22]

Torola IV

The successes obtained by the FAES since the beginning of the year pushed it to continue its advantage. The FMLN was still powerful since, according to the Salvadoran intelligence services, in 1984 it had between 9,000–11,000 combatants, 2,800–3,500 within the FAPL, 3,000–3,500 in the ERP, 1,160–1,325 at the FAL, 1,400–1,550 at the FARN, 700–850 at the FAR-LP and 100 in other organisations. It nevertheless suffered increasingly heavy losses since about 900 fighters deserted and 1,250 were killed between January 1 and August 20.[23]

It was in these circumstances that on 15 October 1984, the first negotiations took place between the government and FMLN in the city of La Palma, Chalatenango department. They brought nothing concrete, but during their unfolding, the military operations were reduced.[24] Lieutenant-Colonel Monterrosa, aware of the weakness of the guerrillas after the failures it suffered at the beginning of the year, knew that this situation would not last long. He therefore wanted to exploit it quickly by hitting the ERP leaders after the end of the discussions. For this, he launched Operation Torola IV.

On the morning of 19 October 1984, 16 helicopters landed, under the protection of fighter-bombers, BIRI Atlacatl, Belloso and Arce troops on an arc of a circle going from San Fernando to the north of Perquin, in the north of the Morazan department, near the border with Honduras. The ERP military school was based in San Fernando while Perquin, which housed the most important FMLN base of operations, had become a nerve centre of the guerrillas in Morazan. Other forces of the 3rd Infantry Brigade and the Centro de Instruccion de Comandos de la Fuerza Armada (Armed Forces Commando Training Centre or CICFA) attacked from the south across the Rio Torola.

In this classic hammer and anvil manoeuvre, airborne troops formed the anvil. The fights were particularly violent. Although the ERP command was not dismantled, the military school was destroyed and an arms depot discovered. The fighting continued for the next few days, but rather than large units, the soldiers then faced small formations of guerrillas who organised ambushes and laid mines.[25]

On October 23, Lieutenant-Colonel Monterrosa, considered the best FAES strategist, was killed when his helicopter was destroyed in flight by the guerrillas along with 14 people including two lieutenant-colonels, two majors and three second lieutenants. The ambush was carried out by ERP special units infiltrated in an area occupied by the FAES near Joateca. Monterrosa's death came as a

Funeral of Lieutenant-Colonel Domingo Monterrosa, on 27 October 1984. (Albert Grandolini Collection)

shock to FAES morale as ERP forces managed to withdraw safely.[26] Whilst some believe that the helicopter was shot down by guerrilla fire, the most accepted version asserts that the ERP intentionally abandoned a booby-trapped transmitter and Radio Venceremos documents that Monterrosa took with him in the helicopter on flying from Joateca to San Miguel. As the latter passed, the guerrillas would have triggered the explosion from a distance.[27]

While Operation Torola IV affected the Morazan department, the FAES also launched a series of military operations in the Cuscatlán and Cabañas departments where localities such as Tenancingo and the surroundings of Cinquera were the object of air attacks and bombings. During these operations, loudspeakers called for the surrender of FMLN fighters and leaflets were thrown from the planes, offering money in exchange for the surrender of arms.[28]

Nevertheless, October 1984 saw a new success for the guerrillas. At Watikitu, about 600 of his fighters attacked a Cazadores Battalion. Despite the FAS bombardments which caused severe losses, the guerrillas managed to destroy the battalion.[29]

Suchitoto – November 1984

Following the defeat of Cerron Grande which demonstrated the new power of the FAS, the FMLN decided to prepare a strong attack against the town of Suchitoto in the north of the country. The latter had been, since the beginning of the war, the target of three FAPL attacks which, each time, succeeded in defeating the FAES. For this new operation, the FMLN mobilised its forces in the sector, those of the FARN and the FAL, but the most important was the FAPL Felipe Peña Mendoza Group, led by Commander Eduardo Linares, whose units participated in the fighting in Cerron Grande. They were reinforced by a support unit from the South Eastern Front with M-60 Browning machine guns, 90 and 57mm recoilless rifles and 60–81mm mortars.

With this operation, the FAPL had several objectives. They first wanted to demonstrate the effectiveness of large-scale military actions mobilising large numbers while strategic and tactical debates

An FAES soldier with an M79 grenade launcher (Albert Grandolini Collection)

FAS was called to provide air support. Five A-37B fighters bombed guerrilla positions while a Hurricane strafed them. Then the A-37Bs returned to Ilopango to load new bombs and took off again. The air attacks lasted for six hours, the A-37B carrying out 42 missions. When the bombardment began to decrease in intensity, the paratroopers launched a counter-attack and captured the trenches held until then by the guerrillas. With fresh troops landed, they secured the area as the fighting ended around 3:00 p.m. During this day, 15 paratroopers died and 45 injured. In Suchitoto, 18 DM-5 soldiers and seven PN agents were killed.

were raging within the FMLN. Next, the attack on Suchitoto had to put an end to the success of the main counter-insurgency tactic of the FAES – the use of airborne troops – by inflicting a defeat to them in an ambush.

On 9 November 1984, the FAL Rafael Aguiñada Carranza Battalion and the FARN Carlos Arias Battalion attacked the Suchitoto garrison, defended by 180 men from the PN Pantera Battalion, the DM-5 and by 40 Defence volunteers civilian who occupied two defensive circles around the city made up of trenches and bunkers. When the guerrillas began to attack with mortars and rocket launchers, the garrison commander warned the General Staff that the outer defences were falling and the town was about to be captured. The FAS then organised an airborne operation to rescue Suchitoto. The planned landing zone was east of the city on the rear of the guerrillas. At the same time, the FAPL organised an anti-aircraft ambush, inspired by the Vietnamese example, which consisted of installing a concentrated anti-aircraft device with five M-2 machine guns to surprise the arrival of airborne reinforcements. Until then, these anti-aircraft facilities represented only a small part of the guerrilla system but were present in any attack after 1982.

At 6 a.m., a first contingent of 120 paratroopers transported by 14 UH-1H helicopters took off from the Ilopango Base. It disembarked half an hour later without encountering any difficulties. Paratroopers did not detect the presence of guerrilla units. They prepared to support the encircled units in Suchitoto and began to advance. It was then that they were violently attacked by an FAPL battalion which prevented them from advancing.

At 6:50 a.m., a second contingent of 120 paratroopers took off from Ilopango. At 7:10 a.m., when the helicopters were on their final approaches, the guerrilla anti-aircraft weapons went into action. Two helicopters managed to land the soldiers they were transporting but the others failed. Many soldiers were hit by gunfire before they could even get out of the helicopters. The few paratroopers who touched down, desperately tried to join the first contingent that arrived earlier. Two helicopters crashed on the other side of Lake Suchitlan, others had to land halfway or manage to return to Ilopango Base.

The FAPL forces, about 300 men, launched assaults against the paratroopers of the first contingent using RPG-2s and machine guns. The anti-aircraft device of the guerrillas also swept their positions and prevented the arrival of reinforcements. At 8 a.m., the soldiers, now isolated, were in a very difficult situation. The

While the FAPL ambush partly failed, it nevertheless demonstrated the vulnerabilities of airborne operations, especially during landing when helicopters were easy targets. In Suchitoto 90 percent of the helicopters engaged were damaged by bullets and there were many victims in the ranks of the FAES. Only the enormous firepower of the FAS could prevent the complete destruction of the paratroopers.[30] On the FMLN side, this operation marked a turning point since it was their last action carried out with troops of the size of a battalion.

The FMLN went on the defensive

The fighting that took place in 1984 indicated that the military situation was reversed in El Salvador. US aid stabilised the Duarte regime while the FAES made notable gains against their undefeated adversary. This situation continued until 1989 and established an unstable balance where the strategic initiative alternated in favour of the FMLN and the FAES, a balance which nevertheless meant the continuation of the misfortunes of the war. The number of displaced civilians continued to increase while aerial bombardments and major military sweeps caused massive upheavals in the Salvadoran countryside.

This balance was the result of the tactical and strategic mutations of the FAES which were showing their first results. The FMLN leaders were aware of these transformations. Carpio, as early as 1981, predicted that American aid would give FAES the advantage of mobility through the use of helicopters. The year 1984 confirmed this prognosis and showed the inability of the guerrillas to face the increase in military forces and their better mobility.

The new and unfavourable military situation could only weigh on the morale of the guerrilla fighters. The ERP thus decided to send a thousand fighters to the camps in Honduras for fear that they would flee during the fighting. Desertions became more important as well as surrenders.[31] The FAPL also experienced massive desertions and recruitment problems. The PCS could not complete its only battalion, nor the PRTC its Luis Adalberto Diaz Battalion. The FARN no longer had enough cadres to form a second battalion. The FAPL interpreted these phenomena, linked to the drop in morale, as betrayals which they ruthlessly repressed. In the Paracentral area, which included the San Vicente and La Paz departments, the FAPL

Intensive deployment of UH-1H helicopters eventually forced the guerrillas into the defensive. (Albert Grandolini Collection)

The lack of combatants forced the FMLN to carry out forced recruitment and start to integrate children as young as this 12 year old boy. (Albert Grandolini Collection)

demonstrated that it was now impossible for it to maintain large concentrations of troops without exposing himself to the greater firepower and increased mobility of the FAES. In addition to this superiority acquired by its adversaries, these concentrations of fighters required a level of financial and logistical resources that proved to be unsustainable while the government was pursuing population displacement policies in areas where the guerrillas were strong, thus depriving it of its sources of support supply and the labour that worked for it.[33]

With the possibility of a short-term military victory beginning to recede, the FMLN prepared for a long war by changing its strategy to preserve its forces. Previously, faced with an offensive by the FAES, the guerrillas would leave a rearguard force and withdraw the others. It only engaged in combat if it saw an opportunity to defeat the opponent or if it had to. The objective was to seek to destroy significant forces of the FAES, both to obtain numerous weapons and to weaken the power of the military. From now on, faced with a military operation, the guerrillas could not flee but divided into small squads of five to eight fighters equipped with sufficient communication and mobilisation capacity to be able to regroup quickly, if necessary. These groups no longer had rearguards and could only rely on the networks of informants and supply they could build, to survive and continue the fight. The latter consisted of trapping advancing soldiers, ambushing them, harassing them with artillery and home-made mortars, rifle grenades, using snipers and landmines.[34]

Thus from 1984, the main objective of the FMLN was no longer to defeat the FAES in short-term decisive battles, but rather to submit it to a war of attrition, a strategy long advocated by the FPL. It was about exhausting the will and determination of the State forces and extending the war to all of El Salvador in an attempt to break the siege of the *retaguardias*. This strategy was part of a lenghty one based on the combination of the armed struggle with the political struggle to weaken the government before launching a large-scale counter-offensive linked to a popular insurrection.

The decision to disperse troop concentrations into small groups was a slow process that met with resistance. The ERP was the organisation that was the fastest to realise this need, especially after its defeat of Ciudad Barrios. It was also subject to an intense military campaign which brought together 10 Cazadores Battalions against its strongholds in the Morazan, San Miguel and La Union departments and which put the BRAZ in a difficult position. The ERP leaders then decided to deconcentrate these units in columns and platoons in the areas of Usulatan, Guazapa and Santa Ana. Elsewhere, it dispersed them and reverted to guerrilla tactics despite the displeasure of BRAZ leaders.[35]

For its part, the FAL decided to concentrate their best forces in the Cerro de Guazapa and dispersed the others. The FAPL were

command executed more than 1,000 combatants and collaborators. The ERP for its part had to resort to forced recruitment, but this process did not resolve the situation since among its recruits, 80–90 percent flew or surrendered to the military.[32] Above all, this practice led to a loss of support in the rural areas where it took place and an erosion of the favourable international image of the guerrillas.

The FMLN was aware of the strategic impasse in which it found itself. The defeats at Ciudad Barrios, Villa Dolores and San Gerardo

The effectiveness of the FAES counter-insurgency units like this one, forced the FMLN to disperse its troops in order to avoid excessive losses. (Albert Grandolini Collection)

the last to accept the principle of the dispersion of forces, only in December 1984. At the end of that year, the leadership of the FMLN met in Chalatenango to ratify the change of strategies. At the beginning of 1985 all the military organisations that it directed would have adopted it, a situation which would only change from 1988. The most important thing now for the FMLN leaders was to preserve its forces in order to continue to remain a movement able to challenge the government for control of the country.

The change in strategy of the FMLN marked its acceptance of the military superiority of the FAES, in particular its air power. During the following years, it therefore tried to find tactics to challenge this domination of the sky by the FAS and always managed to escape the operations of encirclement and annihilation thanked to his intimate knowledge of the ground.

Along with this, the FMLN also intensified its actions of sabotage which affected the transport, communications and economic infrastructure of the country and began to rebuild a political movement in the cities where it had been practically dismantled. Since the January 1981 offensive, it had focused its attention on its *retaguardias* and the organisation of rural guerrillas, abandoning urban centres. The result, according to Spencer, was 'the rapid loss of FMLN popularity and its ever-increasing isolation from national life. The FMLN high command took note of its collision course with disaster and began to formulate a new strategy'.[36]

3

THE FAILURE OF LOW INTENSITY WARFARE, 1985–1986

In order to overcome its defeats in 1984, the FMLN redefined its strategy to simultaneously survive, accumulate forces and be ready, when the time was Right, to return to the offensive. Meanwhile, the FAES continued to deploy the range of counter-insurgency warfare tactics, notably during Operation Fénix in 1986. The military successes they achieved were nevertheless insufficient to definitively break a guerrilla force that showed great resilience.

The FMLN new strategy

Between May and June 1985, the FMLN CG met in the Morazan department to validate the strategic change initiated the previous year. On the military level, the dispersal of forces proved effective, particularly in the face of the FAS power increase, to wage a guerrilla war even if the FMLN still retained its ability to concentrate large troops to launch spectacular attacks. As a 1988 report by four US Army Colonels put it:

> Without a doubt, during the almost conventional phase of the war, the FAS became the big killer. The support of the Air Force with its A-37s and its UH-1M and MD-500 attack helicopters proved to be very effective against the large formations of the FMLN. Once the FMLN opted for a protracted war strategy, lucrative targets almost completely disappeared.[1]

One of the objectives of the new strategy was also to be able to open theatres of operations in the rear of the FAES and to extend the conflict in the Western departments, regions which remained calm during most of the conflict. During this meeting, the CG also approved the new FMLN international line and decided to move forward gradually in the process of unifying the organisations that composed it.[2]

The FMLN new strategy resulted in a tactic of attrition and weakening of the morale of the FAES. For this, it turned to the classic methods of guerrilla warfare including ambushes, harassment and sometimes the attack of fixed positions. Anti-personnel landmines then also began to play a major role in its strategy. Even if the guerrillas used them before, their use increased from 1985. They made it possible to injure or kill enemy soldiers, to weaken their morale, to hinder the great sweeps which generally followed aerial bombardments. The objective was also to limit the mobility of the FAES and prevent it from threatening the *retaguardias* of the FMLN. These weapons, most often home-made, caused more and more losses in the FAES, to the point that in 1986, the CIA estimated that

Different types of makeshift mines discovered by the FAES demonstrated the ingenuity of the FMLN. (Albert Grandolini)

FMLN guerrillas in San Miguel Department, 1985. (Albert Grandolini)

they represented nearly two-thirds of all military deaths. By the end of the war, more than 5,000 servicemen had been maimed by mines.[3] Civilians were also heavily affected by mines which caused a sharp increase in the number of amputees, especially among children and farmers.[4] In 1985 alone, between 31 and 45 civilians were killed by mines and 100 injured.[5]

Having abandoned the objective of annihilating the enemy in a decisive battle of the conventional type, the FMLN began to seek to create the conditions necessary for an armed uprising leading to the seizure of power. Taking up the Sandinista strategy of the accumulation of forces, it therefore concentrated its efforts on setting up the conditions necessary for the launch of a final large-scale offensive, on the model of January 1981. The FMLN then put more emphasis on the political nature of the conflict and adopted more clearly a strategy of a protracted people's war that relied on political organisations and the establishment of close links with the civilian population.

The *retaguardias* played a leading role in this strategy. Each organisation of the FMLN had its own which served it both for the organisation and support of military operations but also for its political work and to undermine the legitimacy of the government. As the war progressed, the guerrillas increasingly expanded their network of rearguards. The FMLN thus established three types of rearguards, each having a different objective. Strategic rearguards, often located in the north of the country, provided support and protection to senior FMLN leaders and key concentrations of guerrilla forces. They also served as a political base, recruitment areas for combatants and material support. Operational rearguards, such as the Guazapa volcano, meanwhile served as forward operating bases with small camps used to support military operations. The third type was the tactical rearguard which provided support during offensive operations and troop rest areas, medical and supply bases.[6] These different types of rearguards could not hide the fact that the Salvadorian territory under FMLN control was reduced from 30 percent in 1984 to 10 percent in 1986.[7]

In addition to their military functions, the rearguards also had an important role in the political struggle. Radio Venceremos, the most popular of the FMLN's radio stations, broadcasted from one of the ERP's *retaguardias* and served as a medium for guerrilla propaganda aimed at national and international audiences. Despite considerable obstacles and numerous attempts to destroy it, Radio Venceremos continued to operate almost without interruption throughout the war. Destroying this radio even became an obsession for Lieutenant-Colonel Monterrosa, who lost his life there.

From 1985, the FMLN also decided to populate its *retaguardias* with displaced persons, particularly from refugee camps in Honduras. According to an American estimate, between 1988 and 1991, the FMLN settled around 16,000 refugees in areas near guerrilla bases. This policy allowed it to expand his rearguards and increase his influence in the Salvadoran countryside. The repopulation of the *retaguardias* also forced the FAES to change their strategy since they were ordered not to enter these repopulated communities and not to carry out military operations within 1.5 kilometres of them.[8]

From these *retaguardias*, the FMLN attacks against the economy grew rapidly. In the first six months of 1985, sabotage actions increased by more than 550 percent compared to the first six months of 1984. Electrical installations were particularly affected. In 1986, the guerrillas destroyed nearly 40 electricity towers, causing long blackouts in San Salvador and in the east of the country. If on the military level, these sabotage campaigns forced the FAES to immobilise troops to protect the infrastructures, this was not the

The FMLN developed a health service to treat its wounded and the *retaguardias* operated several well-equipped hospitals. (Albert Grandolini)

The dispersal of guerrilla forces was one of the most important aspects of the FMLN strategy initiated in 1984. It was supposed to allow the accumulation of forces to regain the military initiative. (Albert Grandolini)

objective that the FMLN aimed for. With total cumulative damage from 1979 to 1985 exceeding $1.2 billion, it sought above all to push the United States to divert part of its aid from the military sector to the economic, to hinder economic recovery and to undermine the popularity of the government.

The economic situation in El Salvador continued to worsen. Since 1981, investment had virtually stopped, industrial production had fallen by 17 percent and unemployment was rampant in construction, trade and transport. In 1985, the unemployment rate was 30 percent, that of underemployment also 30 percent, while inflation was estimated at 22 percent.[9] This situation particularly worried Washington. Since 1981, American aid and credits had prevented the economy from collapsing, but Americans were aware that a real economic recovery was necessary to ensure El Salvador's stability. To revitalise the economy, they advocated for the implementation of classic liberal economic principles, including fiscal austerity, the promotion of private enterprise and the end of social subsidies. This policy was the opposite of Duarte's plans, which promised an economic recovery based on public sector jobs and the maintenance of government subsidies.

Under American pressure, the Salvadoran president launched a liberal-inspired Stabilisation and Economic Reactivation Plan in 1986, provoking opposition on the Right and Left and weakening his popular support.[10] The latter was also shaken by Duarte's inability to effectively implement the prosecution of soldiers who had participated in human rights violations. Added to this, in an increasingly visible way, was widespread corruption among executives and leaders of the Christian Democratic Party.[11]

Alongside its policy of economic sabotage, the FMLN sought to increase its presence throughout the country in order to strengthen its ties with civilians. For this, it put in place the policy of Poder Popular (People's Power) whose objective was to extend its influence from its rural *retaguardias* to the main urban centres. In the latter, it created legal organisations that came into contact with civilians, especially in the Unions, including the Federación Nacional Sindical de Trabajadores Salvadoreños (National Union Federation of Salvadoran Workers or FENASTRAS) and among students. These provided bases and logistics networks, they organised strikes, work stoppages and demonstrations and they spread its propaganda.

At the time of the hoped-for insurrection, they had to be used to mobilise and supervise the populations to take them to fight alongside the guerrillas.[12] Thus, in February 1986, the Union Nacional de Trabajadores Salvadoreños (National Union of Salvadoran Workers or UNTS) was born in San Salvador and in other cities of the country. This new organisation called for a negotiated political solution to the conflict and organised mass demonstrations in San Salvador against the government.[13] Alongside these legal organisations, the FMLN also set up clandestine groups. From these, it formed urban militias whose best militants joined urban commandos.[14]

This return to the cities was, for the FMLN, a kind of step back to the situation of the 1970s when the Salvadoran Left had an impressive set of urban and militant networks. The latter were decimated by years of repression by the security forces and Death Squads, combined with the failed 1981 offensive when most of the FMLN's urban cadres were killed or fled to the campaigns.

The reinvestment of the cities was not only intended to establish itself among the population but also to carry the war in the main urban centres. Military actions in cities targeted officers who were assassinated like José Alberto 'Chele' Medrano, founder of ORDEN (Organizacion Democratica Nacionalista (National Democratic Organization), to commemorate the murder of Archbishop Romero, as well as government officials and US military.

On 19 June 1985, an attack was carried out by the urban commando Urbano Mardoqueo Cruz of the PRTC, under the command of Pedro Antonio Andrade (Mario González) against an open-air restaurant-cafeteria in the Zona Rosa neighbourhood of San Salvador. In the attack, 12 people were killed, four members of the Marine Security Guard of the United States Embassy, two American businessmen and six Latin American civilians. This was the bloodiest attack on American personnel in El Salvador.[15] On 25 July, the FMLN led another spectacular operation enabling it to release seven political prisoners held in Mariona prison. It was the first experience of combining different types of forces in urban conditions with civilian collaborators who provided much of the operational information, militia units, FES and guerrilla units.[16]

FMLN attacks in San Salvador thus increased by 50 percent, from 35 in 1985 to 54 in 1986, and acts of sabotage rose from 54 to 73. The guerrillas also organised artillery barrages in towns against government targets, using home-made ammunition. Extremely inaccurate, these attacks caused civilian casualties, angering some FMLN leaders, especially since these actions never posed a serious threat to the authorities.[17] They nevertheless demonstrated the persistence of the guerrillas at the very heart of the centres of power and contributed to another aspect of the new strategy initiated by the FMLN, to weaken the foundations of the government.

Undermining the government legitimacy

Slowly but surely, the FMLN continued its strategy of accumulation of forces while US and Salvadoran officials saw this as a sign of weakness. In reality, the FMLN widened its targets to weaken the power of its adversaries as much as possible. It was for this purpose that it put in place the Fuego Plan which aimed to dismantle the governmental structures at the local level. During the first six months of 1985, the guerrillas destroyed more than 75 civilian public buildings. It particularly targeted mayors who received death threats, suffered harassment or, in some cases, were kidnapped or killed. The ERP was particularly active in the actions against mayors who appeared to be legitimate targets.[18]

For the FMLN, destroying the political and military apparatus of the central government in the countryside had to prevent the Duarte government from implementing its various policies aimed at combating this and had to make it possible to detach the rural regions from the capital. The US Embassy had to acknowledge that the FMLN's campaign against mayors was having some success, but it was also hurting its popularity, because there were uncorrupted mayors who were trying, through civic action programmes government, to improve the lot of the population. It was also criticised within the FMLN. Nevertheless, it demonstrated both the inability of the central government to protect its representatives and that of the guerrillas to act with complete impunity.[19]

The FMLN also wanted to hit President Duarte directly. The latter was still supported by Washington, which provided him with generous aid. On 10 September 1985, the urban commando Pedro Pablo Castillo, belonging to an unknown guerrilla group, kidnapped Inés Guadalupe Duarte, the president's daughter and one of her friends. The FMLN first declared that it did not know who

If women were absent from the ranks of the FAES, they constituted a significant part of the FMLN personnel, including in the combat units. (Albert Grandolini)

committed this action. A little later, it finally claimed this kidnapping which nevertheless damaged its reputation abroad, particularly in Western Europe.[20]

The kidnapping of Duarte's daughter provoked a crisis within Salvadoran power. The Right opposed concessions being made by the president to the FMLN in exchange for her release. While the FAES command initially supported Duarte, it later became more critical. It believed that the president's wish to respond to the FMLN demands, in particular concerning the release of the guerrilla prisoners, placed the latter in a position of strength.[21] In their view, Duarte was getting too involved in a case that affected his daughter and his eagerness to secure her release, forced him to make too big concessions. For the US Embassy, its handling of the kidnapping weakened its position.

On 24 October, as part of an agreement reached in Panama, the FMLN released Inés Duarte and a group of mayors while the government released a group of political prisoners and authorised the departure of a hundred wounded FMLN to Panama, Cuba, East Germany and Mexico. While this exchange damaged Duarte's credibility with the FAES, the negotiation with the FMLN represented a victory for the guerrillas.[22] More importantly, according to the US State Department, many Salvadorans no longer regarded the FMLN as a terrorist organisation but as a real politico-military power. The concessions made by Duarte also boosted the morale of the guerrillas and strengthened their confidence in their strategy.[23]

The FMLN continued its spectacular actions. The FES and the urban commandos were given the mission of selecting targets of political and military value and hitting them as hard as possible. If the FES targeted the CEMFA installations near La Union, the

FAL urban commandos stood out for a high-profile operation that targeted the commander of the Presidential General Staff, Colonel Omar Napoleon de Jesús Avalos Lopez.

The FAL commandos followed the movements of Avalos Lopez for several months. On 26 October 1985, a commando of eight to 10 men wearing officer uniforms, showed up at the Avalos Lopez ranch in the Cerros San Pedro south of San Vicente. It kidnapped the colonel and took him to a FAR-LP camp in the north of the Morazan department.[24]

A rescue operation was attempted by the paratroopers and the BIRIs Atlacatl and Arce. According to the information obtained, Avalos Lopez was sequestered in the Jocoaitique area. The paratroopers landed north of Cerro Perricon while the BIRI Arce advanced between Carolina and Torola and the BIRI Atlacatl crossed the area passing through Osicala and crossing the Rio Torola towards Jocoaitique. When the latter reached this locality, the guerrillas were no longer there. It then decided to move north towards Perquin, but it discovered suspicious movements towards Cerro Pericon.

On their side, the paratroopers progressed towards the south. In reality, the BIRI Atlacatl was facing paratroopers whom it confused with guerrillas and the paratroopers thought they were facing a guerrilla column. The fight began between the FAES forces. The paratroopers' machine guns prevented the BIRI Atlacatl from advancing. When a Fantasma AC-47, armed helicopters UH-1M and two A-37B arrived, each side was convinced that they were coming to support them. The FAS finally attacked the BIRI Atlacatl positions. Shortly after, the soldiers realised their mistake. It nevertheless resulted in 46 dead and wounded, including 12 dead in the BIRI Atlacatl. Colonel Avalos would not be released until 2 February 1987 during a prisoner exchange.[25]

The FAS air war

If the FAES modernisation, with the formation of the BIRI, the Cazadores Battalions, the PRAL and the Hachas gave it better mobility, the key element to restrict the insurgents movements throughout the territory was the FAS. El Salvador was a very small country and now the FAS was able to reach any part of the territory in a few minutes, depriving the FMLN of any possibility of again accumulating forces large enough to confront the FAES on full equality and forcing it to operate in small units.

Thanks to American support, the FAES had sufficient air force to wage a more aggressive and sustained war against the FMLN. In this aerial arsenal, helicopters played a crucial role, allowing infantry forces to be transported for offensive operations and providing significant firepower. They were increasingly present in the Salvadorian sky. Between 1983 and 1984, the number of flight hours of the UH-1H increased by 60 percent and that of the A-37 by 68 percent.[26] For their part, from February 1984 to April 1985, the A-37Bs performed more than 600 direct support missions for ground units. This came with the increase in firepower. Between February and December 1985, the FAS used 723 750-pound, 1,171 500-pound and 17 250-pound bombs against the guerrillas.[27]

The years 1985 and 1986 marked the height of the FAS air campaign forcing the guerrillas to flee in many sectors. The air intelligence section was reorganised for the needs of counter-insurgency warfare with the formation of the special analysis centre at the Ilopango Air Base. It was based on the air reconnaissance squadron which had the capacity to carry out air photography missions throughout the country, to intercept radio signals and to locate the positions from which they were emitted. For this mission, the light reconnaissance aircraft Cessna O-2, provided by the United States, was particularly effective. It also made it possible to organise Strait Air Support missions which consisted of reaching an area where combat was taking place, contacting ground troops to find out the tactical situation in which they were themselves and then coordinating the

Two Cessna O-2A reconnaissance aircraft at Ilopango Air Base. (Albert Grandolini)

The use of the AC-47 by the FAS made it possible to provide fire support to ground troops against which the guerrillas were powerless. This was one of the examples modified through the installation of modern engines. (Albert Grandolini)

support of other aircraft (A-37, AC-47 or helicopters) to support FAES units. The FAS thus helped various offensives which weakened the main strongholds of the FMLN in Guazapa and Chalatenango by intensive bombardments while the soldiers on the ground evacuated thousands of civilians towards refugee camps thus depriving the guerrillas of their civilian infrastructure.[28]

From 1986, the FAS also began to carry out Lightning operations, a tactic used by the Americans in Vietnam and which the Salvadorans baptised Operaciones de busqueda y destruccion de reductos subversivos a baja altura (Search and destroy operations of subversive strongholds at low altitude). It consisted of a small air force of which one section located and fixed the enemy forces while the other destroyed them. A Hughes-500/E helicopter flew low looking for guerrilla positions while two others assured him cover. When the Hughes-500/E discovered these positions, it threw a smoke grenade to indicate the location and the other helicopters fired their rockets. Then the A-37B fighter-bombers bombarded the area and finally an air assault took place with helicopters carrying paratroopers or special forces.

From May 1985, these operations could be carried out at night through the use of infrared night vision equipments. Faced with the dangers coming from the sky, the guerrillas were obliged to build in these camps wooden anti-aircraft shelters but also anti-aircraft defences equipped with machine guns.[29] These measures were not without effects since in October 1984 a UH-1 was shot down and three in November to which were added four others heavily damaged in the fighting near Suchitoto.[30]

For bombing operations, the FAES used the interception of radio signals to locate guerrilla forces and camps. Thus, in the first days of January 1986, goniometric triangulation made it possible to locate a guerrilla encampment south of San José Las Flores in the Chalatenango department. The FPL commander, Eduardo Linares alias Douglas Santamaria, was present when the FAS fighter-bombers dropped 500 and 750 pound bombs. However, he managed to escape death.[31]

Another operation took place following information transmitted by Colonel James J. Steele of the Milgroup, who warned the FAES of a meeting being held with the FMLN regional commanders east of Tecoluca in the San Vicente department on 18 April 1985. On that day, two UH-1Ms accompanied by an armed Hugues-500 took off from Ilopango. Among one of the crews was a CIA agent, Félix Rodriguez, who played an important role in the adoption of new strategies by the FAS. The helicopters spotted a guerrilla column led by Maria Martha Concepcion Valladares de Lemus alias Nidia Diaz of the PRTC. The column of 50 fighters split into two to escape the helicopters which began to fire their machine guns causing numerous casualties. Rodriguez then asked the pilot to land to take the backpack carried by a rebel lying on the ground and which could contain important documents. When he approached the corpse, it moved. Rodriguez shot and injured Nidia Diaz.

A-37Bs then arrived and bombed the rebels trying to escape. Helicopters landed paratroopers who quickly secured the area and searched for survivors. For his part, Fernandez drove Nidia Diaz in a helicopter to take her to Ilopango. In his bag, the soldiers discovered many documents including the PRTC archives which allowed the arrest of other leaders.[32]

View from the ground as an FAS helicopter is approaching to bring in reinforcements and supplies during one of counter-insurgency operations of the mid-1980s. (Albert Grandolini Collection)

On 15 September 1985, a meeting of the FMLN CG took place in Arambala, south-east of Perquin in the north of the Morazan department. Present were Villalobos and Ana Guadalupe from the ERP, Leo Cabrales and Ivan Portillo from the FARN, Schafik Handal from the FAL and other leaders. In Arambala there was also the ERP political and military school, the Venceremos radio, logistics, propaganda and security teams, altogether about 200 people.

Informed of the meeting of the FMLN main leaders, on the morning of 16 September, UH-1M helicopters appeared and began to fire rockets and strafe the area. An AC-47 also participated in the attack. Soon helicopters approached to land the Parachute Battalion near Arambala but the ERP placed two anti-aircraft positions with six M-60 machine guns nearby. The shots of these machine guns prevented the landing. A-37Bs were then called in to bombard the area with 500-pound bombs.

The guerrillas resisted and the ERP security managed to evacuate the FMLN leaders and the structures of the organisation who took refuge in Los Toriles. The next day, after a short bombardment, the paratroopers finally managed to land and searched Arambala. They retired in the evening. Two days later, the interception of the guerrillas' radio signals enabled the FAS to again bomb the ERP installations while its command, which were in Cerro Gigante south of Perquin, were discovered and attacked by armed A-37s and UH-1Ms, again forcing them to move.[33]

On 21 November 1985, at 5:30 a.m., a huge bombardment began on the southern slope of Cerro de Guazapa. The FAS attacked with three Dragon Fly planes, five Bell UH-1H helicopters and three artillery batteries which targeted the FAL camps where Inés Duarte and her friend had been detained some time before. The FAES had precise information, with the exact coordinates of these camps. However, all the fighters of the latter were able to flee despite the landing of helicopter troops.[34]

The FMLN was aware that it had to break the power of the FAS if it wanted to regain the initiative. The anti-aircraft defences that it had put in place since the beginning of the war and which relied on the concentration of machine guns, turned out to be insufficient for this. From 1985, it began to use home-made rifle grenades to carry out anti-aircraft attacks, several of which took place in the Morazan department. These attacks were the source of rumours of the use of MANPADS (Man-portable air-defence system) SA-7 by the FMLN. They were echoed by Colonel Nelson Hernández who claimed that military intelligence realised that the guerrillas were preparing to introduce new anti-aircraft tactics, which 'consisted of the use of new combat devices, and the appearance [of] special home-made sights, which could be adapted to different types of rifles, in order to turn them into anti-aircraft weapons'.[35] They were also amplified by the discovery (in the documents found on Nidia Diaz) of a training scheme for an SA-7 Strela missile. These fears were, until 1989, unfounded and the FAS could continue to dominate the sky. The rumours certainly disseminated by the FMLN about the presence of surface-to-air missiles were probably aimed at boosting the morale of its fighters and exerting psychological pressure on the FAS.[36]

FMLN offensives in 1985

1985 was a year of strategic transition for the FMLN which, while turning to the employment of small guerrilla groups, still continued to employ battalion-sized units. At the beginning of this year, the two FPL battalions, SS-20 and S-7, were in the Chalatenango department near La Laguna where they detected the advance of the Tehuacan BIAT which reached the locality in the afternoon of 4 January. The same day, the reconnaissance unit, the *Recondos*, of the 5th Infantry Brigade, advanced towards San Jacinto but was spotted by the S-7 Battalion, which was arriving from the Tecoluca-Ingenio Highway. The soldiers settled on the Jaltepeque Hill.

At dawn on 5 January, Tehuacan BIAT left La Laguna and advanced towards Las Delicias and Pozo Azul. It suffered harassing actions carried out by units of the S-7 Battalion but without suffering any damage. Meanwhile, the SS-20 took position on the heights east and south of San Jacinto to attack the *Recondos*, who soon found themselves in a bad position, blocked on the heights of Jaltepeque. It asked for artillery support to avoid being surrounded. The guerrillas then realised that the Tehuacan BIAT aimed to seize the Campana hill while the unit of the 5th Brigade carried out a diversionary operation to move it away from the main objective.

On 6 January, the SS-20 Battalion was on the southwestern slope of the Campania hill while the S-7 was to the north, near the road that ran from San Bartolo to Rio Frio. It was decided that it would attack Tehuacan BIAT when it reached a football field and other disadvantageous places for his defence. However, at noon, BIAT had still not reached the area where the guerrillas prepared an ambush.

As the S-7 prepared for the arrival of the BIAT, the SS-20 began to attack the *Recondos* of the 5th Brigade. Perhaps thinking that the artillery fire had scared off the guerrilla forces, since they had not been attacked during the night, the *Recondos* tried to leave the Jaltepeque hilltop. They were forced to retreat and set up a defensive perimeter on the height of the hill. The guerrillas were preparing to storm it, forcing the military to request air support, which materialised with the arrival of A-37 Dragonflies and UH-1 helicopters. The bombardment of the FAS allowed the soldiers to beat a retreat.

After the fighting against the *Recondos*, S-7 was ordered to seek out the Tehuacan BIAT. When they found it, the guerrillas launched powerful attacks with M-60 machine guns and M-79 grenade launchers. The soldiers regrouped and advanced towards El Naranjal del Chile where they established defensive positions. The guerrilla columns launched an assault on these positions until night fell. The fighting resumed the next day. The soldiers nevertheless managed to break free and reached the crest of the hill where the guerrillas had set up a trap. A few small groups of soldiers managed to avoid the encirclement but most got stuck.

The FMLN command ordered the SS-20 Battalion to support the S-7 while a FAS A-37 bombed and straffed the guerrilla positions, without causing any damage. The fighting continued at night and

Despite the reinforcement of the FAES, the guerrillas remained a formidable force that put the military to the test. (Albert Grandolini Collection)

became more violent with the arrival of SS-20 units. The military resisted attacks in their fortifications with the support of artillery based in Injiboa and an AC-47. On the morning of 8 January, the Tehuacan Battalion was still surrounded, but it received support from three A-37s.

Sometime later, a formation of 12 helicopters arrived along with a Hughes 500 and an AC-47 carrying reinforcements. The fight resumed when they disembarked. Two AC-47s and four A-37s intervened again and another helicopter landing took place to evacuate the wounded. Reinforcements also arrived by road, the Airborne Battalion from San Jacinto and units from the Cañas and Jiboa Battalions from Achiotes. At nightfall, the FMLN withdrew its forces to the Chichontepec volcano.[37]

The biggest FMLN operation in 1985 took place when, on 10 October, the ERP mobilised all its reserves to attack the CEMFA at La Union, the main training centre for recruits. Here, American advisers were stationed with the aim of 'killing gringos, kill seasoned troops and capture recruits'.[38] The attack was carried out by 150 FES fighters supported by 350 BRAZ members who faced the 1st company of the Fonseca Battalion responsible for defending the base where 1,200 recruits then resided. When the BRAZ began to open fire on the defences to the west of the base, the FES attacked their objectives. They opened a breach in the enclosure and reached the barracks where the recruits were, whom they machine-gunned. They ran from building to building, throwing explosive charges inside each one. The soldiers managed to organise a counter-attack and finally drove out the FES, 15 of whom were killed. The attack on CEMFA killed 76 soldiers and injured more than 200, but no American soldiers were killed or injured.

In order to rescue the CEMFA, two combat helicopters arrived at La Union and began to strafe the BRAZ positions to the west of the base while paratroopers and the GOE were transported by 22 helicopters. They remained there for two days to patrol the sector in order to seek the FMLN latecomers. Thus, on 11 October, a retreating BRAZ column fell into an ambush on the Conchagua volcano. The paratroopers, installed on the heights, opened fire on it while the combat helicopters and the attack planes strafed the column.[39]

For its part, the FAES did not remain inactive. In April 1985, they launched Operation Esperanza, which sought to strike the FMLN maritime supply route on the coasts of the La Union department. It mobilised the BIRI Belloso and 67 Naval Commando soldiers. The

A guerrilla fighter in a small town street in 1985. (Albert Grandolini Collection)

FMLN guerrillas in the northern area of El Salvador, 1986. At this time, the FMLN proceeded to disperse its forces into small units. (Albert Grandolini Collection)

latter had to organise an ambush on the El Espino beach in Jiquilisco bay while the BIRI Belloso had to push the guerrillas towards the south and ambush from the hills which surround Jucuaran. As often was the case, the guerrillas managed to flee without significant loss.[40]

The dispersal strategy of the FMLN forces made the FAES large-scale operations less and less effective, which became the target of harassment by small groups that were elusive and evaded the confrontation. On 20 September 1985, the BIRI Bracamonte moved towards El Chile and San Bartolo and found itself facing guerrilla platoons which had divided into squads. They harassed the soldiers with sniping and by laying mines on their way before withdrawing. Hoping that the FAS would send a helicopter to evacuate the wounded, the guerrillas set up an anti-aircraft ambush with five 7.62mm rifles and an M-60 machine gun. However, the helicopter finally landed on the side of a hill and took off out of range of guerrilla fire.[41]

For its offensive operations, rather than large troop gatherings, the FMLN now favoured raids led by its special forces. On 16 March, the FES attacked Cerro Picacho, on the outskirts of San Salvador, where there was an important microwave antenna station defended by a reinforced GN company. The objective was both military–destroying communication equipment used by the FAES – and also media-friendly due to the proximity of the capital. The soldiers resisted the attackers but could not prevent the FES teams from destroying an antenna, several bunkers and the buildings where the garrison was housed. The guerrillas then withdrew to join the north of the Chalatenango department.[42]

In December 1985, after a long period of preparation, the J-28 unit of the FES, commanded by Cruz Carabante, launched an operation against the FAES who were defending the Acahuapa coffee factory, one of the most important in the San Vicente department. It was defended by a platoon of the 5th Infantry Brigade. On 12 December, the FES launched the attack supported by two squads of the SS-20 Battalion. They quickly seized almost all the defensive positions of the military but failed to capture the house where their command post was located. Meanwhile, a group of saboteurs managed to enter the factory. It destroyed machines, spilled gasoline on coffee bags and set fires. The factory was destroyed while the retreat of all the guerrilla forces was carried out without difficulty.[43]

When the FMLN CG met in the Morazan department in September 1985, the strategic turn adopted at the beginning of the year was far from over. Only the ERP had almost completed the dispersal of its large units in the east of the country, but the other groups were still undergoing restructuring. The FALP were still resisting the idea of dispersion and had only dispersed their forces in a few areas they controlled, while the FARN were trying to recompose, not only their military posture, but also their command which had been infiltrated by the FAES. Finally, they sent their troops to the regions of Guazapa, Cinquera, Usulutan and Santa Ana. The FAL, few in number, dispersed their forces quite easily while the FAR-LP were concentrated in the Cerros de San Pedro in the San Vicente and La Paz departments.

When the FMLN leaders who moved in the Morazan department, passed north of San Miguel, the ERP forces in the sector quickly dispersed and avoided contact with the FAES who then launched the airborne operation on Cerro Gigante. The effectiveness of the ERP manoeuvrers managed to convince the FMLN command of the merits of the new strategy and to order the other groups to implement it quickly.

The year 1985 was particularly difficult for the FMLN. The FAES, which had successfully transformed into counter-insurgency warfare and employed around 48 infantry battalions, forced them to adopt a defensive strategy. They could now act deep in areas controlled by the FMLN and organised ambushes on its supply routes. Guerrilla activity declined. At the end of 1985, the results of these actions were 220 ambushes, 700 positions destroyed and 216 weapons captured, which represented only one-fifth of those carried out in 1983.[44] Senior US officials, including Fred Ikle and Southern Command Chief Paul Gorman, believed the FMLN was on the verge of defeat. They thus confirmed the estimate made at the end of 1984 by the Defence Under-Secretary, who announced that the FAES had broken the strategic impasse they had been in since the beginning of the war and could defeat the guerrillas in two years.[45]

Operation Fénix 1986

On 10 January 1986, one of the most important FAES campaigns was carried out against the Cerro de Guazapa, Operation Phoenix, the name being given to symbolise the rebirth of the FAES. This campaign lasted five months before the military concentrated their efforts in the Chalatenango department to carry out Operation Chávez Carreño.

In accordance with the Low Intensity War strategy, Operation Fénix was not only military. As the Reagan Administration increasingly turned its attention to supporting the Nicaraguan Contras, the strategy adopted by the FAES left out civilians, forcing the Americans to again pressure Duarte to launch a larger effort than the NCP (National Campaign Plan) of 1983. The FAES now appeared in a position to prevent the victory of the FMLN and the

Milgroup believed that it was time to redirect strategic objectives towards efforts aimed at obtaining popular support for the government.⁴⁶

Finally, in 1986 with Operation Fénix, the full spectrum of counter-insurgency warfare was deployed. The operation contained a military phase where the FAES had to bombard the targeted areas and then launched large-scale search operations to force the guerrillas to abandon it. Once the area had been secured, civic action programmes deemed necessary to ensure the development of the countryside and the support of the populations had to be put in place to rally the latter and prevent the return of the FMLN after the departure of the soldiers.

The Cerro de Guazapa, located about 35km from the capital, is a geographical area that includes the Guazapa hill, 1,410 metres above sea level. It is also called 'the high zone' and a series of hills and flat lands located to the north of this elevation are called 'the lower zone'. Its limits are to the north, Lake Suchitlan, to the west, the Cañaverales de la Hacienda San Francisco, the Troncal del Norte Highway and the Montaña de Colima, to the east, the road that connected the localities of Suchitoto and San Martin, known as Calle Nueva and to the south, a series of populated hamlets, which extended intermittently to San Salvador.

On a military level, the capture of Cerro Guazapa could allow the FAES to enlarge the defensive belt of the capital, bringing it closer to the FMLN *retaguardias* in the Chalatenango, against which they could strike a second time. Controlling Cerro Guazapa also meant taking away from the guerrillas an area that allowed them to be in contact with the forces of the FMLN in the capital and its surroundings and from where they could carry out concentrations of troops to attack San Salvador.

At the beginning of 1986, the Cerro Guazapa was one of the most important FMLN *retaguardia*. On the north side of the high zone was a camp of about 25 RN fighters, among them three leaders, Leo Cabral, Rubén Rojas and Eduardo Solórzano. About 200 metres to the east was the FES camp, about 25 fighters. To the west there was the FARN general command camp, made up of Fermán Cienfuegos, Chano Guevara, Luisa Jovel and Raul Hércules, with 20 other combatants. A little further down were the hospital, post office, military information system, supply and logistics services. In four or five other more distant places, there were camps of the Carlos Arias Battalion (BCA) and the local guerrillas.

In the lower zone, on the shores of Lake Suchitlan, the FPL, RN and PRTC controlled a fishing cooperative and other production structures. On the southern slope of the hill, the FAL had the BRAC camps, the FES, a hospital, a supply and logistics apparatus as well as an explosives workshop. There were also units from the Felipe Peña Mendoza Battalion and the Luis Adalberto Diaz Detachment which belonged to the FPL and PRTC respectively, a Radio Farabundo Marti repeater, an FMLN propaganda structure and an RN supply camp. On the west side of the hill, in a place called Loma de Ramos, there was an ERP service, logistics and security unit, headed by Commander Armijo, who watched over the correct functioning of the Radio Venceremos repeater. In total, throughout the Cerro, there were some 400 combatants as well as members of the FES, members of the leadership of four FMLN organisations and between 4,000 and 5,000 civilians.⁴⁷

For the operation against Cerro Guazapa, the FAES, in addition to the 150 soldiers of the DM-5 who already occupied the heights of El Roblar and El Caballito, concentrated three BIRI, Atlacatl, Belloso and Bracamonte with 1,500 men each as well as BIATs from the 1st Infantry Brigade and DM-5 from Cuscatlán, the PN

These guerrillas, based in the Cerro de Guazapa posed a permanent threat to San Salvador that the FAES sought to eliminate during Operation Fénix. (Albert Grandolini Collection)

FAES soldiers in a church near Cerro Guazapa in 1986. (Albert Grandolini Collection)

Pantera Battalion, the Airborne Battalion, the GOEs, PRALs, artillery and cavalry units. This artillery support was carried out by three batteries of 105mm howitzers, one in San José Guayabal, the second on the Las Guaras de la Calle bridge which from San Martin led to Suchitoto and the third in Ingenio San Francisco near the Troncal del Norte. Around Cerro Guazapa, GNs and paratroopers patrolled the area while the Navy provided surveillance on Lake Suchitlan. About 6,000 soldiers were thus mobilised and began to comb a territory of 1,500 square kilometres to stay there as long as necessary, as announced by the head of the operation, Colonel Leopoldo Hernández.⁴⁸

The military operation began on 10 January 1986 with an intense and large-scale air attack with the participation of four Dragon Fly, six UH-1H helicopters, an O2 Skymaster reconnaissance aircraft, two Hughes-500 and an AC-47. After this initial bombardment, the

Army troops patrol area around Sesori town, San Miguel Department in 1986. (Albert Grandolini Collection)

BIRIs advanced towards Cerro de Guazapa from the Troncal del Norte Highway and San José Guayabal, while the Pantera Battalion was positioned along Calle Nueva to Suchitoto. In the lower area, a landing of airborne forces was carried out. The fighting began around 10:00 am in the vicinity of Loma Chata.

On the north side of the Cerro, facing the RN forces, led by Chano Guevara, the advance of the military was rapid, the fighting was very brief and had almost always resulted in the crushing of guerrilla units by the power of FAES land and air fire. The progression was more difficult on the southern slope, despite the fact that the territory on which the guerrillas were located, was narrow and theoretically surrounded. It was very difficult for the FAES to advance, as the rough terrain forced them to move over small distances where they were vulnerable to snipers equipped with Dragonóv rifles and also victims of mines laid by the guerrillas. Units of the X21 ERP Battalion, FAL Aguiñada Carranza Battalion and the FAR-LP thus managed to slow down the operations of the BIRI Belloso which succeeded in putting 70 rebels out of action in January 1986.[49] The guerrillas nevertheless, managed to hold their positions for six days. During the nights, 105mm batteries fired for several hours on different parts of the Cerro. About 10 days after the start of Operation Fénix, the FAES finally managed to control most of the villages.[50]

The FMLN responded to the FAES assault by dividing its units and reducing the number of its troops. On 16 January, the FPL and FAL commanders decided to break the encirclement in order to be able to evacuate their command posts, the FES, the wounded and also the units with the weakest combat capability, leaving only the combat units. Command posts were then set up on the outskirts of San Salvador or joined the San Salvador volcano.[51] For its part, the BCA leadership and part of its forces settled in Tenango, from where units were sent to Guazapa and then relieved periodically to return to rest.[52] In order to relieve the pressure exerted on the Cerro Guazapa, the FAL U-24 platoon received the mission to destroy the artillery pieces installed in San José de Guayabal. It went into action on the night of 13 January but was quickly spotted by sentries. RPG fire damaged one of the guns but the others remained intact while the FES were forced to withdraw.[53]

From February, in the northern part of the Cerro, platoons of 30 fighters were divided into units of 12 people including a radio operator and a nurse. They became self-sufficient in supply and able to move more nimbly among enemy patrols, harassing them with ambushes, mines, firing at their encampments, and while on the move. These actions were nevertheless made difficult due to the lack of ammunition and explosives.

The FAES carried out a tactical dispersion on the ground, dividing their battalions into patrols of up to 30 men, which combed each area, relying on their high firepower and good communication that allowed rapid cooperation between them. They carried out a meticulous raking, burnt the foliage, advanced through the fields and along the paths and roads, avoiding any routine in their movements and their camps. At night, some of them laid ambushes, others slept in different places on the mountain and to avoid guerrilla attacks, they changed places 2–4 times a night. Areas raked were usually raked again a few days later. Each patrol sought to collide with the guerrilla units in order to force them to fight frontally or to immobilise them. Then, with the support of other patrols, helicopter and air troops they quickly obtained numerical superiority to annihilate them.

In February, things hardly changed. Planes with loudspeakers flew over the places where the guerrillas were, calling on the fighters to surrender, saying that their lives would be spared. They also dropped thousands of leaflets where they offered money for each weapon delivered – the highest prices being for support weapons. On the southern slope of the Cerro, the BIRI Belloso was still pinned down but guerrilla supplies were running out as the area was left without a population, most civilians having been captured and evacuated by the FAES. In the last days of March, Operation Fénix entered its consolidation phase. The FAES reduced their numbers in the Cerro Guazapa now alternating a BIRI, either Belloso or Atlacatl, as well as two BIATs from the 1st Brigade and the DM-5, in order to maintain a constant presence. They were supported by patrols from the Pantera Battalion, the Navy, soldiers from El Caballito and El Roblar Bases and the GN. There were also 105mm batteries and 120mm mortars at Suchitoto, Colima Bridge and Las Guaras Bridge, as well as permanent air support.[54]

At the beginning of April, the FES carried out a coup de main against a FAES section on the southern slope of the Cerro. It was a minimal operation but the soldiers responded with 105mm howitzer fire before the arrival of the BIRI Atlacatl who engaged in combat against the FAL and the FARN for three days.[55] To definitively remove this threat, between 21 and 22 April, the FAES tried to reach the FMLN camps. The FARN and FAL forces resisted, forcing the soldiers to set fire to part of the vegetation – which at this season, was very dry – and to many trees in order to reduce the hiding places of the guerrillas and uncover the mines that they posed. During the night, about 200 FMLN fighters withdrew, but for six consecutive days there were still clashes between FAES patrols and the new guerrilla positions.[56]

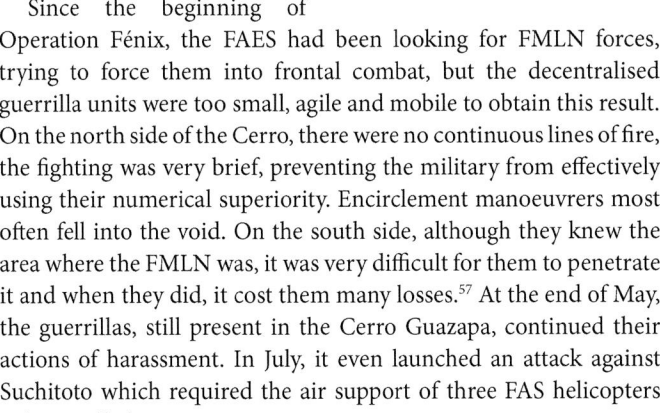
Browning M2 machine gun calibre 12.7mm as used by the FAES. (Albert Grandolini Collection)

Since the beginning of Operation Fénix, the FAES had been looking for FMLN forces, trying to force them into frontal combat, but the decentralised guerrilla units were too small, agile and mobile to obtain this result. On the north side of the Cerro, there were no continuous lines of fire, the fighting was very brief, preventing the military from effectively using their numerical superiority. Encirclement manoeuvrers most often fell into the void. On the south side, although they knew the area where the FMLN was, it was very difficult for them to penetrate it and when they did, it cost them many losses.[57] At the end of May, the guerrillas, still present in the Cerro Guazapa, continued their actions of harassment. In July, it even launched an attack against Suchitoto which required the air support of three FAS helicopters to be repelled.

For nearly 10 months, the guerrillas waged a war of attrition, avoiding unequal frontal combat to carry out night and day attacks, generalising the use of mines and carrying out a few raids with the participation of the FES. At the end of September, it even managed to unite its dispersed forces in the Modesto Ramírez Battalion Group, with a common staff. The RN provided about 75 combatants, the FPL a hundred, the PCS a smaller number.[58] This allowed it to increase its actions from October with the attacks carried out by regular units, which during the day, grouped into platoons of 30 fighters, remained dislocated on the ground to concentrate at night in columns of 60–90 guerrillas and performed actions alone or in combination with FES. If Operation Fénix almost succeeded in driving the FMLN forces out of Cerro Guazapa, the guerrillas never abandoned the area and at the end of 1988, they even succeeded in driving the soldiers out of El Roblar hill.[59]

To relieve pressure on the Guazapa region, the FMLN launched operations in other regions. The most important took place in the San Miguel department, when the FMLN attacked the 3rd Infantry Brigades barracks on 19 June, taking care to avoid having the BIRI Arce present in the garrison that day. The FES broke into the barracks while the PRTC and ERP support groups settled around the garrison and opened fire, RPG gunners aiming at the machine gun towers. Inside, the FES went into action and attacked the Ponce and Leon Battalions barracks. Another FES group destroyed three helicopters which were in the garrison and killed their crews. A last team was in charge of killing the American advisers present but the latter fled from their dormitories, in their underwear, through a tunnel. Outside the base, the battle raged all night. The dormitories of the Ponce and Léon Battalions barracks were completely destroyed, dozens of soldiers were killed while the FES lost about five men.[60] An AC-47 came to support the defenders, but the guerrillas had already entered the El Paraiso base. Finally, the garrison was rescued by BIRI Arce units accompanied by a Mazinger armoured vehicle.[61]

Despite these FMLN operations and the intensity of the fighting in the Cerro Guazapa, the FAES had the means to carry out simultaneous offensives in different regions. In May, they launched Operation Chávez Carreño in the Chalatenango department, where they encountered difficulties against FPL forces that had adapted to its counter-insurgency strategy. During the remainder of 1986, three operations were also launched in the north of Morazan department and in the Usulutan and San Vicente departments in order to reduce the *retaguardias* of the FMLN in the central and coastal strip of El Salvador.

Operation Fénix, like those that followed during 1986, was accompanied by the implementation of the civic action programme Unidos Para Reconstruir (United to Rebuild or UPR) which was understood throughout the territory. Aware of the objective behind the UPR, to rebuild a local government framework in its *retaguardias*, the guerrillas responded by intensifying their campaign of terror against the mayors who formed the local base of this framework. Nevertheless, the government, grappling with a serious economic crisis, could not support costly programmes despite American aid. In October 1986, when San Salvador was rocked by an earthquake that caused enormous damage, the already thin funds intended for the UPR were redirected to disaster relief and reconstruction. Operation Phoenix therefore ended with the failure of the Low Intensity War strategy, allowing the FMLN, two years later, to move to a higher level of the revolutionary war process.

4
THE STRATEGIC BALANCE 1987–1988.

The failure of Operation Fénix demonstrated the limits of the Low Intensity War strategy in a country on the verge of economic collapse, despite the importance of American financial aid. However, this observation did not change the military situation. The superiority acquired by the FAES remained intact, forcing the FMLN to maintain its strategy of dispersing its forces, spectacular raids and economic sabotage. The strategic balance which appeared in 1984 led to an impasse, no side having the means to defeat the other, a situation which led to the continuation of a war which seemed hopeless, particularly in the eyes of the civilian population who were paying the hard price and which was increasingly responsive to calls to begin peace negotiations.

The FMLN on the defensive 1987–1988

1987 was a difficult year for Duarte's government. The earthquake that hit San Salvador at the end of 1986 highlighted its incompetence while the economic malaise increased the discontent of the population. On 19 January 1987, big business and the Salvadoran Right, led by ARENA, called a business strike against the government's decision to establish a new 'tax for defence of national sovereignty'. The strike succeeded in paralysing the country while the Supreme Court of Justice declared the 'war tax' unconstitutional. It was a political defeat for Duarte, while on the Left, the UNTS and the rest of the social movement succeeded in bringing together more than 70,000 people in San Salvador during the May Day demonstrations. Yet, despite the growing fragility of the Duarte government, on 5 January 1987, US Secretary of State George Shultz announced that El Salvador would receive $319 million in military aid and $121 million in civilian aid.

The continuation of this American support for Duarte rested in large part on the positive evolution of the military conflict at a time when the FAES sought to dismantle the FMLN *retaguardias* in the centre of the country. The next objective was the destruction of the *retaguardias* in Morazan and Chalatenango departments in 1987 and 1988 with the hope of ending the war in 1988. These optimistic prospects seemed realistic since, on the military level, the supremacy of the FAS, the growth of FAES and their ability to operate for longer periods reduced the effectiveness of the FMLN whose decline in large-scale operations was compensated only by the spectacular actions of the FES and urban commandos and whose forces continued to decrease.

While in 1983 the guerrillas numbered, according to estimates, around 10,000 combatants, this figure fell to around 7,000 in 1985 after the losses and desertions that marked the period 1984–1985.[1] The policy of forced recruitment, a practice that greatly harmed the popularity of the FMLN in the countryside, was proving ineffective. The peasants preferred to flee and the numbers of the guerrillas continued to decline, reaching around 4,000 combatants at the end of 1987. At the same time, FAES losses continued to decrease, dropping from 865 dead in 1985 to 756 in 1986, 826 in 1987 and 783 in 1988. The soldiers regained the initiative and were more aggressive in areas dominated by the FMLN. In 1988, guerrilla attacks and ambushes against the FAES fell by 12 percent and 14 percent compared to 1987, while sabotage increased by 50 percent.[2] It seemed obvious that it was only a matter of time before the FAES would definitely prevail over a guerrilla in decline.

A family collect the body of their daughter, killed during an air strike by the Salvadorean Air Force outside the town of Carolina in northern Morazan department. (Albert Grandolini Collection)

The US-made M60 machine gun calibre 7.62mm was used by each side during the civil war, here in the hands of an FAES soldier. (Albert Grandolini Collection)

In reality, the FMLN strategy of dispersing its forces and the means taken against air attacks prevented the FAES from finding concentrated targets to attack. If the guerrillas no longer had the same strength as before 1984, they nevertheless remained more powerful than the American and Salvadoran leaders believed. Moreover, at the end of 1986, the FMLN CG considered that the conditions were met to go on the offensive again. On the political and social level, the objective was to provoke the radicalisation of the population in order to isolate and weaken the government. Then, when the situation was favourable, the activity of the FMLN had to culminate in a military offensive joined to a general strike and the armed insurrection in the cities, in a pattern which reproduced that of the January 1981 offensive.[3] In this perspective, from the end of 1987, the guerrillas began a phase of concentration and training of their forces for the preparation of the future strategic offensive.

The FMLN remained no less active militarily and was once again targeting the El Paraiso Military Base in the Chalatenango department. Since it was attacked at the end of 1983, this base had seen its defences reinforced, in particular with the installation of outposts on the heights which surrounded it. The FMLN nevertheless had a spy within it, an artillery sergeant who provided it with a lot of information. Despite this, in early 1986, a commando from the FES F-30 unit was captured during a reconnaissance mission of the base, the spy sergeant arrested and the security of El Paraiso tightened. Shortly afterwards, the FPL infiltrated new sympathisers inside the base and prepared a new attack whose plans were carried out in February 1987. As it appeared too dangerous to concentrate regular forces to carry out this attack, it was entrusted to the FES whose mission was to enter the base and cause as much destruction as possible before leaving.

The FES crossed the defensive perimeter with three groups composed of 10 guerrillas on the night of 30–31 March and attacked at 2 a.m. El Paraiso was then full of soldiers, many returning from a military operation – about 2,000 men. RPG rockets, machine guns and mortars fired from outside the base against the guard towers while inside FES teams launched explosives into each building or bunker. In total, between 30 and 40 charges were launched in order to annihilate the soldiers in the buildings. Nevertheless, some soldiers survived, notably First Sergeant Gregory Fronius, an American special forces adviser.

When the FES attacked, Salvadoran officers left their troops in a panic, choosing to flee. Fronius on his side, came out of his defensive position and began to gather the soldiers present. He then tried to do what many other special forces members had done before him and he mounted an effective counter-attack. This was when he confronted the guerrillas who shot and killed him. Fronius would later receive the Purple Heart posthumously.[4]

The officers of the base finally managed to regroup soldiers and organised a defence. Around 5:30 a.m. the FES retreated to the hills surrounding El Paraiso while combat helicopters fired on their positions. The entire base was on fire and almost all vital structures were destroyed or badly damaged.[5] During the attack, in addition to Fronius, the guerrillas also killed 79 Salvadoran soldiers. In May 1987, another military base in the Morazan department was attacked by guerrillas.

Nevertheless, despite successes such as the destruction of the El Paraiso base, the weakness of the FMLN was visible in April 1987, during the Easter weekend when it threatened to paralyse all road traffic in the country. A squadron of the Cavalry Regiment with Cashuat armoured vehicles, based on armoured and armed 100 Dodge three quarter-ton diesel trucks, left San Salvador, protecting a convoy of buses and civilian vehicles, for San Miguel. Infantry units patrolled along the road while helicopters flew over the area to detect possible ambushes. The convoy encountered no obstacles and returned to the capital without problems.[6]

In October or November 1987, the guerrillas launched raids from their stronghold in the Morazan department, crossing the Rio Torola to strike FAES positions on Osicala, Cacaopera and

The bodies of two people killed during a military operation in the northern department of Cabañas lie in a field. (Albert Grandolini Collection)

Altos del Aguacate hills, before returning to its bases in El Mozote, Joateca and on the Volcancillo hill. The FAES commandos were then responsible for setting up ambushes along the paths taken by the guerrillas, but one of these teams was surprised by an FMLN patrol near Volcancillo and a short fight ensued. Finally the commandos were ordered to join the rest of their unit eight kilometres to the south-west. Once reunited, the commandos set up camp near Cerro Pando and lighted fires to be spotted. This was a trap since as soon as night had fallen, the soldiers moved two kilometres further west to Villa El Rosario.

As expected, the guerrillas launched an attack on Cerro Pando with large forces that encountered no adversary. The commandos then called on the FAS, which sent an AC-47 to strafe the guerrilla forces.[7] The various raids carried out by the FMLN in 1987, either against El Paraiso or in the Morazan department, in addition to their possible media repercussions, aimed to preserve the *retaguardias* of the north of the country where the future strategic offensive was beginning to be prepared.

The 1988 fights

At the end of 1987, in accordance with the instructions of the FMLN leadership, the FAPL on the Chalatenango department began to concentrate their units with the objective of carrying out major attacks in order to test the troops and cadres for a future offensive. By doing this, they made themselves more visible and more vulnerable as the BIRI Atlacatl operated in Chalatenango, sometimes supported by paratroopers, to strike command centres and guerrilla concentrations.

One of these operations, called Halcon 2-88, began on 18 January 1988 when a paratroopers squadron landed in Cerro El Sauce southwest of Santa Rosa Guachipilin in the Santa Ana department. Another landing took place in Cerro Duraznillo on 21 January, north-west of Agua Caliente in Chalatenango. Two hours later, fighting broke out against the FAPL. From Santa Ana, 40 paratroopers embarked in five UH-1H to come and support them. At the end of the operation,

Trained by the US Special Forces, the BIRI Atlacatl was the oldest counter-insurgency unit of the FAES and one of the most effective. (Albert Grandolini Collection)

FAES special forces struck a major blow to FMLN suggesting the Salvadoran conflict could be resolved with military victory. (Albert Grandolini Collection)

which carried out search and destruction operations in the areas of Concepcion Quezaltepeque, La Laguna, El Carrizal and Comalapa in the Chalatenango department. For fear of the rebels who were in the Cerro El Volcancillo, the paratroopers, reinforced by the PH Libertadores Battalion, were transported by truck from Chalatenango to Concepcion Quezaltepeque then Comalapa. The progression north to La Laguna was on foot. In this locality, the paratroopers occupied defensive positions. The 1st squadron was at La Cuchilla to the north-east, the 4th between Cerro Cuatro Pinos and San José township to the north, and the 5th between Loma Las Delicias and Aldea Vieja. These squadrons sent patrols to Petapas, Petapitas, Potrerios, Crujiletas and El Carrizal. PH agents from the Libertadores Battalion covered La Laguna on their side, while the 1st Squadron then moved south to del Carrizal. The paratroopers set up ambushes on the roads that led to the positions they were defending.

The Direccion Nacional de Inteligencia (National Intelligence Directorate or DNI), with a listening post in La Laguna, identified the presence of three FAPL columns each with 150–200 men in the areas where the paratroopers were deployed. Added to this was a platoon of 20 men from the FES which was near the Honduran border in the north of Carrizal, as well as a unit of J-28,[8] directed by Amadeo Martinez Menjivar (Tino). The latter began to carry out reconnaissance of the positions of the soldiers, in particular those of the PH and the Cobra Battalion in the Cerro Las Delicias.

In the early hours of 18 February, the FES infiltrated PH positions in La Laguna and planted explosive charges on the barracks that housed the command post. Other guerrilla forces reached the entrance of the locality while the J-28s were ready to attack the command post of the paratroopers. The guerrillas went on the attack, the barracks held by the PHs were taken while the fighting against the paratroopers was violent. At Loma Las Delicias, the J-28s used M-60 machine guns, Law anti-tank rockets, and the new RPG-7s. They seized part of the positions of the paratroopers who only controlled a small elevation. The latter launched a counter-attack and overwhelmed the guerrilla positions. Eventually, the J-28s began to withdraw towards La Montañosa.

The FAS could not support the soldiers because of the weather conditions. The guerrillas then continued to approach more and more lines of the paratroopers and sometimes seemed on the point of overwhelming them. To break out of this situation, forces from the 4th Squadron moved north and north-east of La Laguna to attack the FAPL rear, while units from the 5th Squadron executed a double envelopment of the guerrilla lines of attack. This manoeuvrer disorganised the latter who finally preferred to withdraw. The paratroopers command drew the conclusion from this operation, that military actions were not enough to defeat the guerrillas and recommended increasing civic actions in the region to obtain the

the latter destroyed a guerrilla camp from which 15 fighters were killed. In the FAS ranks, a pilot was injured and three planes were hit by enemy fire.

On 13 February 1988, the Airborne Battalion was placed under the command of the 4th Infantry Brigade to relieve the Cobra Battalion

A gunner of an FAS UH-1 helicopter seen while underway over the Rio Lempa. (Albert Grandolini Collection)

The FMLN militias were made up of civilians who would protect the local population and took part in local actions. They were not full-time fighters and continued their professional activities the rest of the time (Albert Grandolini Collection)

had to return to Ilopango for repairs. On the ground, the paratroopers had to repel the attacks of the guerrillas, then fought their way between the minefields and the actions of harassment, to finally reach Suchitoto while the guerrillas withdrew.[10]

Despite the resumption of FMLN large-scale operations, the FAES, as in previous years, tried to expel the guerrillas from their *retaguardias*. In June 1988, they continued their actions in the Chalatenango department. Thus, the BIRI Atlacatl was responsible for occupying the small town of Las Vueltas. The BIRI commando company received the mission to reach Cerro La Laguna, then the south of Las Vueltas, in order to organise an ambush. Meanwhile, BIRI units were advancing from the north and south-east towards Las Vueltas, whilst others remained in the La Laguna sector. During their night march, the commandos were discovered and attacked by the guerrillas. They asked for the support of the FAS. The AC-47s, thanks to night vision devices, spotted the FAPL positions they were attacking. The fighting lasted 14 hours and only the support of helicopters and AC-47s prevented the commandos from being overwhelmed. The fighting stopped after three days and the commandos managed to enter Las Vueltas.[11]

To relieve the pressure the FAES were placing on the FMLN *retaguardias* in the Chalatenango department, on 22 September 1988, the ERP attacked FAES positions at Altos del Aguacate, Corinto and Morazan defended by the Morazan Battalion. Again, only the intervention of armed helicopters and the landing of GOE units prevented the Battalion from being defeated. It nevertheless had 15 dead and 38 wounded while the ERP counted 11 dead.[12]

Despite these actions, the FAES continued to harass the *retaguardias* during the end of 1988. In September, during Operation Perquin I, Commandos Domingo Monterrosa of the 3rd Infantry Brigade, had to penetrate the FMLN *retaguardias* in the Morazan department to conduct reconnaissance, set up ambushes and strike at the FMLN in the territory between Perquin and Honduras. The commandos were divided into three patrols armed with M-60 machine guns, M-16 rifles, M-203 grenade launchers and LAW anti-

support of the population, in particular by organising health and telephone services in order to thwart the FMLN influence.[9]

In the winter of 1988, the FPL returned to major operations with a full-scale attack on the town of Suchitoto, which lay on the southern shore of Lake Suchitlan. If the city was defended by the Pantera Battalion formed by members of the PN, the objective of the guerrillas was not to seize it but to inflict losses on the reinforcements which would be sent to defend it. The city was attacked by large forces causing the Pantera Battalion commander to call reinforcements to prevent the city from falling. The Airborne Battalion left Ilopango Air Base by helicopter with the objective of landing south of Suchitoto to hit the guerrillas. When the helicopters tried to land, they came under heavy fire. The same misfortune happened to them when they tried to land on other areas. A dozen affected helicopters

A close-up view of an FAS UH-1H in the process of delivering supplies to forward-deployed troops. (Albert Grandolini Collection)

tank rockets. They were flown to the border with Honduras and had to progress south towards Perquin. Even if they only moved at night, they were quickly spotted and harassed by FMLN militia units. A commando patrol set up defensive positions on Cerro Gigante but quickly found itself surrounded.

Due to the weather, the FAS could not come to support them and the only help available was that of the two other patrols which were in the region but which were also quickly attacked by guerrilla squads. One of them managed to reach the Llano del Muerto, a flat plain near Perquin and received supplies by helicopter. It then moved to Cerro La Crucita, crossed the Rio Negro and reached Ojo de Agua. It was there it had to face a violent attack from the guerrillas which it managed to repel.

The next day, this patrol joined the village of El Carrizal and found the third patrol. The latter, which was installed on a hill, attacked and surrounded them. The patrol coming from Ojo de Agua came to its aid. The fighting was violent but the guerrillas ended up withdrawing. The next day, the weather being better, the encircled patrol on Cerro Gigante, was evacuated by UH-1 helicopters supported by A-37 Dragonflies. Around the El Carrizal hill, two A-37 bombarded the positions of the guerrillas while helicopters evacuated soldiers. The others took advantage of the bombardment to slip between the positions of the FMLN and continued their initial mission.[13]

At the end of 1988, the DNI learnt that an FAPL regional leaders meeting was being held in Cerro El Caballete, near San José Las Flores in the Chalatenango department. The FAES decided to organise an operation led by the 2nd Airborne Squadron. The latter was divided into two groups, one landed in the north-west of Flores and the other in the south-west. During the night, they had to gather and prepare an assault against the FAPL meeting. However, the lack of coordination prevented the success of this plan.

The paratroopers who landed near El Caballete, indeed faced the guerrillas near Las Flores. The FAS then had to intervene with A-37s and UH-1Ms, while the FAPL reinforced themselves, aware that the paratroopers, divided into two groups, were more vulnerable. The fighting lasted 11 hours and with the help of the FAS, the paratroopers held firm. The two groups finally managed to reunite and left the area under cover of night.[14] The guerrillas demonstrated once again that they were still a formidable adversary. This resistance sometimes pushed the FAES to reconnect with the practice of reprisals against the civilian population. Thus, on 21 September 1988, a dozen villagers from the hamlet of San Sebastian in the department of San Vicente, were massacred by the troops of the 5th Infantry Brigade.[15]

The FAES strategy nevertheless, proved to be effective and greatly reduced the operational capacities of the FMLN. Between 1986 and 1988, the FAL lost nearly half of their fighters, a large number during Operation Fénix. During this operation, the support bases of the RN in the Cerro Guazapa were destroyed, which led to the loss of 10–13 percent of the fighters of this organisation, between 1986 and 1988.

The PRTC was also hard hit by the FAES operations in its Cerros de San Pedro base and also by the destruction of these urban commandos and the loss of infrastructures in the Guazapa region. From 1985 to 1987, it lost 30–40 percent of these fighters, which forced them to evacuate what remained of their forces to Cerro Guazapa at the beginning of 1987. Only the ERP and the FPL, the two most important organisations, suffered less from the blows of the FAES and gathered, at the end of 1988, two-thirds of the FMLN combatants.[16] The unequal balance of power that had settled in El Salvador did not favour the search for dialogue. The FAES believed that they could defeat the guerrillas in the medium or short-term, while the FMLN knew that in a weak position, negotiation would mean nothing less than surrender.

Negotiations attempts

Since the start of the civil war, various international actors had sought to find ways to end the conflict in El Salvador. A few weeks after the 10 January 1981 offensive, the Office for Central America and the Caribbean of the Socialist International (SI) met in Panama, under the auspices of General Omar Torrijos, and invited a delegation from the FMLN. Villalobos, Fermán Cienfuegos and Ana Guadalupe

A patrol of government soldiers, supported by a M38A2 jeep with a pintle-mounted Browning M2 machine gun. (Albert Grandolini Collection)

Martinez proposed mediation and the search for a political solution to the conflict. The meeting was attended, at the request of Willy Brandt, by a leader of the German Social Democratic Party, Hans Wishniewsky.[17] From Panama, the latter went to Washington to meet State Department officials, then on to San Salvador to see Duarte. The mediation proposals were nevertheless, rejected everywhere, including within the FMLN where Carpio was against it, believing that the guerrillas had to first develop and strengthen before entering the political game.[18]

A new mediation effort was made in May, on the initiative of the Canadian Edward Broadbent, vice president of the SI, who had good relations with the Mexican and US governments. Again, Duarte and the State Department rejected this proposal, as they considered the defeat of the FMLN was only a matter of months and that any attempt at dialogue would hinder this objective. In June 1981, a new approach to talks was made by European parliamentarians worried about the possibility of direct American military intervention. When they met Duarte, he asked them to demand that the FMLN first lay down their arms.[19]

The JRG's refusal to open negotiations led the SI to support the FMLN, especially since the MNR, a member of the FDR, belonged to the SI and its leader, Guillermo Ungo, enjoyed the respect of the social democrats of the whole world. It was in this context that the FDR conducted negotiations with the Mexican and French governments during the summer of 1981, which resulted in the Franco-Mexican declaration of 28 August, which granted the FMLN the status of a belligerent.[20] This declaration was important since it gave a beginning of international recognition to the FMLN but also an implicit sovereignty on the territories which it controlled and which France and Mexico wanted to protect from a direct intervention of the United States.[21] The statement received support from many SI and Left parties.

Following this diplomatic success, FMLN-FDR delegations settled in 15 countries, alongside those of the legal government.[22] In reaction, Rafael Caldera, Social-Christian president of Venezuela supported Duarte and undertook an international tour to put an end to the FDR diplomatic offensive. Caldera achieved some success in having nine Latin American governments and so approved, at the beginning of December, the Caracas declaration, which harshly criticised the Franco-Mexican declaration.[23]

In October 1984, President Duarte, at the request of Archbishop Romero's successor, Arturo Rivera y Damas, took a bold first step by deciding to hold talks with the FMLN. This was the first time that the government had seriously offered to engage in dialogue. The meeting took place on 16 October 1984 in the La Palma village. The hope for peace provoked a lot of enthusiasm among the population but the discussions did not yield any tangible results.[24]

In November 1984, FMLN representatives and the Salvadoran government again met in Ayagualo. While in La Palma, Duarte promised to discuss measures to 'humanise the armed conflict', under pressure from the FAES and the Reagan Administration, he backtracked and demanded that the FMLN lay down their arms, accept an amnesty General and take part in elections. The guerrillas rejected these proposals and demanded a power-sharing agreement, a gradual de-escalation of the fighting, followed by a ceasefire, then the formation of a new government, the drafting of a new Constitution and a FAES reorganisation, before the holding of elections.[25] The talks were a failure.

While the US government still wanted a military victory in El Salvador, regional countries, Venezuela, Panama, Colombia and Mexico, sought to end the various conflicts ravaging Central America. Their efforts led to the Contadora Accords, a plan to demilitarise the region, which were nevertheless, scuppered by the White House, which did not want peaceful coexistence with the Sandinistas. Despite the American veto, the peace process resumed its march, under the aegis of the President of Costa Rica, Oscar Arias, who sought to promote the democratisation of the region through electoral processes and also through the end of external support for the different belligerents.

On 24 and 25 May 1986, the presidents of Guatemala, El Salvador, Honduras, Nicaragua and Costa Rica, meeting in Esquipulas, Guatemala, jointly signed a declaration that launched a peace process. They announced the formalisation of the meetings of Central American presidents as the main forum to analyse and seek solutions to problems related to peace and development in the region. They held the desire to reaffirm democracy as the only process, allowing each person to determine freely and without foreign country interference, its economic, political and social situation. Although military issues and regional conflicts, such as the Salvadoran Civil War, were not addressed, Esquipulas I was the first political agreement of Central American countries in which the search for peace was the central element.

In February 1987, Arias presented a new plan which foresaw a series of steps leading to regional ceasefires and the demobilisation of the armed forces.[26] This plan resulted, after intense negotiations, in the elaboration of the document 'Procedure to establish a firm and lasting peace in Central America', better known as Esquipulas II, which was signed on 7 August 1987 by Central American presidents.

Guerrillas from the FPL during a rally with a banner that read FMLN. (Albert Grandolini Collection)

One of the missions of the FAS helicopters was the supply of the troops which operated in the combat areas. This one was photographed only seconds short of landing with a load of bagged food. (Albert Grandolini Collection)

It called on governments of countries in conflict to initiate dialogue with all unarmed, internal political opposition groups. It also asked that the international community not provide any form of support or solidarity to insurgent movements. The novelty of this plan was that it wanted to include the regional insurgents in the political processes through democratic elections supervised by international actors. In addition, it defined a timetable for the execution of the agreements.[27]

The Reagan Administration first tried to sabotage the Esquipulas peace process and less than a month after it was signed, announced aid to the Nicaraguan Contras. However, this time, the rejection of regional peace efforts was met with opposition from the US Congress, opposed to the continuation of Reagan's proxy war against Nicaragua. Furthermore, President Arias refused to be intimidated by Reagan's threats and continued to plead for dialogue and peace. In El Salvador, despite his mistrust, Duarte ended up signing the Esquipulas II agreement. He did so because of his desire to end the conflict and also because the he recognised the legitimacy of the governments in place and did not give any formal status to guerrilla organisations.[28]

For its part, the FMLN showed itself to be very cautious in the face of the solutions advocated by Esquipulas II, which resulted in a change in Nicaragua's attitude towards them. Indeed, if the Sandinistas continued to support it with military and logistical aid, their acceptance of Esquipulas II obliged them to transform this hitherto official support, into a more hidden practice. On the other hand, the Esquipulas II agreements equated the FMLN and the Nicaraguan Contra with insurgent and illegitimate forces, a parallel that the Salvadoran guerrillas could not accept politically.[29]

Despite these mistrusts, the FMLN had been pursuing episodic talks which, since 1984, had remained fruitless, in particular because each side gave this discontinuous dialogue a secondary role in favour of victory on the battlefield. On 26 October 1987, when the human rights defender, Herber Ernesto Anaya Sanabria, was assassinated near his home, his murder caused great protests for four days in San Salvador and other cities. The Federal Republic of Germany and France asked Duarte to investigate the crime. For its part, on 29 October, the FMLN announced, in protest, the temporary suspension of the dialogue and accused government agents of being responsible for the murder.[30]

Nevertheless, Esquipulas II, by proclaiming democracy as a political model for resolving disputes and giving space to the various actors in the conflict regardless of their ideological position, pushed the main Salvadoran political forces to consider participating in the peace process to protect their interests and seek peaceful means to end the conflict. In the second half of November 1987, the FDR main leaders, Guillermo Manuel Ungo and Rubén Zamora, returned to El Salvador and founded the Democratic Convergence, an alliance of three parties from the centre and the Left in order to participate in the elections of March 1989.[31]

In February 1988, American diplomats clearly perceived a change within the Salvadoran opposition and saw in the decision of the FDR leaders, the sign that the FMLN was beginning to recognise that it could not win militarily and a political solution was the only way to achieve its goals. This evolution was consistent with that of American policy towards Central America. At the end of 1988, George Bush became President of the United States. Rather than seeking a military and political victory in El Salvador, the new administration wanted above all to end the conflict in the best possible conditions. For this, it had different advantages.

The success of the 1982 and 1984 elections ensured legitimacy and political stability for the Salvadoran government, whilst the collapse of the Soviet bloc considerably reduced anti-communism as a factor influencing American policy. Freed from the supposed threat of Moscow and Havana, the Bush Administration was now pursuing a more flexible approach to the conflict that was no longer tied to the Cold War context. The US began to subordinate the continuation of their aids to the will of Duarte to carry out serious negotiations with the FMLN.[32] It was without counting on the will of the latter to reverse the balance of power by a new offensive which it hoped would be decisive in its long march towards power.

The FMLN rearmament

Despite the decline of its forces, between the end of June and the beginning of July 1987, the FMLN CG decided to enter a more active phase in the preparation of its future offensive. It first made the decision to set up the command post of this offensive outside the country but very close to the borders. This was in order to lead the military, political and social forces in a concentrated, direct and unique manner, contrary to what had happened in January 1981. Above all, it decided to increase the number of guerrilla units and their armament, particularly by equipping them with automatic rifles and artillery, as well as weapons capable of neutralising FAS air hegemony.

The FMLN still had various sources of supply for its armament, in particular on the arms markets of Western Europe and Florida, on the expensive black markets of Central America or thanks to the weapons captured or bought from the FAES. The rebels apparently had enough funds from 'war taxes' and collections in Western Europe and the United States, which were said to represent 80 percent of the FMLN budget, to be able to afford purchases through these networks.[33]

Nevertheless, the bulk of guerrilla weaponry came from countries in the socialist bloc, including North Korea, East Germany and Cuba. The Defence Under-secretary Fred Ikle, estimated that half of the guerrillas' arms and a fifth of their ammunition was captured from Salvadoran troops and that the US-made M-16, had become the FMLN's standard weapon.[34] This last remark, if it was true for the first years of the conflict, was no longer so from 1988 onwards when the FMLN received mainly Soviet-made weapons, AK-47 rifles, Dragunov sniper rifles, RPK and PKM machine guns, RPG-18 and RPG-7 individual anti-tank weapons.[35]

These weapons entered El Salvador in different ways. Some would have arrived by air or land from the southern United States and via private farms in northern Costa Rica. During 1989, several shipments of weapons were thus discovered, one in a van loaded with weapons, largely of Soviet manufacture, intercepted in Honduras in mid-October and others, in two light aircraft coming from Nicaragua in November.[36] The Gulf of Fonseca was also widely used for the maritime transfer of weapons aboard *pangas* or long boats that travelled at night and were not detected by maritime radars. They disembarked on the beach at the edge of the coast of the

This photo shows the diversity of guerrilla weaponry; the young boy with his US M-16 rifle and his neighbour with a Soviet AKM-series assault rifle and an RPG-2. (Albert Grandolini Collection)

Jucuaran mountain, where their journey began along the internal logistics corridor of the guerrillas to the *retaguardias*.

At the beginning of 1989, the FMLN remained well established in the country, particularly in the Chalatenango and Morazan departments. In the centre of El Salvador, around the main roads, the Pan-American and Litoral Highways, its situation was more precarious, since the FAES tried to recover and defend the economic zones of this central band. Therefore, the Cerro Guazapa, close to the capital, was the last dangerous *retaguardia* for the Salvadoran power and it was from this latent threat that the strategic surprise would come. The evolution of the war in the west was still unfavourable to the guerrillas. The Sonsonate, Santa Ana and Ahuachapán departments had been controlled by the FAES since 1981, with the exception of the rear flank of the Chalatenango department, while the north-eastern area of the country was lost to the military.

While the Salvadoran and American authorities convinced themselves that the FMLN was on the verge of being defeated, Villalobos, the ERP leader, considered at the end of 1988, that the time had come to accelerate the preparation of the strategic counter-offensive. This decision signalled both the confidence that the FMLN maintained in its operational capacities and also the failure of counter-insurgency strategies.

5

1989 – THE DECISIVE YEAR

If in 1989, the eyes of the whole world were fixed on the Orient in full transformation, the Western hemisphere was not spared the march of history, especially in Central America. Nicaragua was well on the way to peace, while the situation was changing in El Salvador. The largely discredited Duarte presidency ended as the FMLN military activity continued to decline, suggesting that its defeat was only a matter of time. This certainty, which was partly based on illusions, was shattered before the end of the year.

The end of the Duarte presidency

Since 1984, American aid to the FAES had been the main factor that had prevented the FMLN from launching large-scale offensives threatening the existence of the government. At the beginning of 1989, American leaders believed that this trend was not reversible and had to lead to a military victory against the guerrillas. Nevertheless, certain elements worried the Bush Administration such as the renewed activity of the Death Squads, the continuation of the guerrillas actions and the FMLN propaganda as the 1989 presidential elections approached and the Duarte regime sunk into unpopularity.

The assessment of the Duarte presidency was not, however, totally negative. After the failure of the UPR civic action programme, the latter did not completely abandon this aspect of the counter-insurgency war and even sought to improve its implementation. The result was the Municipios en Acción (Municipalities in Action or MEA) programme, which began in 1988. The programme provided US funding to Salvadoran mayors to carry out development projects. Its novelty was in the fact that the population decided on the use of these funds during public meetings organised by the municipalities. This mechanism should make it possible to eradicate corruption and ensure that the beneficiaries received a major part of the funding. Unlike other civic action programmes, the MEA was considered a success and continued until the end of the war, increasing the government's presence in the countryside and the support of the population.[1]

The MEA successes could not, however, erase the poor results of the Salvadoran economy, the fruits of the war which continued its destructive work. This situation was aggravated by Duarte's American advisers who pushed him to adopt austerity measures. These ended up being harmful while the various reforms implemented to stabilise the economic and political system and to attack the root causes of the conflict failed, in part because of elite intransigence.[2] While unemployment continued to rise, reaching 50 percent of the active population in 1986, GDP grew on average by less than one percent between 1984 and 1989. In 1988, it remained 6.5 percent lower than its 1980 level. During this same period, GDP per capita fall by 16 percent compared to 1980, agricultural production collapsed by 32 percent and food production per capita was at 85 percent of its level from 1980.[3] This situation led to the rise of poverty in the population and in 1989, about 10 percent lived in squalid squatter camps.

The growing poverty stimulated popular protest. Already, in 1984, a series of strikes had begun against the wage freeze and the loss of purchasing power, which lasted until 1986. In this renewed social protest, the FMLN saw an opportunity to radicalise the population, which, duly guided by them, could result in an insurrection, supported by a nationwide guerrilla military offensive.[4]

However, a few months before the presidential elections, on 23 January 1989, the FMLN proposed new peace talks to the Salvadoran government and the Bush Administration. It indeed wanted to use the presidential elections as a 'step towards peace'. It announced that it recognised the validity and legitimacy of the next election and its willingness to participate in it, but asked that it be delayed by six months, to have time to prepare and to present itself as a viable party.[5] Salvadoran military and government officials believed this was purely a ploy to buy itself more time to rearm and prepare for future military campaigns.

In fact, this proposal demonstrated that the end of the Cold War was a blow for the FMLN. It found itself in a new environment which, combined with the difficulties of the Sandinistas in Nicaragua, favoured within it the supporters of negotiations. These people also believed in the FMLN electoral potential.[6] Through this approach, the FMLN aimed to weaken support for the government in the country and abroad, while strengthening its own legitimacy. Its ultimate goal was to obtain a power-sharing agreement that would allow it to be part of the government.

One from a battery of Yugoslav-made, Zastava M55 anti-aircraft automatic guns (also designated '20/3-mm-M55'), deployed by the FAS for the defence of Ilopango AB. (Albert Grandolini Collection)

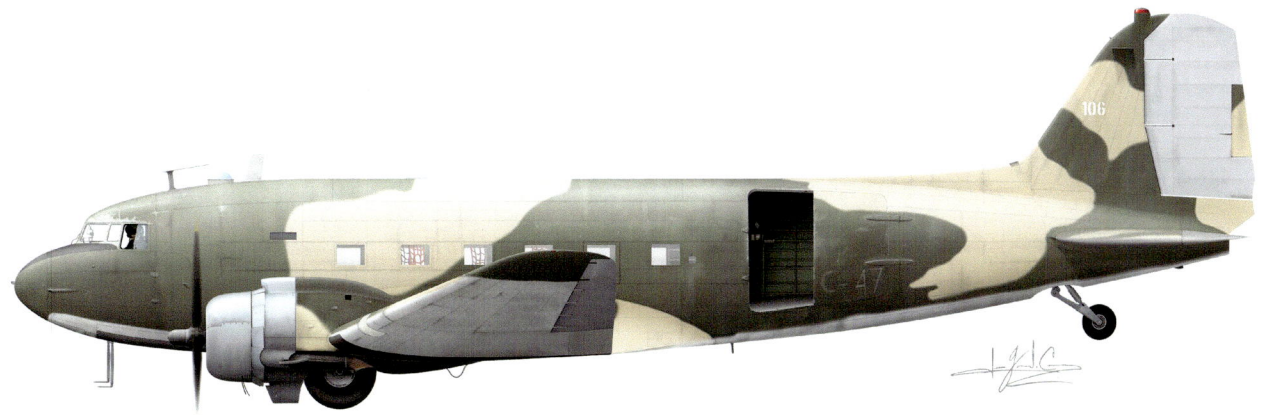

One of oldest aircraft of the 1980s operated by the FAS during the war in El Salvador, was this Douglas C-47A-1DK Dakota (colloquially known as 'Fantasma' within the FAS personnel). Its original construction number was 11867 and US Air Force serial 42-92104. El Salvador received it in September 1967 and it served with the Escuadrón de Transporte, FAS, throughout its career. It is shown as around 1989, in a disruptive camouflage pattern of tan and olive drab on top surfaces and sides and (quite worn out) light aircraft grey on undersides. Other insignia was limited to the serial number 106 on the fin. (Artwork by Luca Canossa)

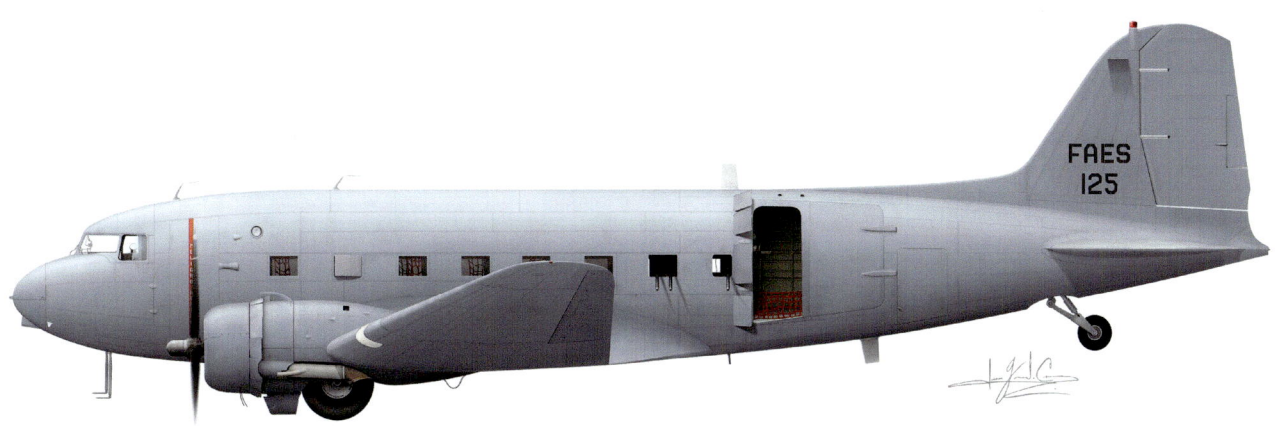

By 1989, most other Dakotas of the FAS were re-equipped as gunships, including the installation of three 12.7mm machine guns in two of the port-side-windows. This was valid for this C-47A-1DK: construction number 13364, US Air Force serial 43-93451, which received the FAS serial number 125. The aircraft was painted in light gunship grey overall. On 4 December 1990, this Fantasma was shot down by an insurgent-operated SA-7 MANPAD while over La Laguna, in Chalatenago. The crew – including Captain PA Reynaldo Martin Nochez Morroquin, Lieutenant PA Ricardo Humberto Guzman Lara, Airman Héctor Antonio Mata and soldiers Jaime Iván Zelada, Yohalmo Cruz, and Isaac Neftaly Hernández, were killed. Airman Carlos Zaldana managed to jump out on time and land safely under a parachute. (Artwork by Luca Canossa)

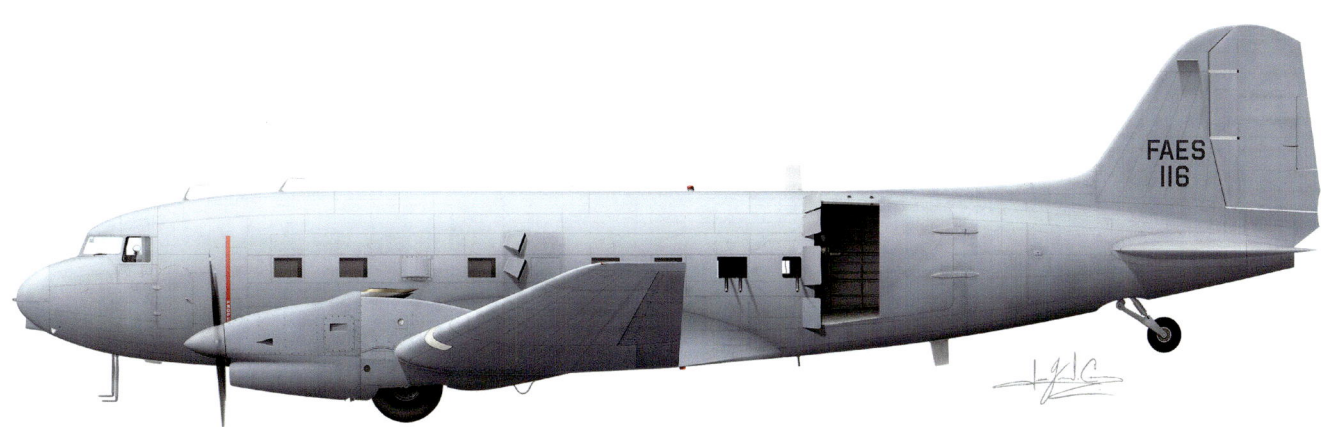

In the early 1990s, several of FAC AC-47s underwent conversion to the Basler BT-67 standard, which included re-engining to modern turbines and installation of new wings to stretch their operational life. One of the Salvadorean examples to receive such modifications was the 'Fantasma' with serial number 116: former C-47B-35-DK, construction number 16534, US Air Force serial 44-76950. It was delivered to El Salvador on 31 August 1990 and promptly entered service with the Escuadrón de Transporte, FAS, as a gunship armed with the usual three Browning M2 machine guns calibre 12.7mm. (Artwork by Luca Canossa)

The FAS continued operating its surviving Aérospatiale SA.315B Lama helicopters through the 1980s. One of these, delivered in 1974, was construction number 2441: it received the serial FAS 11 and served with the Escuadrón de Helicópteros from the Ilopango AB. Although designed as light utility and liaison helicopters, Salvadorean Lamas were frequently deployed as 'bombers', usually armed with two Mk.82 bombs (calibre 250kg), or one M117 (calibre 375kg), or four bombs (calibre 70kg). This capability became available through the installation of bomb shackles from disused Cavalier F-51D Mustang piston-engined fighters. (Artwork by Luca Canossa)

Surviving Aerospatiale SE.316B Alouette IIIs remained operational throughout the 1980s. This example – FAS serial number 22, construction number 2373, acquired in 1973 – is shown in livery as around 1984, while re-assigned to the Escuadrón de Helicópteors, at Ilopango Air Base. (Artwork by Luca Canossa)

This was the Schweizer TH-30 helicopter (nicknamed the 'Hálcon', or 'Falcon' by the FAS) construction number S1223, acquired by the FAS in 1986. It served with the Escuela de Aviación Militar, Centro de Educación e Instrucción Militar Aeronautico, at the Ilopango Air Base, for elementary and basic training of future helicopter-pilots. It is shown in livery and markings of around 1989. (Artwork by Luca Canossa)

The Hughes/McDonnell MD.500D helicopters were nick-named 'Guardiancillo' in service with the FAS. This one was acquired in 1983, by the defection of Commander Bravo from Nicaragua. He landed at the headquarters of the 6th Infantry Brigade in Usulután (city), sold it to the Salvadoran armed forces for US$ 700,000, then travelled directly to the Ilopango Airport and took the first aircraft to Miami in the USA. As of 1984, this MD.500D was painted as illustrated here: in tan and olive drab, with a white serial number 30. Meanwhile, it was armed with a mini gun calibre 7.62mm. It served until 21 January 2005, when it crashed due to engine failure. (Artwork by Luca Canossa)

In 1983, the FAS received nine MD.500Es. Assigned to the Escuadrón de Helicópteros, at Ilopango AB, they were meant to serve for scouting and liaison. Nevertheless, all were armed with (six-barrel) mini guns calibre 7.62mm (usually with a big ammunition box in the rear cabin) and frequently deployed as gunships for fire-support operations. This was the MD.500E construction number 0213E: it received the FAS serial 41. It survived the war, but crashed during a rescue mission on Suchitlan Lake, on 8 March 1993. (Artwork by Luca Canossa)

Bell UH-1Ms (an upgraded the Bell UH-1B, with a more powerful engine, protected by armour plating and exhaust diffuser) were nicknamed 'Guardián' in FAS service. This example – construction number 1764, US serial number 66-15036 – was delivered in September 1985 and received the FAS serial number 230. While serving with the Escuadrón de Helicópteros, it crashed on 12 March 1991. It is shown as armed with a pod for unguided rockets and a mini-gun calibre 7.62mm. The insert shows a similar, though slightly older installation of a similar nature with the red protective cover over the barrels of the mini gun. (Artwork by Luca Canossa)

Another of UH-1M Guardiáns to see service with the FAS was the example with construction number 1898, US serial 66-15170. Delivered to El Salvador in September 1985, it received the serial number 228 and is shown (as of 1988) in the 'Armagedón' configuration (used also as a call-sign during such operations): armed with a mini gun and a Mk.82 bomb calibre 250kg. This example saw intensive combat deployment until it crashed on 12 March 1991. (Artwork by Luca Canossa)

The Cessna O-2A received the nickname 'Martillo' in service with the FAS. This example – FAS serial number 613 – had the construction number 337M-0395 (former US Air Force serial number 68-11170): it was delivered to El Salvador in October 1984, and assigned to the Gurpo Caza y Bombardero, FAS. It was foremost flown by Captain Salvador Palacios and by 1991, received the corresponding cartoon – a condor with the aircraft designation O-2A and pilot's family name – on the left forward fuselage. (Artwork by Luca Canossa)

This Cessna O-2B – construction number 337M-0106: formerly 67-21400 of the US Air force – received the serial number 614 upon delivery to the FAS, in October 1984. The aircraft served with the Gropo Caza y Bombardeo at Ilopango air base and is shown as of 1990, while painted in dark green, with some olive drab in addition and armed with a GPU-2/A gun pod (inboard pylon) and a LAU-3A pod for unguided rockets calibre 68mm. (Artwork by Luca Canossa)

EL SALVADOR VOLUME 2: CONFLAGRATION 1984–1992

This Fouga CM.170 Magister (construction number 49) was one of three acquired from France and delivered to El Salvador on 26 April 1979. It was powered by Marbore VI engines and received the FAS serial 511. While serving with the Escuadrón Caza y Bombardeo, at the Ilopango Air Base, it was armed with two nose-mounted machine guns calibre 7.62mm. It is shown as of around 1990, by when most of the airframe and wings were painted in dark tan colour, with some traces of dark green on the lower rear fuselage and engine nacelles. The jet was written off in 1992. (Artwork by Luca Canossa)

As described in the Volume 1, Dassault MD.450 Ouragans were originally acquired to serve both as fighter-bombers and interceptors. This example was delivered on 24 January 1974, and received the serial number 702, but its original construction number remains unknown. Nicknamed the 'Planeta', all the Ouragans served with the Escuadrón Caza y Bombardeo of the Grupo de Combate, home-based at Ilopango. It was foremost piloted by Lieutenant Roberto Leiva (chief technician was Aristides Flores), and is shown in colours as of 1979 and armed with an Israeli-made Shafrir Mk. II air-to-air missile. Insert shows a typical configuration for ground attack, including two pods for unguided rockets calibre 68mm. '702' was written off on 27 January 1992. (Artwork by Luca Canossa)

Delivered to El Salvador on 15 June 1984, this Cessna A-37B Dragonfly had the construction number 43533 and used to wear the US Air Force serial 73-1085, before becoming the FAS 424. In service with the Grupo Caza y Bombardeo, all the A-37s were nicknamed 'Dragón'. The jet is shown as around 1984: wearing the (quite weathered) Europe One wrap-around camouflage pattern in Euro 1 Gray (FS36081), medium green (FS34102) and dark green (FS34079) – and equipped with no drop tanks but armed with six Mk.82 bombs calibre 250kg. (Artwork by Luca Canossa)

The A-37B Dragón that received the FAS serial number 427 (shown here as of 1990, already re-painted in dark grey overall), was delivered in February 1985: its construction number was 43397 and the former US Air Force serial was 71-0862. As with all jets of this type, it was assigned to the Grupo Caza y Bombardeo and is shown here equipped with (from inboard pylons outwards) two drop tanks with capacity of 100 US gallons, a SUU-11A mini gun pod, and a LAU-59 pod for four unguided rockets. (Artwork by Luca Canossa)

This A-37B Dragón – construction number 43229, former US Air Force serial 69-6384 – belonged to the batch delivered to El Salvador in February 1985. It arrived still painted in South East Asia wrap-around camouflage pattern, in (worn out) tan (FS30219), medium green (FS34102), and dark green (FS34079). The jet was shot down on 18 November 1989 while flown by Captain P. A. Andrade. The pilot was on a suppression mission in the area next to the Urbina Bridge, near San Miguel, when hit – and seriously wounded – by an insurgent sniper armed with a Dragunov rifle. Andrade ejected and was recovered by an UH-1H helicopter. The payload illustrated here included four LAU-3 pods for unguided rockets calibre 68mm. (Artwork by Luca Canossa)

This OA-37B was delivered to the FAS in 1989, as an attrition replacement. Its construction number was 43460 and the US Air Force serial number 73-1094. Indeed, the aircraft spent some time at the AMARC storage facility (AS AB0004) before it was overhauled, repainted in European One wraparound camouflage and sent to El Salvador. It is illustrated in weapons configuration used for nocturnal operations as of 1991, including (from inboard stations outwards) an ALQ-123 countermeasures pod (useful against SA-7 and SA-14 MANPADs), Mk.82 bomb, and Mk.24 pod for deployment of illumination flares. (Artwork by Luca Canossa)

As the civil war began raging all over the country, in 1980, the FAES found itself critically short on armoured vehicles. One of solution was the development of Mazzinger-Z armoured trucks. These were based on commercial chassis (usually that of the International Harvester truck), outfitted with armour. Although packing autocannons calibre 20mm in the turret installed atop of the driver's cabin, they proved big, heavy, and slow and had an open-topped combat compartment: as such, they were far from ideal and many were lost in combat. However, they have offered a vehicle suitable for convoy escort and patrol duties. (Artwork by David Bocquelet)

A much better solution – developed with help of US technical advisors – proved the Light Assault Vehicle (LAV): this was based on the Dodge M37B truck, which was cheap, easy to maintain, available in sufficient numbers and had the same engine like the standard M35 REO trucks of the FAES. The first prototype emerged in 1985 in the USA and was then shipped to El Salvador for assembly. On the negative side, LAVs lacked air conditioning and were still open-topped. A total of 66 were completed and they became known as Cashuat (Horse in the indigenous Nahuat language). Ultimately, they proved to offer insufficient protection against RPGs even after having a screen fitted, inadequate off-road performance, and too little firepower. (Artwork by David Bocquelet)

The MAN 630 was a five-ton lorry made by the Maschinenfabrik Augsburg Nürnberg (MAN) from 1953 to 1972: the L2 was the military version, with a switchable front-wheel-drive, and by far the most widely available. El Salvador purchased several dozen and the FAES used them as its standard truck throughout the 1980s. The 630L2 was 7.9 metres long, weighed 7,980kg when empty, powered by a MAN D1246 diesel engine of 96kW and could carry a load of up to 5,000kg. (Artwork by David Bocquelet)

This was an infantryman of the 5th Infantry Brigade, in central El Salvador as of 1984. By then, the FAES began receiving large amounts of US military aid, including uniforms and personal gear. He is shown wearing the traditional green uniform but already with a cap in woodland camouflage and Vietnam-style jungle boots. The belt, combat suspenders, and backpack were of the US-made M1957 standard, but the magazine pouch was from the ALICE system for M16A1 assault rifles. Notable are bandoliers for extra magazines across his torso. (Artwork by Anderson Subtil)

Colonel Nicolás Carranza, former Deputy Defence Minister and Director of the Treasury Police, as seen in 1984. Most of FAES officers wore local copies of M1942 (khaki) and M1957 (green) uniforms, with black rigid caps and light blue shirts, with the brass three-star insignia on shoulder straps and the General Staff insignia on the lapel. Identification plate, unit patch and different decorations were worn on both pockets or above them, while the crest of the Policia del Tesoro (Treasury Police) was worn on the left shoulder. (Artwork by Anderson Subtil)

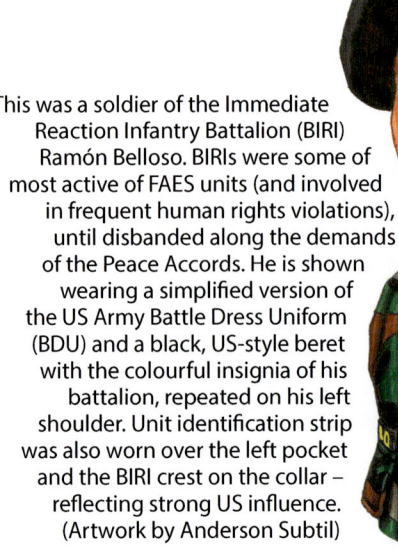

This was a soldier of the Immediate Reaction Infantry Battalion (BIRI) Ramón Belloso. BIRIs were some of most active of FAES units (and involved in frequent human rights violations), until disbanded along the demands of the Peace Accords. He is shown wearing a simplified version of the US Army Battle Dress Uniform (BDU) and a black, US-style beret with the colourful insignia of his battalion, repeated on his left shoulder. Unit identification strip was also worn over the left pocket and the BIRI crest on the collar – reflecting strong US influence. (Artwork by Anderson Subtil)

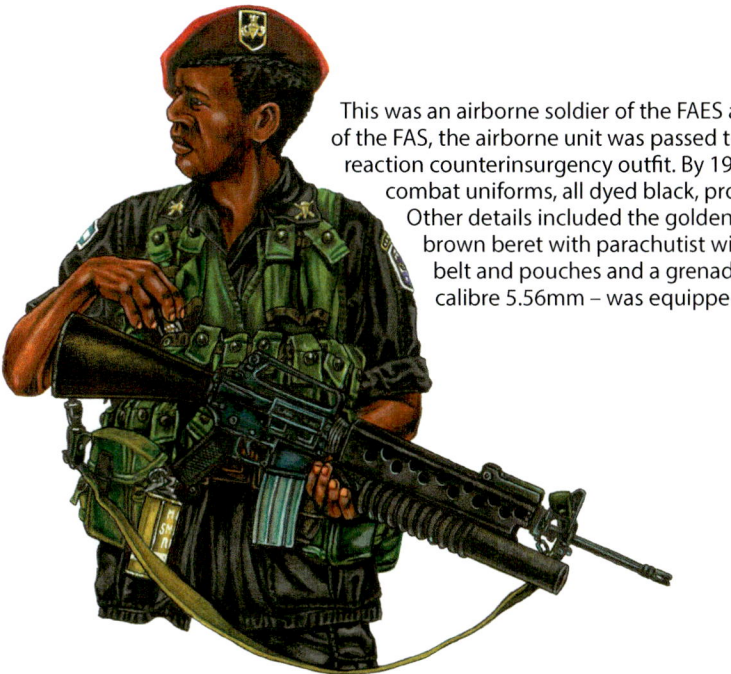

This was an airborne soldier of the FAES as of 1989. Originally established as Escuadrón Paracaidista of the FAS, the airborne unit was passed to the army and expanded into a battalion, trained as a quick-reaction counterinsurgency outfit. By 1989, troops of the Parachute Battalion wore US-style tropical combat uniforms, all dyed black, probably to increase their impression and denote their elite status. Other details included the golden collar emblems, striking patches on both jacket sleeves and the brown beret with parachutist wings. Combat equipment included an ALICE system ammunition belt and pouches and a grenade carrier vest. The weaponry – including the M16A-2 assault rifle calibre 5.56mm – was equipped with an M203 grenade launcher. (Artwork by Anderson Subtil)

This guerrilla was a member the Rafael Arce Zablah Brigade (BRAZ), part of the ERP, the most active organisation within the FMLN and certainly the most audacious in combat. The BRAZ was a result of ERP's effort to abandon the warfare of scattered guerrilla units and form a professional, manoeuvrable force capable of countering the FAES in conventional battles (eventually adopted by the entire FMLN). The BRAZ eventually evolved into a special forces asset, trained in infiltration. This combatant is shown while demonstrating techniques developed in Cuba and Viet Cong, while wearing only shorts and having his skin camouflaged with mud. His sole equipment was a Soviet-made ammunition bag and one of rare AKMs (contrary to other insurgent movements in Latin America, the FMLN predominantly used M16s and Heckler & Koch G3 rifles). (Artwork by Anderson Subtil)

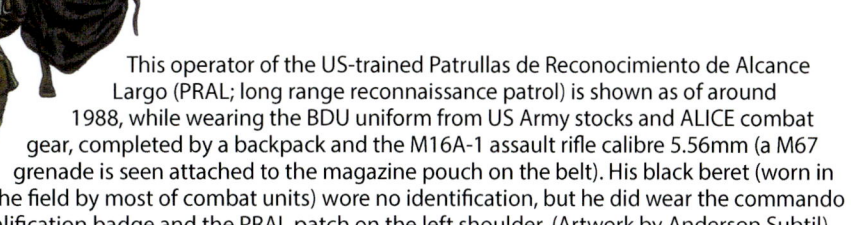

This operator of the US-trained Patrullas de Reconocimiento de Alcance Largo (PRAL; long range reconnaissance patrol) is shown as of around 1988, while wearing the BDU uniform from US Army stocks and ALICE combat gear, completed by a backpack and the M16A-1 assault rifle calibre 5.56mm (a M67 grenade is seen attached to the magazine pouch on the belt). His black beret (worn in the field by most of combat units) wore no identification, but he did wear the commando qualification badge and the PRAL patch on the left shoulder. (Artwork by Anderson Subtil)

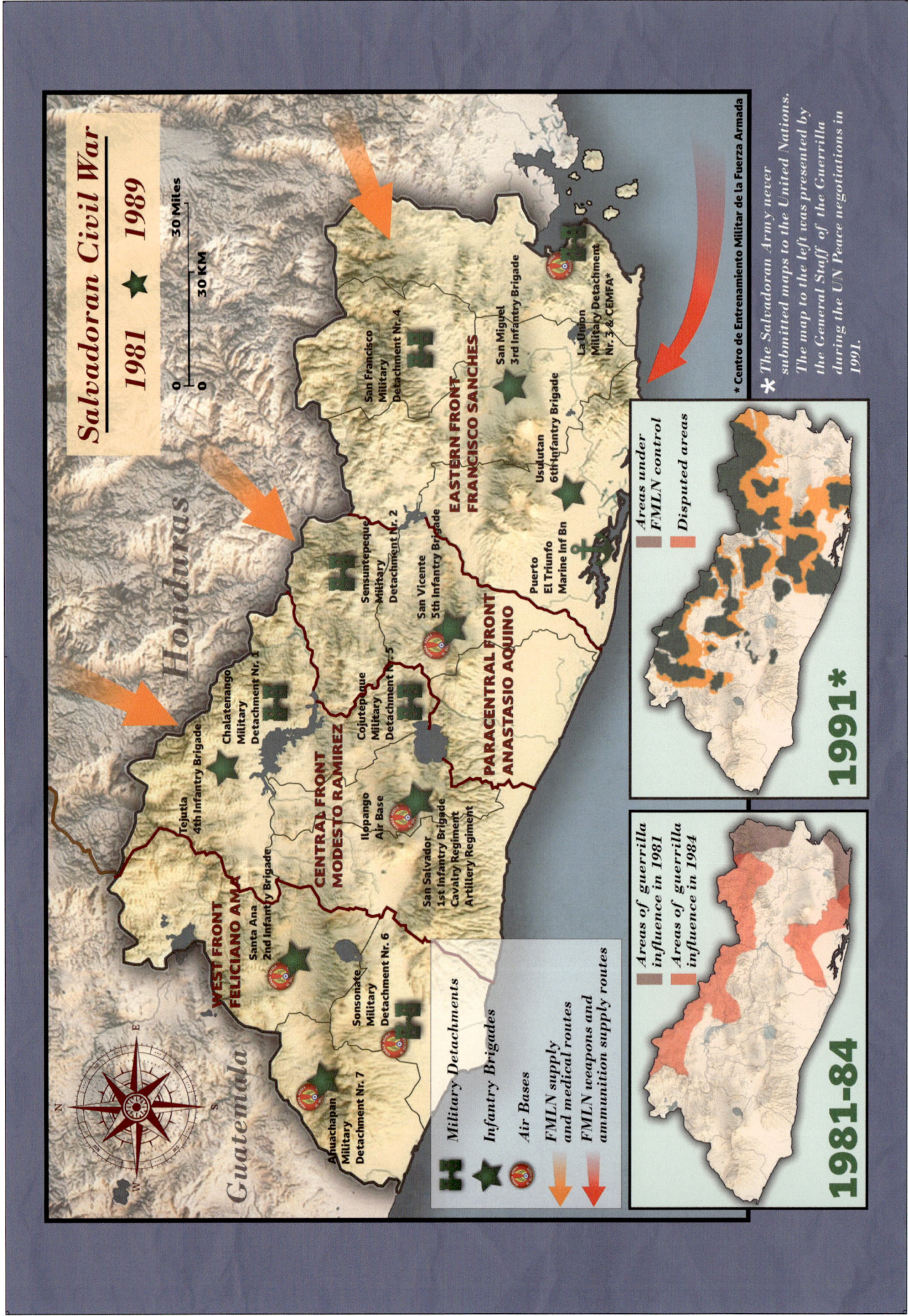

(Map by Anderson Subtil)

Salvadorean troops trained in the United States ready to return home. (Albert Grandolini Collection)

For this new elite, the continuation of the war was a brake on economic development while the demands of the FMLN on the agrarian question, no longer represented a threat to their survival. This modernist bourgeoisie was gradually gaining the upper hand within ARENA, which had been led by Alfredo Cristiani since 1985, who precisely represented this moderate wing. This change was expressed in the 1988 legislative electoral campaign when ARENA, which had always called for the annihilation of the FMLN, now presented itself as favourable to a dialogue to bring peace to El Salvador.[7]

As Duarte slowly died from stomach cancer, his party split, victims of infighting and corruption, with economic policies which weakened him, even within his traditional base. Meanwhile, the population was more and more convinced that the situation could only improve when the war was over.[8]

At the end of 1987, the Christian Democracy in power found itself in a difficult situation, dialogue with the FMLN was broken off and the population was dissatisfied. It was also only tolerated by the FAES under the pressure of the Americans who still believed it was the only solution to defeat the FMLN and get El Salvador out of the crisis it was undergoing.

The PDC loss of influence benefited ARENA which, in 1988, won the Assembly elections. The CIA therefore predicted Cristiani's victory, a prospect that resented Washington, which feared that ARENA extremists, particularly D'Aubuisson, would advocate policies opposed to those of the United States. In El Salvador, some, like the Universidad Centroamericana (Central American University or UCA) rector, Father Ignacio Ellacuría, feared that on the contrary, an ARENA defeat would radicalise its hardest wing which could dispute the result of the election. Even Villalobos, the ERP leader, was in favour of an ARENA victory which could allow his organisation to appear more moderate and occupy the centre of the political scene by attracting the PDC base.[9]

An FMLN guerrilla with an M67 recoilless rifle. (Albert Grandolini Collection)

This goal did not seem utopian when El Salvador was undergoing a profound political change.

The PDC, which won the 1982 and 1984 elections, was threatened by ARENA for those of 1989. ARENA, formed by Roberto D'Aubuisson in September 1981, was a conservative Right-wing party close to the Death Squads and who represented the interests of the big landowners. Nevertheless, the effects of Duarte's reforms and especially the consequences of the war, weakened the traditional foundations of this economic oligarchy. This was to the benefit of industrialists, merchants and financiers who profited from the development of the service sector, the *maquila* industry, non-agricultural exports.

As the elections approached, the FMLN intensified its military, political and diplomatic activities, which only increased concern in Washington. In order to create the necessary conditions for its strategic counter-offensive, it promoted social protest. In 1987–1988, it sent political agitators to urban centres where popular protest was developing.[10] This return to the cities was producing results. In January 1989, a strike led by construction workers, paralysed 177 companies while the week of the presidential elections was marked by a transport strike.[11] Above all, the FMLN continued its policy of executions of former allies, government officials and civilians.

At the beginning of January, it resumed his campaign of assassinations of mayors, even if it mainly took place in areas under the ERP control. During 1989, 214 of the 262 mayors of the country were threatened by the FMLN, 20 were killed and 80 resigned.[12] In February 1989, the guerrillas assassinated Miguel Castellanos,

A private security guard for Roberto D'Aubuisson, centre, spoke with FAES soldiers about potential guerrilla attacks in Suchitoto. ARENA, the party founded by D'Aubuisson was very close to the military as well as to the Death Squads. (Albert Grandolini Collection)

a former FMLN guerrilla who had defected and written a book about his experience. After the March elections, it still assassinated figures such as Francisco Peccorini, José Roberto García Alvarado, attorney general, and José Antonio Rodrigo Porth, Chief of Staff of the new president.[13] During the first half of 1989, killings of civilians by the FMLN, including mine deaths, 'outstripped assassinations by uniformed government forces for the first time in the course of the war'.[14]

This renewed activity of the FMLN in the cities provoked a reaction from Right-wing extremists. While killings by Death Squads and large-scale massacres by FAES and security forces, characterised the early years of the conflict, these practices declined thereafter, especially from 1984 under pressure from Washington. From then, the number of victims killed by these different groups dropped considerably.[15] It went from 225 in 1984 to 136 in 1985 and 45 in 1986.[16]

While the political killings had never completely stopped, they had just become more selective and the Death Squads continued their actions, threatening trade union activists and journalists. Nevertheless, the resurgence of their activities was more and more noticeable from 1987.[17] New Death Squads appeared like Comandos Domingo Monterrossa and Comandos Suicidas Salvadoreños. According to American Watch, during the first six months of 1988, the number of civilian deaths attributed to the military, increased by 44 percent compared to 1987.[18] As early as January 1989, the American embassy noted this return to violence and practices that reconnected with those of the beginning of the war. The CIA, for its part, feared that the revival of the Death Squads would further discredit the Duarte government and increase sympathy for the FMLN.

FAES strengths and weaknesses

The renewed activity of the FMLN did not however seem capable of endangering the Salvadoran government, as the FAES had been strengthened and modernised in a few years. At the end of 1988, they had about 43,000 men, organised into 22 medium and 14 light BIAT, gathered in six Infantry Brigades, nine Infantry Regiments, a motorised Cavalry Regiment, an Artillery Brigade, an Engineers Battalion, six BIRI, seven DM. Added to this was the Airborne Battalion and the Anti-Aircraft Artillery Battalion which depended on the FAS.

Artillery had tripled since the beginning of the war and communications and logistic support services had improved. The 1980 small Navy had 1,500 men in 1988, organised into a Marine Infantry Battalion with 600 men, a Marine commando unit of 330 men. The fleet consisted of three 100-foot radar-equipped Cam Craft Point cruise boats, four American-built outboard-powered 36-footers, two World War II-vintage 40-footers, two 75-footers delivered in the mid-1970s, a 65-footer and 30 patrol craft Piranhas.[19]

A view of the second in formation of two (out of 15) A-37 Dragonflies of the FAS, during a training flight over the sea. Notable is the big drop tank under the underwing hardpoint; bombs, pods for unguided rockets and other equipment, were usually installed on one of two outboard pylons. (Albert Grandolini Collection)

The FAS transformation was even more spectacular with, in 1987, 2,500 men, an Air Support Battalion, a Security Group, five Aircraft Squadrons and a large force of helicopters. The Combat Squadron, based in San Miguel, included eight Ouragans, the Counter-Insurgency Squadron 10 A-37Bs and two AC-47s. The reconnaissance squadron had 11 O-2As, the transport squadron had five C-47s, one DC-6, three Arava and two C-123Ks, the training squadron had a T-41 and six CM 170 Magisters.

The Helicopter Squadron included nine Hughes 500 MD attack helicopters, 14 UH-1H combat helicopters, 38 UH-1H service helicopters, three SA-315 Lamas and three SA-316 Alouette IIIs, making a total of 67 helicopters. This expansion of the FAS even allowed it to conduct operations overseas. Thus, at the end of 1983, six O2-As armed with 28 Heat rockets attacked the fuel depots in the Corinto port in Nicaragua. The following day, a new attack hit arms depots in Managua.[20]

In 1989, the FAES were therefore no longer the traditional and inefficient army of 1981, essentially repressive. They had become modern, cultured and trained, but still unable to defeat the FMLN. Their rapid growth posed problems. To mentor larger troops, the number of officers was increasing but their training time had been reduced dramatically and many went through North American military schools where the counter-insurgency warfare curriculum was minimal. As far as NCOs and troops were concerned, training times were limited while the excessive turnover of soldiers slowed down the accumulation of experience.

To add to these weaknesses was the persistence of a military tradition characterised by non-subordination to the civil authorities, the disrespect of human rights and the logic of internal structuring of the officers corps based on the *tandas*, a system which, in the opinion of American military advisers, constituted the main obstacle to the true professionalisation of officers. Military commanders continued to favour a conventional approach: employing battalion-sized units in operations backed by close air support and heavy artillery to chase down small bands of guerrillas. A more lenient US military adviser noted, 'The Salvadoran Army has been thoroughly trained in US counter-insurgency tactics and they can do them well – the problem is getting them to actually use these tactics'.[21]

A 1988 report, written by four American Colonels, pointed out the recurring weaknesses of the FAES. While highlighting the effectiveness of the PRALs, they added, 'With the exception of these instances, the Salvadorans attempted to adopt small unit tactics which were not effective'. An American trainer disparagingly referred to these units in an interview as 'search and avoid patrols'. Another trainer compared Salvadoran security posts at night to 'a gathering of young explorers with campfires and transistor radios'. More generally, US Colonels noted the FAES failure to adopt US counter-insurgency tactics:

> US trainers continued to push the FAES to adopt counter-insurgency tactics such as: small unit patrols, ambushes and night operations. They have even offered incentives that constitute personal advanced equipment for Salvadorans, such as night vision devices, and even then their progress has been limited. The FAES continue to devote too much force to unnecessarily securing fixed sites such as barracks, bridges, industrial facilities and coffee plantations. In the field, unmanageable battalions continue to expend too much energy, without aim or result.[22]

The FAS used six Fouga CM.170 Magister jet trainers since 1970 (three from Israel and three from France). Based at Ilopango AB, they were deployed for ground attack and thus armed with two nose-mounted machine guns, before being withdrawn from service in 1984. (Albert Grandolini Collection)

Added to this were coordination problems between the ground forces and the FAS, which continued to act with excessive autonomy.

The CIA also discussed the government's problems, unable to provide security in the countryside where Civil Defence units were poorly trained and armed. At the end of 1987, out of the 240 existing detachments, only a hundred were deemed fit to receive M-14 rifles or M2 carbines. Moreover, during the same period, there was only one Civil Defence detachment in the Morazan department, seven in that of Chalatenango and five in that of La Union; all regions where the guerrillas were the most active.[23] In addition, some of these units were close to Death Squads and violated human rights, such as Los Patrióticos, made up of wealthy citizens who provided security for some of the most privileged neighbourhoods in San Salvador.[24]

The Bush Administration and El Salvador

In February 1989, the CIA director presented the report 'El Salvador: Government and Insurrectional Prospects' in which he analysed the general situation in that country. He pointed out that between 1987 and 1988, the FMLN intensified its protracted war strategy based on sabotage and small-scale attacks in the main urban centres, with more visible and violent actions, particularly in San Salvador, day and night. Thus, on 21 February 1989, FMLN urban commandos blew up a car in San Salvador near the 1st Infantry Brigade headquarters while guerrilla units attacked Apopa and Zacatecoluca. However, the director noted that the FMLN was only able to partially mitigate the effect of FAES incursions into its *retaguardias*.

With regard to the FAES, the CIA report indicated that they were able to carry out more frequent and more effective sweeps on a large scale, as well as operations throughout the country. He pointed out that the development and use of tactical intelligence had also improved considerably, contributing to greater efficiency in military operations and he nevertheless, qualified the FAES' short-term prospects for victory. The latter could continue to put pressure on the FMLN, prevent preparations for the most important attacks, gradually reduce the military effectiveness of the guerrillas but without drastically reducing their range.

On this point, the director only confirmed the criticisms expressed by the American military specialists present in El Salvador. He added that civic action programmes, important in US counter-insurgency warfare doctrine, had never received sufficient government or military support. William H. Webster, therefore, concluded by acknowledging that if the FAES had the necessary power to continue to contain the guerrilla forces, the FMLN could still 'fight a protracted war, relying increasingly on terrorism, sabotage and small-scale attacks. The guerrillas, even if they cannot take power, will continue to seriously threaten the security and stability of the country'.[25]

This report by the CIA director could only reinforce the doubts of the new administration on the continuation of American involvement in El Salvador. It thus began to wonder about the sums of money spent in this country while the FMLN defeat seemed to be constantly moving away. Despite all the changes made to its structure, the training received by the military in the field of counter-insurgency warfare, the modern military equipment and weapons provided by Washington, the FAES ultimately only managed to contain the guerrillas and prevent us from seizing part of Salvadoran territory. Even in 1988, FMLN forces still posed a real threat to the State.

In turn, Cold War conditions were changing very rapidly and the major powers were already taking steps to reduce direct and indirect conflict among themselves. External conditions were putting pressure on Salvadoran actors to resolve the conflict through negotiations. If the aid granted by the Reagan Administration influenced the development of the counter-insurgency war in favour of the FAE, but without obtaining the military defeat of the FMLN, it also made it possible to build a democratic system, however imperfect it might be. It was on the achievement of the previous administration that President Bush wanted to break the Salvadoran conflict impasse in order to find the way to a negotiated end to the war.

The 1989 presidential elections

While the FMLN called for a boycott of the presidential elections of March 1989, the Central Elections Council suspended voting in 22 municipalities which were under the control of the guerrillas whose units prevented voting in 20 other municipalities and disrupted them in 42.[26] Nevertheless, the elections were taking place normally in the rest of the country with the participation of the Democratic Convergence formed by the parties stemming from the FDR. This presence of a Left-wing organisation provoked the anger of the FMLN, which qualified these former allies as traitors but gave additional democratic and pluralist legitimacy to the ballot.[27]

It was finally the ARENA candidate, Alfredo Cristiani, who won the presidential elections with 53 percent of the votes, promising economic recovery and negotiations with the FMLN. He thus rallied an urban vote of the middle classes whilst the PDC achieved its best results in rural areas.[28] Despite his election, Washington's doubts about Cristiani persisted.

The PDC defeat, a staunch American ally, indeed sounded like a disavowal and the United States feared that the new government would lift the constraints imposed on the Death Squads and that violent repression would resume. These fears were not unfounded since the ARENA had been for many years the place of confrontation between a reactionary wing, embodied by D'Aubuisson and a more moderate and reformist sector – a balance of power which nevertheless tilted in favour of the latter.

The ARENA reformists wanted to rebuild the Salvadoran economy, which required the end of the war and therefore the need

The Dassault M.D.450 Ouragan was a French-made fighter-bomber designed and manufactured in the 1950s. Intensively deployed early during the war in El Salvador, it was eventually replaced by the US-made A-37B Dragonfly. Surviving Ouragans were withdrawn from service before the end of the conflict. (Albert Grandolini Collection)

The Cessna T-41 Mescalero was a military version of the popular Cessna 172, operated by FAS as a pilot training aircraft. (Albert Grandolini Collection)

The election of Alfredo Cristiani as president, opened a new era despite causing fears in Washington. Above all, it demonstrated the possibility of a democratic alternative in El Salvador (Author Collection)

to integrate the FMLN into the political system if it agreed to lay down its arms. Quickly, Washington was reassured by Cristiani who launched economic reforms and knew how to keep the FAES in obedience. Above all, he showed himself ready to negotiate with the FMLN and to put an end to the conflict without obtaining a military victory.[29]

Paradoxically, ARENA's victory first produced an increase in tensions. One officer said before the election, speaking of guerrilla-held areas: 'Let's hope ARENA wins. We can bombard all these populations at will'. For his part, Colonel Orlando Zepeda, commander of the 1st Infantry Brigade, formed, on 7 May, the first contingent of the Patriotic Civil Defence, composed of Right-wing militants while the soldiers injured several students during the dispersal of a demonstration on 17 July.

On 5 September, the FENASTRAS trade union, close to the FMLN, suffered a dynamite attack and on 16 September, riot police dispersed a march by this organisation, arresting many demonstrators. The press was also the target of the soldiers who assassinated several journalists including a photographer from Reuters and a cameraman from Dutch television. For their part, the Death Squads murdered around 150 people in the two weeks following Cristiani's election.[30]

The replacement, of Colonel Blandon by Colonel Ponce at the head of the FAES General Staff, also indicated a more aggressive attitude against the guerrillas.[31] Faced with what appeared to be a hardening of the regime, the FMLN intensified its actions. It called a nationwide transport strike on election day and attacked BIRI Belloso facilities in Ilopango on 15 May. On 9 June, urban guerrillas assassinated the Minister of the Presidency, Rodriguez Porth and on 30 June, Edgar Chacón, a Right-wing ideologue.[32]

While the political conditions of the Salvadoran conflict evolved, military operations did not diminish in intensity. The FAES continued to operate against the guerrillas as in the San Vicente department with Operation Rayo which aimed to eliminate the PRTC forces in the El Tortugal region. During this operation, on 15 April, two A-37s bombed an FMLN mobile hospital. They were followed by three UH-1M rocket launchers and six helicopters carrying special forces. The soldiers landed near the hospital and captured five people including an Argentinian doctor and a French nurse who were executed.[33] In Chalatenango, Morazan departments, in the west of Usulutan and in Cerro Guazapa, the FAES launched the Atlacatl campaign, which consisted of search and destruction operations which, according to the military, led to the death of 200 guerrillas.[34]

In September 1989, the BIRI Atlacatl 3rd Company made a risky landing on the top of Campanario hill, in the Guazapa volcano, in a desperate attempt to help another unit ambushed further south. Eight UH-1H helicopters landed 60 soldiers under enemy fire. Fierce fighting broke out, forcing the FAS to maintain constant close air support and launch one of its strongest and most sustained bombing campaigns of the entire war. Severely beaten but with few casualties, BIRI Atlacatl units managed to reach San José Guayabal.

Despite the blows of the FAES, the FMLN continued to prepare its strategic offensive. In the clandestine workshops, weapons were manufactured while the political work extended in the zones known as expansion, in particular in the cities, districts and suburbs of San Salvador where the urban commandos prepared all the logistics necessary for an important operation. At the same time, the FMLN continued its negotiation efforts, without concrete results. In July 1989, Cristiani proposed to start discussions in Mexico but the FAES command categorically opposed it.[35]

The guerrilla preparations did not go unnoticed. On 8 November 1989, a note from the FAES intelligence services reported an increase in guerrilla actions. According to this report, the FMLN planned to launch an attack imminently with an 'unusual concentration of rebels in and around San Salvador'. The FAES also feared that the FMLN would assassinate government officials and provoked reprisals from 'Right-wing elements or renegades in the army'.[36]

Salvadoran security forces became militarised during the war. Here a class of students from the CETIPOL police school during a military operation (Author Collection)

Since the presidential elections, repression against Centre-Left activists, including trade unions, had in fact continued to intensify throughout the country. These actions culminated in a new bomb attack against FENASTRAS on 31 October 1989. This was the third time this union, closely linked to the FARN, had been the target of an attack since the beginning of the year. While the previous attacks did not claim any casualties, this one claimed nine lives, including the union general secretary, Febe Elizabeth Velásquez, and injured 40. In reaction, on 2 November, the FMLN CG published a statement announcing the suspension of negotiations with the government, accusing them of having no desire for peace.[37]

Above all, the FMLN took this attack as a pretext to launch an offensive, the largest since the beginning of the war. This should allow it to get out of the impasse in which it found itself at the end of the year. Peace talks failed and repression escalated against Centre-Left political parties, popular organisations and trade unions as the idea that the guerrillas were defeated militarily and politically, expanded in the FAES and that the only point to negotiate, was their surrender. The FMLN leadership, aware that it could not prevail by force of arms, knew that it had no other possibility than to consider a process of negotiation and its incorporation into the Salvadoran political system, but for that it had to assert itself militarily in order to show its strength and hold sway at the negotiating table.

6
THE NOVEMBER 1989 OFFENSIVE

On the morning of 11 November 1989, two days after the fall of the Berlin Wall, the FAL urban commandos set up mortars in the vicinity of the Colonia Atlacatl which soon fired on the GN headquarter in eastern San Salvador. This action marked the beginning of the Final Offensive, known as Hasta al Tope (to the top). This major operation represented the culmination of the strategy initiated by the FMLN in 1984, aimed at producing a decisive battle and a massive uprising against the government.

The FMLN managed to gather a large force which, during the first days of the offensive, surprised the FAES and overwhelmed them. Just when the military thought the guerrillas were about to disappear, they were shaken by the power they were displaying. The FAES nevertheless succeeded in modifying their arrangements, gathering elite units in the capital and concentrating all their firepower on open ground. For its part, the ease with which the FMLN managed to position its forces in the big cities gave it a false sense of confidence which collapsed when it realised that the population did not give it the expected support.[1]

The FMLN plan
At the beginning of November 1989, the FMLN was ready for the strategic offensive it had been preparing for years. The guerrillas were then completely re-armed with weapons supplied by the Soviet bloc.[2] The plan, prepared by the CG, was discussed by the five leaders of the FMLN member organisations in Managua, in the presence of Cuban officers. From a military point of view, it looked like the 1968 Tet Offensive in Vietnam, while the desire to articulate the guerrillas actions with a popular insurrection, was inspired by the Sandinista conceptions of July 1979. It was based, as in January 1981, on the idea that the FAES were weakened by a process of moral decomposition and that the population, dissatisfied with the economic and social situation, would trigger an insurrection and would join the guerrillas causing the collapse of the government.[3]

This plan provoked intense discussions within the FMLN. Some were more in favour of a series of attacks on strictly military objectives, but Villalobos defended the idea of triggering an insurrection in working-class neighbourhoods, thanks to the presence of the guerrillas. This opinion was shared by Handal while the FPL were opposed to it. Nevertheless the CG choose the

In 1989, the leadership of the FAES was convinced that the guerrillas were in irreversible decline. It therefore continued its military operations against the *retaguardias* of the FMLN. (Albert Grandolini Collection)

Villalobos strategy, despite the reluctance of Fidel Castro as told by Fernando Jovel :

It was thought that with an effort of that magnitude, it was highly probable — almost certain — that the people would launch an uprising. It was then that Fidel Castro let it be known that he did not want to be seen as a pessimist. Still, despite the general enthusiasm and optimism and the fact that we were the ones who could best anticipate the reaction of the people, he thought that we needed to be prepared for the eventuality that our military effort would not lead to victory, but would instead improve the possibility of a negotiated agreement. And he also had other things to say about the guerrillas' specific military plans. For example, he was very insistent about military units needing to be deployed in order to prevent the government troops from mobilising. And he said he thought that the current plans were deficient in terms of providing adequate control of the roads, something about which — and I say this in the spirit of self-criticism — he was entirely Right.[4]

The FMLN offensive searched several objectives. The most modest was to support the fight in the cities for 72 hours in order to tip the balance of power in FMLN favour. The latter believed that the moment was favourable since the newly elected Cristiani government was still weak and inexperienced and it could still count on the support of Cuba, Mexico, Venezuela and Panama. It was therefore up to it to force the government and the military to begin serious negotiations. In this perspective, the offensive had to also bring about a qualitative change in the correlation of forces, in order to be in a better position before resuming the process of negotiations still at an impasse.

Some sectors of the FMLN gave a more ambitious objective to the offensive, that of winning a decisive victory.[5] Thus, Salvador Samoya, member of the FMLN Politico-Diplomatic Commission declared: 'There is no longer a possibility to back away. Now, the only possible negotiation is on the basis of the overthrow of the Cristiani government'.[6]

Contrary to the January 1981 offensive, the FMLN plan was to concentrate its actions in San Salvador, the nerve centre of the country where many FAES troops were located and also the political leadership of El Salvador. Additionally, an attack on the capital would have great international repercussions and would show that the guerrillas were far from being defeated. In the rest of the country, the plan only provided for smaller-scale actions.

The Eastern Front, dominated by the ERP, concentrated its forces in the north of the Morazan department to seize San Miguel. The South Eastern Front had to gather forces in the Cerro El Tigre and the San Agustin-Tres Calles area to attack Usulutan, without necessarily seeking to conquer it. Another secondary action targeted San Francisco Gotera in the Morazan department to fix the FAES forces. Within the Paracentral Front, the FAPL had to attack the Destacamento Militar de Ingenieros de la Fuerza Armada (Military Detachment of Engineers of the Armed Forces or DMIFA) in Zacatecoluca and carry out secondary actions on the Litoral Highway and in the San

One of FMLN's columns setting off in direction of San Salvador. The majority of insurgents during that campaign were equipped with weapons of Soviet origin. (Albert Grandolini Collection)

Vicente department where the 5th Infantry Brigade was located. Finally, it was up to the ERP and the FPL to launch actions in the Santa Ana department against the 2nd Infantry Brigade.

Most of the FMLN forces therefore, had San Salvador as their objective, where they were divided into five groups. The ERP had 300 fighters concentrated in the Guazapa and San Salvador volcanoes who had to advance to the areas of Nejapa and Finca Colombia to then enter the capital, take control of the western part of the Colonia Zacamil and attack the PN post there. They also had to occupy San Ramon, the Colonia Universitaria Norte and launch urban commandos against the 1st Infantry Brigade in the San Carlos barracks. This force was led by commanders Claudio Rabindranath Armigo (Chicon) and Jaime Alberto Campos Melara (Jaime Beltran).

The FAL were also in charge of attacking the north of the capital through San Laureano, from the slopes of the Guazapa volcano. Under the direction of José Luis Merino (Ramiro Vasquez) and Dagoberto Gutiérrez (Logan), 250 men had to take control of Ciudad Delgado while a smaller force of 150 men, led by Dagoberto Sosa (Lucio Rivera), had to support the FARN in Soyapango. Another force of 100 FAL men, under the orders of Captains René Armando and David Pereira, were tasked with blocking the Troncal del Norte Highway towards Apopa by setting up ambushes.

South of San Salvador, a column of 80 to 100 FAL fighters, accompanied by the urban commando U-24, had to infiltrate San Marcos under the orders of Rafael Benavides (Ramon Suarez) and captains Mauricio Rivera and Benito Lara. In San Salvador, the FAL also had urban commandos Amilcar Mendoza, which had only about 50 men and was reinforced by the arrival of the FES U-24 unit. In total, the FAL mobilised about 600 combatants for the offensive in San Salvador.

The FARN forces were divided into two groups. The first, with about 150 men under the orders of Misael Gallardo, were responsible for attacking the capital from the south, towards San José Villanueva, Zaragoza, La Libertad. From the San Salvador volcano, they were to attack towards Antiguo Cuscatlán, the Estado Mayor Conjunto de la Fuerza Armada (Joint Staff of the Armed Forces or EMCFA) complex and the Ministry of Defence, with the support of 100 militiamen.

The second, which was the most important, had to attack San Salvador from the north towards Soyapango sector, – in particular, the Ilopango Air Base – and cut the Pan-American Highway. This force, commanded by Dimas Rojas, had 300 men as well as the four columns, bringing together 300 men from the Carlos Arias Battalion, led by Raulito and stationed in Guazapa. There were also 20 members of the FES and the column of 250 combatants, led by Francisco Montes, who arrived from the Cabañas department. The FARN urban commandos, led by Herberth Soriano Flores, which had about 50 men, were also mobilised. With approximately 860 combatants, the FARN were, after the FAPL, the most numerous forces to attack San Salvador.

The FAPL, with approximately 1,300 to 1,500 men, were the most numerous to take part in the assault on San Salvador. They were directed by Nicolas Hernan Solórzano Sanchez (Dimas Rodriguez), Facundo Guardado (Esteban Cabrales) and José Ricardo Ruiz (German Serrano). Part of the units attacked from the San Salvador volcano to the popular districts north of the capital, Ayutuxtepeque, Cuscatancingo and Mejicanos. They were reinforced by FES units who had to destroy the installations of the 1st Infantry Brigade.

A smaller force of 200 men, led by Carlos Ildefonso Castillo (Ramon Torres) and coming from Cinquera was responsible for

A guerrilla, armed with an AKM assault rifle, seen in the suburbs of San Salvador during the November 1989 Offensive. (Albert Grandolini Collection)

supporting the FARN in the east of the city. Finally, a column of 80 men led by Eduardo Alfonso Linares (Douglas Santamaria) had to descend from the southwestern slopes of the San Salvador volcano to head towards the President's Residence, the Feria Internacional Convention Centre, approach the EMCFA from the west and mortar attack the Centro Técnico de Instruccion Policial (Police Training Technical Centre or CETIPOL) in Santa Tecla, in the La Libertad department.

The PRTC was also taking part in the offensive on San Salvador with 400 FAR-LP fighters led by Pedro Antonio Mira Hernandez (Camilo Turcios) and Manuel Melgar (Rogelio Martinez) who had to fight in the western area of Soyapango alongside the FAL and then supported the FARNs against the Ilopango Base.

The attack against San Salvador was designed in three phases. During the first, the guerrilla forces occupied the popular neighbourhoods. The second was that of the FAES counter-attack which, according to the FMLN, would be violent and would provoke a popular uprising. The last was when the guerrillas, reinforced by the massive rallying of the population, would gain the advantage over the defeated FAES.[7]

The Battle of San Salvador, 11–16 November 1989

The offensive on the capital began at 9 a.m. on the morning of 11 November when a truck stopped in Ciudad Delgado. FMLN urban commandos members got out and shot the GN headquarters with a home-made mortar. This action was actually a message that confirmed to the other guerrilla forces the start of the offensive.

In the suburbs, to the north and east of the capital, sabotage plunged these neighbourhoods into darkness while the FMLN forces, already infiltrated in San Salvador and posing as civilians, took out hidden prepositioned weapons and supported the arrival of the columns descending from the San Salvador volcano a few kilometres west of the capital. Winding through ravines and along streams under the cloak of darkness, these forces evaded FAES patrols to reach their areas of operation.

They then infiltrated the northern and eastern suburbs of Soyapango, Zacamil, San Jacinto, Ayutuxtepeque, Cuscatancingo,

Ciudad Delgado and Mejicanos. In these localities, they erected barricades in the streets, shot at cars and buses to paralyse transport and entered houses, breaking down the walls of separation between them to facilitate mobility and communication.

In Soyapango, RN forces entered the neighbourhood around 10:00 p.m. to cover a wide line of fire to the centre of the municipality. FAL and PRTC troops also entered the city and advanced towards its centre, controlling the heights of the La Coruña water tank. Throughout the night of 11-12 November, fighting in Soyapango intensified.

In Ciudad Delgado, urban commandos attacked Civil Defence units while FAL forces advanced and established positions with urban commandos in the centre of the city. In Mejicanos, the FPL fighters entered the locality from different directions supported in the Colonia Metropolis by the ERP urban commandos. In Zacamil, the ERP urban forces began the attack on the PN headquarters while further south, in the Colonia Layco, other ERP urban commandos established positions near the University of El Salvador, where they placed a 60mm mortar piece to attack the San Carlos barracks.

While the FMLN focused its main effort on the working-class neighbourhoods in the north and east, the offensive also allowed it to take position in the wealthier western suburbs of the capital. One of the first actions of the guerrillas was to attack the CETIPOL of Santa Tecla and to deploy between this locality and Ciudad Merliot to the west of San Salvador. The inhabitants of privileged neighbourhoods were, for the first time, confronted with both war and guerrillas. For many whose homes were occupied by the rebels, the experience was less difficult than they might have thought since the latter often treated them with respect and did not steal or vandalise their property.[8]

Among these wealthy neighbourhoods, several guerrilla columns entered Colonia Manuel José Arce and almost simultaneously, attacked President Cristiani's official and private residences and the respective residences of the Legislative Assembly president and vice president. Cristiani was not present in any of these buildings. In front of his personal residence, the presidential security detail repelled guerrillas who animated a block in the Colonia Maquilishuat. After a fierce exchange of gunfire, the guerrillas fled.

Three guerrillas and a government corporal were reportedly killed in the assault on the president's official residence. Another three guerrillas were also reportedly killed at the home of the vice president of the Legislative Assembly. Meanwhile, the two policemen guarding the home of the Legislative Assembly's president were wounded repelling a 45 minute guerrilla attack. The Legislative Assembly president was exfiltrated with his family to a nearby house.

South of San Salvador, in San Marcos, the FAL forces were trying to take control of certain areas of the locality and engaged in combat with the Centro de Instruccion de Transmisiones de la Fuerza Armada (Armed Force Transmissions Instruction Centre or CITFA) forces. In the Colonia San Jacinto, the FARN took control of several streets and attempted to advance along the San Jacinto hill to the Colonias Amatepec and Ciudad Credisa.

One of the FMLN main targets was the Ilopango Air Base east of San Salvador. 'We think they wanted to take Ilopango because it would prevent us from using air power against them, and also because

With the November 1989 offensive, the FMLN demonstrated its ability to organise a large-scale operation at the heart of the enemy system. Its fighters carried the war to the heart of the capital, which became the scene of violent combat. (Albert Grandolini Collection)

FAES troops moving with their 'Pig' armoured personnel carrier into a neighbourhood held by FMLN guerrillas in first days of the November 1989 offensive. (Albert Grandolini Collection)

Government soldiers disembarking from an armoured personnel carrier in the wealthy suburb of Escalon. Guerrillas had taken over a number of houses during the November offensive. (Albert Grandolini Collection)

they would use our own planes against us and send reinforcements from Nicaragua', said Major René Alcides Rodriguez Hurtado, commander of the paratroopers.[9] To accomplish this mission, the FMLN had to first control Soyapango, a task for the FARN and one of its oldest and most notable commanders, Dimas Rojos.

Reconnaissance of the area targeted by the attack had begun six months earlier, allowing the guerrillas to install weapons, equipment and ammunition. During the day of 11 November, a force arrived from the Guazapa volcano southern flank to the north of the Ilopango Base main runway. It had to attack with mortar fire and then set up a command post in Soyapango.[10]

At 5:30 p.m., the first shots hit the north and west sides of the Ilopango Base. A 20mm anti-aircraft artillery piece repelled the attack. The next day, in Los Conacastes, the FARN installed two 81mm mortars to fire the helicopters stationed in the Airbase, but the shots were too short and did not do any damage. The guerrilla forces who then tried to storm the base, were repelled by the Security Battalion in charge of its protection which received support from a UH-1M helicopter and which managed to take off.[11]

The guerrillas thus proved incapable of neutralising the FAS. Patrols were sent to locate these mortars, but they came up against strong defences. The fighting lasted all day while the paratroopers held positions at Los Conacastes, in the Colonia San José, facing the Rio Las Cañas. At 11 am, a paratrooper and armoured vehicles column succeeded in approaching the FAL command post in Soyapango. The fighting was very violent but at 4 pm, the FAES had to withdraw. Despite the intervention of two armed UH-1Ms and two Hughes-500s, the FARN managed to penetrate the positions of the paratroopers, particularly in the Colonia San José and reached the Colonia Guadalupe.

In the Colonia Los Conacastes, the 3rd Airborne Squadron was also quickly overwhelmed, with FARN fighters even managing to reach the entrance to the FAS base before being pushed back by an M-55A2 artillery piece. To the west, PRTC forces established positions in the Colonia Villa de Jesús, near the centre of Soyapango. On 12 November, while the FAS carried out three reconnaissance and 27 fire support missions in the San Salvador metropolitan, five UH-1H, two UH-1M and four Hughes-500 helicopters were hit by enemy fire in the Soyapango sector.[12]

In the rest of San Salvador, north of the city, the BIRI Atlacatl 'Alfa' group was advancing from the Carretera Troncal del Norte towards Ciudad Delgado. Meanwhile, in that city, PH agents established blocking positions in the Institute of Cartography area to attack the FAL positions. The BIRI Bracamonte, which was heading on the road to Comalapa for a counter-insurgency operation, received the order to deploy to the military hospital of the Metropolis colony of Mejicanos. For their part, BIRI Atlacatl 'Bravo' and 'Charlie' groups began their movement towards Ayutuxtepeque through the eastern slope of the San Salvador volcano, a goal they reached at nightfall on 12 November. West of San Salvador, the FA withdrew in a disorganised manner from San Marcos while fighting continued between CETIPOL students and FPL forces in Ciudad Merliot.

Despite calls from Radio Venceremos, the local population did not join the guerrillas' ranks, nor provoke an insurrection. On the contrary, it abandoned the dangerous zones and the places where the guerrillas were. The government and all the institutions continued to function; the private companies – with difficulty – did not cease their activities while the factory workers of greater San Salvador, sympathisers of the FMLN, did not answer these calls. If the reluctance of the population prevented the guerrillas from increasing their numbers, which were, according to Herard von Santos, 3,660 fighters, they had a sufficient supply of weapons, thanks to the work of their clandestine infrastructures in the capital. Countless arms depots were in fact, set up in the main urban centres before the start of the offensive, precisely to be able to equip insurgent civilians.[13]

On 13 November, in Soyapango, the fighting was intense, especially in the neighbourhoods located on the foothills of San Jacinto and San Marcos hills, more precisely in the neighbourhood of Santa Marta, where the guerrillas established a command post. At times, the Pan-American Highway was even cut off by barricades. A few reinforcements, from BIRI Belloso and GOE units, were sent to support the paratroopers holding the sector north of the Ilopango Base, which allowed them to begin to put pressure on the guerrilla forces. However, the paratroopers did not manage to break the FARN lines and only the fire support provided by the helicopters, the AC-47s and the A-37Bs, prevented them from being defeated. To the south, guerrilla forces threatened to unite with those of the FARN and FAR-LP to attack the Air Base from the south-west. It was the GOEs, who settled in the Amatepec colony, who succeeded in blocking this advance.

The FAR-LP command, in coordination with that of the FARN, decided to make a new effort to isolate the Ilopango Base to tie-in with the units to the south-east of the capital. On the night of

13–14, the FAR-LP infiltrated the lines defended by the paratroopers west of Colonia Guadalupe while the FARN attacked from Ciudad Credisa with the aim of penetrating the FAS defences. The guerrillas were nevertheless hard hit by the BIRI Atlacatl and the CEAT, which even succeeded in attacking the command post of Misael Gallardo, which was shot down, along with almost all of his staff.

The survivors tried to join Soyapango in difficult fights where the losses were numerous. The FAR-LP who were fighting the GOE, the BIRI Atlacatl units and the CEAT teams at the same time, were finally forced to withdraw from Antiguo Cuscatlán. Meanwhile, other FAES units attacked the FAL in San Marcos, forcing them to retreat to Cerro San Jacinto, Panchimalco and Rosario de Mora.

The FAS had six Hughes/McDonnel MD.500D and nine additional 500Es were delivered in 1983. They were armed with 7.62mm machine guns and unguided rockets and served as a gunships. They were also used for reconnaissance and liaison missions, especially during the November 1989 offensive. (Albert Grandolini Collection)

In the middle of the day of the 14th, the PH Libertadores Battalion attacked in the direction of the Loma del Tanque and confronted the FAR-LP and the FAL forces in Prados de Venecia, a district of Soyapango. In the rest of the city, the fighting was still as violent as Cessna O-2s and UH-1M helicopters strafed the guerrilla positions. The command of the latter decided that the FAL installed in the Loma del Tanque sector had to withdraw to reinforce Ciudad Delgado, which was under pressure from the BIRI Atlacatl. This decision left the FAR-LP and the FARN alone in Soyapango.

Paratroopers and special forces eventually managed to halt the guerrilla advance towards Ilopango Air Base at least a kilometre from its perimeter. At the same time, the BIRI Atlacatl and other BIRIs from bases outside the capital arrived to reinforce the heavily stretched local forces, thus halting the guerrilla push towards the northern part of the capital, the San Jacinto Volcano slopes, the Presidential Palace and the CITFA in south-east San Salvador. The inability of the guerrillas to block these FAES reinforcements was probably the biggest tactical error they made, to which had to be added their inability to neutralise the Ilopango Base. The most difficult thing still remained for the FAES, however, was to expelled the guerrillas from the densely populated neighbourhoods of the San Salvador metropolis.

Mobilising up to 7,000 soldiers, led by the BIRI Atlacatl, the FAES began a vast movement from west to east of the capital to dislodge the guerrillas from the positions they held. The FAS was also beginning to come into action in urban areas. From 2 p.m. on the 13th, rocket bombardments and machine gun fire were carried out with O-2As, Hughes-500 and AC-47 attack helicopters, with the main targets being the FMLN command posts and its logistics lines. The military's first objective was to eliminate guerrilla resistance at the Metropolitan Technological Institute in Zacamil, where the FMLN had set up a command post in a building reinforced with concrete and sandbags. It was also a choke point for guerrilla reinforcements coming from the San Salvador volcano, a few kilometres to the west.

On the morning of the 13th, the ERP urban commando which installed a 60mm mortar in the Colonia Universitaria Norte, withdrew with great difficulty and considerable losses to join the FPL positions near the Mejicanos cemetery. From there, they headed to the command post of Dimas Rodriguez located in Colonia Buena Vista, in order to re-establish contact with the ERP troops in Zacamil. In the latter, the BIRI Bracamonte advanced with armoured vehicles and began the siege of the buildings where the ERP forces were entrenched. While helicopter gunships chased the rebel snipers from the upper floors, the soldiers crushed the stubborn guerrilla resistance with 90mm recoilless rifles, LAW rockets, .50 calibre machine gun fire and finally seized the Technological Institute building on 16 November.

In the impoverished town of Mejicanos, the layout of concrete and adobe houses and the hilly terrain, provided guerrillas with an abundance of perfect sites to stage ambushes. In addition to this favourable geography, the guerrillas hindered the action of the FAES by erecting numerous barricades which blocked the advance of armoured personnel carriers. However, artillery and support from 81mm mortars allowed the military to progress.[14]

Further north, on 13 November, the BIRI Atlacatl 'Bravo' group attacked the positions of the FPL FES in Ayutuxtepeque. The fighting lasted all day, and in the afternoon, it took a bayonet attack by the BIRI 3rd Company to dislodge the rebels from their positions.[15] The soldiers then received the order to reinforce the PN in the eastern sector of Zacamil.

At Cuscatancingo, the FAES had less success as the troops of the 1st Infantry Brigade, unable to advance, withdrew, after suffering heavy losses. According to a US military observer, 'This was the place the security forces learnt their lessons in urban warfare. The local police station was captured but the police retook it two days later. Unfortunately they did not secure every house and the guerrillas came back to retake the station'.[16]

On the morning of 14 November, the FMLN still controlled the northern area of San Salvador, including the towns of Apopa, Ayutuxtepeque, Zacamil, Mejicanos, Cuscatancingo, Ciudad Delgado and Soyapango. Ciudad Delgado was seriously threatened as the BIRI Atlacatl and the units of the 1st Infantry Brigade, despite violent clashes, fail to defeat the guerrillas in this area. On November 14, the BIRI Atlacatl positioned themselves on the Troncal del Norte

The FMLN offensive against San Salvador forced FAES soldiers to adapt to urban warfare. (Albert Grandolini Collection)

The FMLN assault in San Salvador marked the irruption of war in the daily lives of tens of thousands of civilians. (Albert Grandolini Collection)

Highway and began, with the support of the Cavalry Regiment, to advance towards the centre of Ciudad Delgado, where they encountered strong resistance. At night, the FAL forces in Soyapango withdrew to Ciudad Delgado to join the troops resisting the BIRI Atlacatl advance.

On the morning of the 14th, the paratroopers still could not advance into Soyapango in the face of guerrilla resistance. The FAS command then decided to bombard their defences with two A-37s. The mission was a success and the paratroopers began to advance. The 3rd Squadron attacked the guerrillas at Reparto Guadalupe while the GOEs and a BIRI Belloso company, advanced towards the Colonia Montes de San Bartolo but were blocked by the guerrillas.

In Los Conacastes, the fighting was still strong between the 2nd Squadron and the FAR-LP. Throughout the day, helicopters and AC-47s provided support to the military. When guerrilla columns tried to advance from Cerro Tecomatepeque, north of Oratorio de Concepcion to reinforce FMLN lines north-east of San Salvador, they were attacked by A-37s which disrupted their advance.

On the morning of 15 November, the paratroopers who had been fighting for several days, were relieved and replaced by other paratroopers from Comalapa, thanks to an airlift with C-123s and four C-47s. The '12 de Octubre' Marine Battalion also arrived by truck to reinforce the paratroopers. Its mission was to advance to Ciudad Delgado to establish contact with the BIRI Atlacatl and attack the FAL troops. The 4th Airborne Squadron, which was in Colonia Guadalupe, had to advance to regain its positions at Los Conacastes while the 1st Squadron was responsible for advancing on the roads that went to El Limon and Tonacatepeque township. The GOE were to attack Colonia Guadalupe from the north, while the Marines advanced from the west, directly towards the Soyapango town hall.

From San Martin, Carretera de Oro and Colonia San Bartolo, BIRI Belloso and DM-5 forces were also to attack Soyapango.

The BIRI Atlacatl continued its advance towards the Ciudad Delgado centre against the FAL forces who reinforced their positions with troops coming from Soyapango and the district of San Sebastian. During the morning, the BIRI succeeded in making progress at various points in the city. An infernal battle began in the municipal street market. The guerrillas set fire to some of the abandoned market stalls and demolished the foundations to make barricades.

In Soyapango, the PRTC forces were expelled from the vicinity of the market by FAS troops and fell back towards the INCO factory and the Las Flores district. In the afternoon, a fire broke out at the INCO plant due to aerial rocket and machine gun fire from the Air Force. The BIRI Atlacatl 'Bravo' group attacked the blocking positions of the FPL FES in the area of the YKK factory with the support of armoured vehicles, allowing the rest of the BIRI to progress, dislodging the snipers located in the surrounding buildings and freeing the PN forces entrenched in their barracks.[17] The fighting lasted all day. The security forces pushed the guerrillas back to their command post in a cemetery and advanced from tombstone to tombstone, with the support of helicopter gunships.

After reaching the centre of Soyapango, the paratroopers advanced towards Los Conacastes with the Marine Infantry on their Right. The GOEs on their side progressed from the east to Los Conacastes, Los Santos and La Guadalupe. The guerrillas withdrew, crossing the BIRI Belloso lines further east. The Marine Infantry Battalion continued its progress in Soyapango and reached the Rio Acelhuate which it crossed during the night to approach Ciudad Delgado. This situation made it more difficult to defend the FARN positions which were attacked from the morning of the 16th, by paratroopers supported by an AC-47 and UH-1M. The FARN leadership then decided to withdraw its forces to the east, under the protection of snipers using Dragunov SVD rifles.

At 4 p.m. on 15 November, a series of FAES General Staff meetings were convened to assess the situation and act. It was decided to coordinate a simultaneous all-unit, counter-offensive at dawn on 16 November, in which all available resources and men would be utilised. To ensure its success, the FAES leadership authorised the use of infantry support weapons, 90mm recoilless guns and 81mm mortars, armoured vehicles and also aerial bombardments to dislodge the guerrillas from the areas it controlled, at the risk of causing numerous civilian victims.

Rather than join the ranks of the FMLN, the inhabitants of San Salvador preferred to flee the fighting. (Albert Grandolini Collection)

At dawn on 16 November, the FAES launched their counter-attack on FMLN positions in the greater San Salvador region. Fighting continued all day on all fronts. In Ciudad Delgado there was for the first time, a fight with tear gas between the BIRI Atlacatl and the FAL.[18] The latter's command post and field hospital were attacked by planes and helicopters, forcing the evacuation and relocation of these structures. At around 10 a.m., at the entrance to the Dolores neighbourhood in Mejicanos, near the YKK factory, the BIRI Atlacatl 3rd Company, with the support of armoured vehicles and O-2A planes, attacked the FPL forces. The fighting lasted until late afternoon when the military finally took control of this area. For its part, the BIRI Belloso progressed in Mejicanos, with the support of the Hughes-500 helicopters and the O-2A and AC-47 planes, which attacked the buildings where the guerrillas were entrenched.

Despite the continuation of intense fighting in other parts of the capital, most of the FAES action on 16 November took place in Soyapango where the RN forces were fighting in three directions, in particular near the Pan-American Highway and in the Colonia Guadalupe, while FAS and BIRI Belloso troops managed to complete their encirclement. The FAS even authorised the use of an A-37 fighter-bomber to attack an RN strong point in Colonia Guadalupe with two 500-pound bombs. The guerrillas fought fiercely, throwing blocks of TNT with lit fuses at the advancing soldiers with the support of AML and UR-416 armour.[19] However, as in the other *barrios* reoccupied by the armed forces, the rebels did not resist to the FAES counter-attack. During the night, the RN commanders took the decision, despite the enormous risk involved, to break the FAES encirclement and headed towards the Tonacatepeque road. At nightfall, the FMLN prepared its retreat.

Fighting in San Salvador was particularly violent and deadly, as typical of urban fighting. This situation was aggravated by the use of the FAS to bombard working-class neighbourhoods, resulting in civilian casualties, although estimates of their number were hotly disputed.

The Jesuits Assassination
In addition to the bombardment of residential areas, a murder committed by the FAES damaged the credibility of Cristiani's government, as well as its international reputation. On 16 November, the BIRI Atlacatl entered the campus of the Universidad Centroamericana José Simeón Cañas and assassinated six Jesuit priests including Ignacio Ellacuría, rector of the university.[20] The soldiers also killed the governess of the Jesuits and her daughter. Wanting to make it appear to be a guerrilla action, they organised a mock machine gun fight and wrote on a piece of cardboard 'FMLN executed those who informed on it. Victory or death, FMLN'.[21]

In reality, Jesuit priests had long been considered suspect by the authorities. According to reports, Colonel Inocente Montano, Deputy Minister of Public Security, even publicly stated that they were 'fully identified with subversive movements'.[22] It was true that the UCA Jesuits maintained contact with the FMLN, in particular Father Ellacuría, who met on several occasions with Villalobos, the ERP leader. For the FAES, this was proof of collusion between the FMLN and the Jesuits, although the latter were critical of the guerrillas. Throughout the war, Father Ellacuría sought to persuade Villalobos to negotiate a peace agreement. According to the United Nations Truth Commission for El Salvador, the decision to assassinate the Jesuits was taken the day before by the FAES' highest leaders, including Colonel René Emilio Ponce and General Juan Rafael Bustillo. The unit chosen for executing the murder was the BIRI Atlacatl who had raided the university a few days earlier. Despite initial denials and attempts to cover it up, it quickly emerged that the Jesuits were killed by the American-trained Battalion.[23]

The murder of the Jesuits embarrassed the Bush Administration and angered Congress, which was increasingly reluctant to fund the war in El Salvador. On Capitol Hill, Aronson asked to 'negotiate an end to the conflict in El Salvador and ensure a safe space in the democratic process for all'. This was the first time a US official had explicitly acknowledged that he favoured settling the war through political negotiations.[24] While American Watch accused the administration of covering up human rights violations committed by the FAES, Congress decided to suspend aid, despite protests from the Bush Administration. Finally, it adopted an amendment that halved aid to El Salvador.[25]

The FMLN retreat, 17-19 November 1989
On the 17th, the fighting moved north of Soyapango towards Prados de Venecia and La Margaritas where the guerrillas tried to regroup. The 5th Airborne Squadron was sent to Colonia Guadalupe where FMLN forces were forced to withdraw.[26] Meanwhile, an airborne operation was organised north of Tonacatepeque. It had to cut off the guerrillas' retreat route while other FAES forces pressed the rebels to the north. The paratroopers landed at the planned location and awaited the retreating guerrillas.

On the morning of the 17th, the ERP forces finally left Colonia Zacamil and crossed San Ramon to the slopes of Picacho, in the San Salvador volcano. In Ciudad Delgado, PH troops continued to advance while BIRI Atlacatl forces reached the centre of the town, supported by armoured vehicles and aerial fire from O-2A aircraft. During the afternoon, intense fighting took place during which the guerrilla forces finally withdrew.

Soyapango, east of the capital, was the last municipality where the FAES had to face a large concentration of guerrillas. The day before, Dimas Rojas announced to his commanders the CG's decision to retreat. This had to be carried out by the sector of Colonia

From 16 November, the FAS received the authorisation to carry out bombardments on San Salvador in order to expel the guerrillas. Even old Magisters were pressed into action again, together with UH-1H helicopters. (Albert Grandolini Collection)

On the 18th, the main guerrilla forces, those of the ERP and the FAPL, followed by those of the FAL, withdrew from the north of San Salvador to partly regroup on the slopes of the San Salvador volcano. Meanwhile, in northern Soyapango, FARN reinforcements launched an attack to relieve pressure on FAR-LP and FARN units in Venecia and Prusia cantons.

On the 19th, the guerrillas tried to withdraw through the townships of San Laureano and San José Cortez south of Tonacatepeque. In the Colonia Los Conacastes, the RN forces also fell back near the Las Caña River in the direction of San José Guayabal, towards the camps of Santa Inés en Piedra and Labrada, where they fought with destructive helicopter troops. During the night, the withdrawal of FPL and ERP forces from Mejicanos and Cuscatancingo began. The Commander Dimas Rodriguez command post maintained in Colonia Buena Vista, was dismantled and headed for the San Salvador volcano slopes. All guerrilla forces finally abandoned the northern area of Soyapango and those occupied in the east of the capital, retreated towards the Guazapa volcano passing south of Tonacatepeque.

By the morning of the 20th, the withdrawal of guerrilla forces from San Salvador was complete. Almost all managed to reach positions on the outskirts of the capital. The operational commanders coordinated among themselves and the FMLN CG to decide on the follow-up to the offensive. The decision was finally made to remain on the outskirts of San Salvador to attempt a series of raids on strategic points in the capital.

At around 9 a.m. on 20 November, American Green Berets, who were in the country giving counter-insurgency training to the BIRI Atlacatl commando unit, a mission suspended due to fighting in San Salvador, rented rooms at the Salvador Sheraton Hotel. At 1 p.m., OAS Secretary General, João Clemente Baena Soares, checked into the same hotel.

An FMLN fighter resting during the fighting in San Salvador. (Albert Grandolini Collection)

Los Santo I. The retreat began on the night of the 16th, while the vanguard formed by about 20 FES fighters and a regular force of 30 men, had to open the way and break the encirclement. The FARN were in charge of attacking a section of the BIRI Belloso between the Colonia Guadalupe and the Colonia Los Santos I to be able to continue advancing, while the FAR-LP fell into an ambush which caused heavy losses.

The fighting was particularly intense, but around 8 a.m. the vanguard managed to reach the old street of Tonacatepeque, breaking the encirclement near Los Santos I and opening the way to retreat. The FARN then managed to cross the lines of the FAES and reached the area of San José Guayabal with the objective of taking refuge in the Cerro Guazapa. About 60 FMLN fighters died during this fighting. At noon, the FAES secured Soyapango and authorised the civilian population to bury the bodies of the guerrillas in a mass grave.

The FMLN Raids on San Salvador, 21 November – 12 December

The fighting was far from over following the guerrillas' retreat. For days, the latter launched actions of harassment in the northern suburbs of the capital and in Soyapang. Using their mobility, they did not hesitate to effectively strike the wealthy neighbourhoods of the west of the city, where they carried out one of the most spectacular actions of the entire war.

On 21 November, the FAPL (800 to 1,300 men), FAL (400 men) and ERP (100 men) forces, who had regrouped on the San Salvador volcano, attempted an incursion into the west of the capital, in the sectors of Colonia Escalon, San Benito and the Masferrer roundabout. About 250 FAPL men, led by Ramon Torres, had to enter Ayutuxtepeque and Mejicanos for a diversionary manoeuvrer while preparing the assault against the Sheraton Hotel, which was carried out around 6 am. The buildings of the latter consisted of two towers, a main tower of six floors and a new tower called VIP, in which the third floor was rented to house American officials and military.

The hotel was protected by GN units who were both inside the buildings and on the outskirts. A platoon of around 20 ERP fighters entered the VIP tower which dominated the hotel while the FPL forces, whose objective was to capture the main tower, could not enter but maintained control of the streets surrounding the hotel.

Inside the VIP tower, the ERP fighters learnt of the presence of the American Green Berets of which they previously knew nothing. The ERP commander, Claudio Armijo, installed at his command post located near the hotel, informed the FMLN CG in Nicaragua, as well as the politico-diplomatic commission in Mexico. The latter gave the order not to try to capture the American soldiers whose presence would be an asset for negotiations. A few minutes later, Armijo learnt the OAS Secretary General was in the VIP tower. He tried to establish telephone contact with him, but without success. He then decided to send a verbal message, via a call to the hotel manager, to inform him that the diplomat should not fear for his safety and that he was not the target of the operation.

AML-90 Panhard armoured cars fitted with the D921 F1 90mm gun were widely used to drive FMLN fighters out of San Salvador. (Albert Grandolini Collection)

Faced with the FMLN daring raid, the FAES organised the operation 'Rescate' from the Ilopango Air Base. A CEAT force prepared to conduct an aerial assault on the Sheraton Hotel roof. At the same time, the Pentagon gave the order to send a Delta Force detachment to El Salvador, in order to be ready to carry out a rescue mission.

At 10 a.m., a direct telephone line was established between the FMLN political-diplomatic commission in Mexico City and the State Department in Washington to negotiate the release of the American soldiers and civilians present in the hotel. These discussions had the support of the Apostolic Nuncio in San Salvador and the Mexican government as Delta Force landed at Comalapa airport and established a forward position in Ciudad Merliot, ready to execute its rescue mission if necessary.

At 12:30 p.m., the CEAT, commanded by Captain Chavez Garcia, launched Operation Rescate on the hotel, an airborne assault using 17 men, two UH-1H helicopters for transport, two UH-1Ms and two Hughes-500s for protection. During the assault, the guerrillas prevented one of the UH-1Hs from approaching but the second managed to land on the hotel roof to disembark the soldiers. Half an hour later, they came out through the hall with Baena Soares and a few civilians who accompanied him. They got into an armoured vehicle to be taken to safety at the EMCFA. An hour later, the Apostolic Nunciature announced the conclusion of a ceasefire agreement to allow the hostages to be evacuated. It stipulated the maintenance of FAES armoured vehicles at a safe distance and the non-intervention of other forces, including American ones. At around 3:00 p.m., the ERP forces withdrew from the VIP tower and soon after, the Green Berets left the hotel in armoured vehicles.

At the end of the day, the FAPL, coming from the San Salvador volcano, moved towards Colonia Escalon to protect the retreat of their comrades. A section then headed towards the volcano slopes while another retreated towards the wooded area of Finca El Espino in Antiguo Cuscatlán under FAS harassment. In the evening, all FPL forces left Colonia Escalon.

The FMLN continued its raids against the capital in the following days, whilst the FAES carried out operations to drive the guerrillas away from San Salvador. Thus, on 22 November, the PRTC forces, who again tried to enter Soyapango, suffered some losses against the soldiers who had secured their positions. They chose to withdraw to the Plan del Pino camp to await further instructions.

On the 22nd, the FAES High Command, which feared that the FMLN was capable of launching large-scale operations against key points in the capital, wanted to take advantage of the withdrawal of guerrilla forces to intercept and destroy them. It decided to launch an airborne operation carried out by GOE soldiers transported by nine UH-1H helicopters and protected by two UH-1H and three Hughes-500, which had to land north-east of San José Guayabal. The assault had to be preceded by the attack of three A-37Bs.

The operation took place on the 23rd and the special forces confronted FARN troops. The fighting was violent and required the landing of an airborne squadron while the BIRI Belloso 5th Company attacked from the canton of Plan del Pino towards the west to confront the units of the FAL, coming from the Sheraton Hotel, who preferred to fight in retreat north of Maniguas where FAR-LP forces were located.

The day of the 23rd saw many fights scattered north of the capital. Due to the large concentration of guerrilla forces in the San Salvador volcano, the FAS landed GOE units in the highest part of the volcano, while part of the FPL forces near Cerro El Carmen, were heading towards the volcano.

The following day, FAL and PRTC forces, located in Plan del Pino, advanced north towards Cerro Guazapa. They encountered GOEs and paratroopers advancing south of Guazapa with A-37B air support from Comalapa. The guerrillas were ambushed, the FAL

Two locally-made Cashuat APCs during operations in an urban neighbourhood. (Albert Grandolini Collection)

received the reinforcement of forces coming from Chalatenango to confront the BIRI Belloso 4th and 5th companies and resisted all day before withdrawing, in difficult conditions, to the north, in the canton of San José Cortez. They had to nevertheless, remain in the northern outskirts of San Salvador to support the FAL and FAPL who were preparing to enter the Escalon and San Benito districts again. In the San Salvador volcano, fighting continued on the 25th and 26th, with the FAES ambushing the FAL columns. The latter managed to evade the BIRI Atlacatl and the GOE, by joining the ERP and FPL forces who carried out a raid in the Colonia Escalon in the north-west of San Salvador.

On the 27th, ERP and FAL troops entered the Colonia Lomas Verdes, a residential area, and attempted to attack the presidential residence located about 500 metres away. At the same time, FPL forces entered San Salvador from two directions. The first from the forest area of El Espino and the second by Antiguo Cuscatlán, the Colonias La Sultana and Lomas de San Francisco with the objective of carrying out a pincer manoeuvrer towards the EMCFA.

FPL troops set up forward positions near Rond-Pont Masferrer and Ciudad Merliot, to support those entering the city through Antiguo Cuscatlán and Colonia San Benito. On the morning of the 29th, fierce fighting took place in Colonia San Benito which adjoined the community of Las Palmas, which was part of the EMCFA security perimeter. The forces entering through Antiguo Cuscatlán, Colonia Sultana and the San Francisco heights failed to reach Colonia Los Héroes and had to retreat against BIRI Bracamonte.

While the FAPL attacked from the south towards the EMCFA, other FAPL and FAL troops left the San Salvador volcano and occupied the neighbourhoods of San Benito and Escalon south-west of the capital. Around 10 a.m., they were attacked by troops and armoured vehicles from the CEBRI Battalion, which were stopped by rocket launchers and an attack by FAL special forces. A Cashuat armoured vehicle was destroyed by RPG-7 fire and the troops following its advance, retreated with a significant number of casualties.

At around 3:00 p.m., FAL fighters clashed with members of the government communications team, causing the death of five of the group, a fact that the Cristiani government denounced as an 'attack on journalists'. The situation required the dispatch of the BIRI Atlacatl 3rd Company, a Cavalry Regiment squad and a Marine Infantry company who managed to surprise the guerrillas with a pincer movement. It was only at night that the FMLN forces withdrew from all the combat zones of Antiguo Cuscatlán, San Benito and Lomas Verdes and retreated to the San Salvador volcano and the forested areas of Antiguo. Cuscatlán.

That same day, 48 GOE soldiers, transported by six UH-1Hs and escorted by two UH-1Ms, landed on the Picacho Military Base, on the top of the San Salvador volcano. They had to attack the rear of the rebel forces resisting at San Benito and Escalon. However, poor coordination prevented the GOE from accomplishing their mission and it was ultimately the BIRI Atlacatl that forced the guerrillas to withdraw.

Although expelled from the capital, the FMLN maintained significant forces around San Salvador, which posed a real threat to the FAES. On 1st December, it again made a new incursion into the Soyapango sector where it faced the paratroopers who were supported by two UH-1M helicopters and a Hughes-500. The guerrillas finally withdrew in the night.

In the San José Cortez canton of Ciudad Delgado, BIRI Belloso units attempted to defeat the FAL forces defending their positions. On 2 December, the latter launched an attack but suffered heavy losses. Finally, they retreated in the night towards the east. On the night of 4 December, FAL forces carried out a new raid in the Miramonte district, from the San Salvador volcano via San Antonio Abad. There they confronted the PN forces and then retreated.

These latest FMLN raids on San Salvador could not stop the inexorable decline of its offensive. At the beginning of December, it ran out of steam and the capital returned to its usual activity. Gradually, the FMLN forces that participated in the offensive against San Salvador joined their *retaguardias*, but they did not hesitate to launch attacks during their journey. Thus, on 8 December, RN forces coming from the Tonacatepeque region attacked the FAS military positions and the Artillery Brigade in San José Guayabal, in their retreat towards Cerro Guazapa. However, this retreat was not without risk.

On 6 December, the intelligence services detected the presence of three concentrations of guerrillas, one north of Soyapango, another north of Santa Tecla and the last south of Antiguo Cuscatlán. The High command decided to attack these three concentrations. An Airborne squadron was to land south of Tonacatepeque while two A-37Bs bombarded the rebel positions south of Cerro Guazapa and the BIRI Belloso attacked the rear of the guerrillas. The fighting lasted until 9 December.

At the beginning of December, the FAES were given the task of driving out the FMLN forces which could still pose a danger to the San Salvador security and which continued to strike at military positions on the outskirts of the capital. On the 11th, the paratroopers were sent near Tonacatepeque where the Civil Defence positions were attacked by FARN forces coming from the Guazapa volcano.

An FMLN fighter during urban combat in November 1989. (Albert Grandolini Collection)

On 15 December, the BIRI Belloso was tasked with destroying the guerrilla concentrations south of Guazapa. On the 17th, it left San José de Guayabal and progressed in the Cerro Guazapa with the support of the FAS. The next day, the fighting was very violent against the FAL troops. While the BIRI Belloso was in difficulty, the paratroopers landed north-east of its positions while the A-37Bs bombarded the area. The paratroopers attacked the rear of the FAL, but the latter resisted and the fighting lasted several more days. On the 21st, the guerrillas launched violent attacks against the positions of the paratroopers and the BIRI Belloso, forcing the landing of the 3rd Airborne squadron north of San José Guayabal, to progress towards Suchitoto and join those who were already fighting on the eastern flank of Cerro Guazapa.[27]

In early December, fighting continued for control of the San Salvador volcano, north-west of the capital. On 11 December, the FPL who were in the northern area of Ayutuxtepeque and Mejicanos, climbed the volcano to reinforce the troops who participated in the incursions into the Colonia Escalon. In the afternoon, the FAL and FPL engaged in combat against BIRI Belloso and GOE units who were looking for guerrilla concentrations on the volcano.

On the morning of the 12th, a new landing by helicopters of GOE units was carried out. The fighting lasted several hours and the military received air support from A-37 planes and helicopters. Under intense bombardment, a burst of aerial fire killed Commander Nicolas Hernán Solórzano Sanchez (Dimas Rodriguez), who led FPL troops during the November offensive. Eventually, the FMLN commanders decided to send the guerrilla forces present on the San Salvador volcano to other *retaguardias*.

Part of the FAL, RN and PRTC forces returned to Cerro Guazapa, particularly to the El Quemado camp. The region was also subjected to intense bombardments by the FAS on 13 and 14 December. PRTC forces marched towards San Vicente, where they arrived on 25 December in the camps of Cerros de San Pedro. Those of the FPL reached their various camps in the Chalatenago department at the end of the year. Part of the forces that broke up towards Antiguo Cuscatlán, filled up towards the Cordillera del Bálsamo in the La Libertad department to found a 'southern front' that would exist until the end of the war.

Two groups of BIRI Atlacatl were sent to the Cinquera region to persecute the last guerrilla columns retreating towards the Chalatenango department. Another group from the same unit joined the San Salvador volcano to maintain patrols while an another remained in Santa Tecla in order to protect the capital against a new guerrilla incursion.

The November 1989 Offensive outside San Salvador

If the FMLN main effort during the November offensive focused on San Salvador, the rest of the country was not spared. San Miguel, the third largest city in the country, appeared to be particularly vulnerable at the time of the November offensive. When the guerrillas began their operation against this commercial city of approximately 150,000 inhabitants around 8 p.m. on 11 November, most of the FAES forces based there were dozens of kilometres away, operating in the mountains. They had nevertheless, been informed of an imminent FMLN assault on San Miguel and were on their way back, still a few days from the city, when the guerrillas attacked. The armed forces present in San Miguel had to therefore repel it whilst being largely outnumbered.

As in San Salvador, the FMLN struck the poor neighbourhoods on the northern and eastern outskirts of San Miguel. However, it complicated the military's defence by also trying to capture the power plant and the hospital south-west of the city. The immediate concern of Colonel Vargas, who commanded the 3rd Infantry Brigade, was to ensure the security of the Vice President, Francisco Merino, who was in San Miguel on an official visit. When he learnt that guerrillas were trying to seize the hotel where he was staying, Vargas, accompanied by an escort of only eight men, left the 3rd Brigade garrison and fought his way to the hotel. As his soldiers pushed back the guerrillas, he reinforced the security of the building until he could evacuate the vice president to San Salvador the next day.[28]

The guerrillas had penetrated many neighbourhoods, but Colonel Vargas skilfully manoeuvrered his weak forces to prevent them from capturing the hospital, power station, 3rd Brigade garrison and other important military and economic installations. The guerrillas tried to enter the city centre, but the FAES units managed to push them back. In less than 48 hours, the military contained the threat of the guerrillas in the south-west of the city and began to concentrate on its north-eastern outskirts, in particular facing the Colonia Milagro de la Paz where there was a guerrilla command post. The latter was attacked by FAS helicopters, a 3rd Brigade company and a motorised cavalry unit.[29]

On 15 and 16 November, the defenders were reinforced by the return of the 3rd Brigade units which had been patrolling dozens of kilometres to the north when the offensive began, as well as the arrival of reinforcements from other towns. With these 1,800 to 2,000 additional men, the military overwhelmed the guerrillas, who were forced to retreat. The final action took place in eastern San Miguel where the FMLN had set up its rearguard but where there were also thousands of civilians. Air support, which had a limited range in San Miguel, was then widely used to destroy its positions, forcing the guerrillas to flee.

Southwest of San Salvador, Zacatecoluca, which then had a population of around 20,000, was also a target for the FMLN. Some 500 guerrillas attempted to invade it on 11 November. The next day, they managed to occupy the Santa Teresa Hospital, blowing up and burning part of one of its floors. However, the guerrillas underestimated the fighting spirit of the Engineer Battalion defending the city. After several days of fighting, they finally withdrew from the city.

At the end of October, in the Usulutan department, troops of the 6th Brigade ambushed a guerrilla column and captured 1,000 pounds of TNT. Seeing that the rebels were moving from north to south, towards Usulutan, the 6th Brigade was put on alert, awaiting an assault on the town. On 10 November, an informant from the FAES made known the approach roads planned by the guerrillas. It

FMLN guerrilla commander Jehová Márquez Lizama, aka Comandante Cirilo, killed in Santa Ana during the November 1989 offensive. (Albert Grandolini Collection)

was under these conditions that the FMLN attacked Usulutan on 11 November. The assault was halted outside the city, about a kilometre to the west, in the cemetery. It seemed that the only success of the FMLN was to install a home-made mortar which managed to hit the 6th Brigade headquarters with an explosive shell, causing material damage and injuring two soldiers. After four or five days, the guerrillas withdrew, to return on 29 November with a lesser force of about 180 men who were again, arrested on the city outskirts.

El Salvador's second city with more than 250,000 inhabitants, Santa Ana was also attacked by the FPL on 11 November with some 250 guerrillas. They infiltrated several neighbourhoods close to the 2nd Infantry Brigade to try to prevent the troops from leaving to reinforce the FAES in San Salvador, before withdrawing on the 14th.

Other smaller actions were taking place in the rest of the country. The guerrillas attacked the Comalapa Air Base, 50km west of San Salvador where three O-2 Martillos planes and an AC-47TP were hit by bullets but could still fly. In Morazan, they tried to take control of the airstrip located three kilometres north of the city but failed.

The November 1989 Offensive was an occasion of particularly violent fighting which claimed many victims. During the months of November and December, the FAES had 556 killed, 1,703 wounded and 27 missing, while the FMLN had 600 dead, 1,485 wounded and 788 prisoners.[30]. For the FAES, the year 1989 was particularly difficult with 1,358 dead – a level not reached since 1982.[31]

The offensive consequences

The November 1989 FMLN offensive came as a surprise to the US Embassy. The night before, it even hosted the Marine Corps Ball, an event that would never have happened had it known of an impending attack. Perhaps more importantly, in the days following the start of the offensive on the capital, the situation in San Salvador appeared uncertain. The Bush Administration first tried to minimise its impact and presented it as a desperate action by an organisation on the verge of defeat. Secretary of State James Baker insisted that 'there is no threat to the Salvadoran government'.[32] There was a great fear that the working-class neighbourhoods would switch to the side of the FMLN. The offensive also frightened the FAES command which, according to Ambassador Walker, was 'panicked'.[33]

For their part, the FAES suffered a total loss of credibility. The offensive demonstrated that they had not defeated the guerrillas despite the efforts of previous years, while the Sheraton Hotel action revealed their inability to ensure the security of sensitive places. A senior US military officer at the US Embassy thus stated that the FAES was well organised but:

> ... there were inherent command and control problems in the confusion of combat – cases of battalions firing on each other's flanks. A lack of detailed maps complicated the situation. You have to remember, too, that there hadn't been pitched battles in the capital since the 1981 offensive and most of the soldiers did not have experience in urban combat.[34]

The murder of the Jesuits also affected the government's credibility, which was losing some of the legitimacy it had acquired over the past few years.

As the Cold War receded, the November offensive forced the world to turn its gaze to El Salvador. Hundreds of journalists began to arrive in San Salvador on the 12th to cover the fighting in the capital and capture photographs of the clashes. The Intercontinental Hotel, the one preferred by the international press, was rapidly running out of rooms. The conflict was no longer, strictly speaking, an internal problem in El Salvador.

Domestically, the vast offensive launched by the FMLN brought the theatre of war to the capital, San Salvador, with its aftermath of death, suffering and destruction. Political leaders, businessmen and other influential sectors of society for whom the war had no concrete realities, found themselves confronted with its violence and joined the many supporters of a political solution. Thus, the offer of peace talks that President Cristiani had formulated the previous 1st of June, when he took office, took on new validity.

The FMLN, by leading the largest urban guerrilla operation in the modern history of Latin America, demonstrated its strength but also its isolation since it did not receive the support of the population. It also showed its military weakness since it was unable to have sufficient reserves that would have allowed it to exploit its initial successes.[35] While it failed in its goal of overthrowing the government and failed militarily, it nevertheless won a political victory. Within its own ranks, those who still believed in the possibility of military victory began to see the end of the war as the result of a negotiated settlement. Abroad, its military prowess bolstered its credibility and drew international attention to El Salvador. Above all, they demonstrated to its adversaries that the war was impossible to win, reinforcing the argument that American aid to the government was ineffective.

For Washington, the offensive demonstrated that the FMLN retained its ability to carry out a daring operation when most

The November 1989 offensive was a shock for the FAES which was forced into realisation that the guerrillas were far from defeated. (Albert Grandolini Collection)

analyses claimed it was impossible. The power of the offensive shattered the illusion that the FAES were winning the war. The senior American officer responsible for Latin America believed that negotiations were the only way to settle the conflict. During his testimony on Capitol Hill, General Maxwell Thurman, head of the Southern Command, asked about the likelihood of the FAES defeating the FMLN and replied bluntly, 'I think they won't be able to do that'.[36] This opinion was shared by politicians like James Baker who wrote in his memoirs, 'on the one hand it ended any illusion among the guerrillas that the civilian population was ready to follow their call, but it also shattered the military's hopes that the guerrillas were a spent force. And the Jesuit massacre galvanised Congress like never before to cut aid'.[37] For all the actors in the conflict, the FMLN, Washington, the FAES and the Salvadoran government, the only way to peace in the country was through dialogue.

Despite many differences, the November 1989 Offensive had similar characteristics to that of the Vietnamese Tet in January – February 1968. Similarly, it was massive and powerful, it reached the urban areas of the big cities, and as in Vietnam, if the guerrillas did not win, the offensive changed the course of the war.

7
THE PATH TO PEACE

The November 1989 FMLN offensive did not lead to a rapid return to peace. It was a long process to arrive at this conclusion. Although negotiations began at the start of 1990, the FMLN and its adversaries wanted to end them in a position of strength to impose their points of view, an issue that was mainly played out in the military arena. Therefore, the fighting continued until the end of 1991 and it needed constant pressure from the international community for each side of the Salvadoran civil war to gradually make concessions. It was only days after the demise of the Soviet Union that the last iconic conflict of the Cold War finally came to an end.

The new international situation
In 1989, the Cold War ended and the strategic importance of El Salvador decreased for Washington. The FMLN offensive in November definitively shifted the Bush Administration to the side of regional and international actors working to end the various conflicts in the region, abandoning Reagan's objective of winning a decisive victory. From now on, the administration was ready to tolerate a negotiated settlement in the new international context. The task was delicate since it had to have this new orientation accepted by the FAES. For this, it could count on the support of President Cristiani, who also believed that a military victory was impossible and that peace was necessary to get the country out of the economic and social slump into which years of war had plunged it. The Salvadoran president also understood growing war-weariness and people's desire for peace.[1]

Washington also had to convince the FMLN that if it continued the war, the United States would not abandon the Cristiani government. For this, it received support from Moscow. Since the failure of the January 1981 offensive, the Soviets had reconsidered the validity of armed struggle in Central America and reduced their aid to the FMLN as the chances of guerrilla success seemed to be diminishing.[2] This trend was accentuated with the coming to power in 1985 of Mikhail Gorbachev, who sought to improve his country's relations with the West. Faced with the deterioration of the Soviet economy, he also sought to reduce the aid, including military, that Moscow provided to its various allies, such as Nicaragua and Cuba. In a speech at the UN in December 1988, Gorbachev announced the end of support for national liberation movements in the Third World, providing the Bush Administration with an opportunity to rethink its rivalry with Moscow in Central America. This process of disengagement was nevertheless gradual and was accompanied by calls from Gorbachev for the two superpowers to end their intervention in the affairs of other countries, in particular in the Third World. Regarding El Salvador, he believed that the FMLN had to negotiate with the government.[3]

While Cuba continued to support the FMLN, including obtaining arms and coordinating international support for the guerrillas, it was also in favour of a negotiated settlement. Castro was indeed

ERP fighter in Perquin, Morazan department in 1990. (Albert Grandolini Collection)

FMLN on their territory, pushing the latter to set up these offices in Mexico City in 1984.⁴ This desire of the Sandinistas to normalise their international relations and save their regime explained why, during the Central American presidents conference in San Isidro, in December 1989, Daniel Ortega joined his colleagues in condemning the warmongering attitude of the FMLN.⁵

This convergence between the various international protagonists in the Salvadorian conflict in favour of a negotiated peace, placed the Central American question at the heart of the discussions at the Bush-Gorbachev summit in Malta on 2 and 3 December 1989. The FMLN offensive in November appeared, in effect, as an obstacle to further Detente between the two superpowers. A week earlier, a Cessna carrying SA-7 MANPADS from Nicaragua was discovered in El Salvador, angering Moscow, which blamed Cubans and Nicaraguans for ignoring its demands not to send more weapons to the FMLN. Although it appeared that this batch of weapons came from Cuba and transited through Nicaraguan territory with the complicity of the Sandinistas, Managua and Havana denied that the delivery took place.

Furthermore, Moscow suspected that the November offensive was timed to coincide with preparations for the Malta summit.⁶ The USSR Ministry of Foreign Affairs, commenting on the 1989 offensive, for the first time, publicly criticised the FMLN as well as the FAES. While the latter were denounced for their indiscriminate use of bombardments, the former was criticised for having carried out offensives in densely populated urban areas. In Malta, Bush asked Gorbachev to stop supporting the FMLN through Cuba.⁷

The message was heard by Moscow and throughout 1990, the Soviets repeatedly insisted that the FMLN negotiated with the Salvadoran government in the presence of the United Nations. They even suggested that if the United States stopped supporting the Salvadoran government, it should unilaterally lay down its arms.⁸ Despite the progress of the peace process in Nicaragua resulting from the cooperation of the superpowers, the resolution of the Salvadorian conflict was proving more difficult. Nevertheless, Gorbachev continued to support efforts to resolve the crisis by peaceful means, relying on the UN and the OAS but also by putting pressure on Cuba and Nicaragua.⁹

aware that the FMLN could not prevail against the importance of Washington's aid to the Salvadoran government. Added to this was the intention to normalise Havana's relations with the Americans as Soviet protection receded.

Nicaragua already diminished its support for the FMLN after the January 1981 offensive but continued to offer it political and moral support. The fear of a direct American military intervention against them also pushed the Sandinistas to stop supplying ammunition to the Salvadoran guerrillas and to restrict the activities of the

By the end of 1989, the international environment was no longer favourable to the FMLN, a situation which worsened the following

A UH-1H helicopter armed with a mini gun and rocket launcher, as seen at Ilopango AB. (Albert Grandolini Collection)

year with the loss of support from Cuba and Nicaragua. Under the terms of the Arias peace plan, Managua held elections in 1990 which saw the unexpected defeat of the Sandinistas who were driven from power. Nevertheless, the latter still retained key positions within the Armed Forces and thus continued to support the FMLN clandestinely, by supplying it with new weapons, in particular surface-to-air missiles.[10]

The FAS losing Control of the Sky
Since 1984, the FAS firepower and mobility, acquired thanks to American support, had forced the guerrillas to remain on the defensive. It gave yet another demonstration of its ability to give the FAES the advantage during the November 1989 Offensive. A US military officer who observed the FAS counterattacks said:

> The air force was crucial in turning the tide against the guerrillas and defeating them on the offensive. The AC-47 gunships and M model Hueys were very effective. But the guerrillas feared most the helicopters the Salvadoran Air Force calls the Hughes 500, probably since it was so fast and manoeuvrable and could pursue them in difficult terrain.[11]

The FMLN understood the impact of the FAS evolution in the development of the war and with the advice of its allies in Vietnam, Cuba and Nicaragua, it tried to counter this. From 1985, it had snipers, equipped with the semi-automatic Dragunov SVD rifle, tasked with shooting at vulnerable parts of helicopters or at pilots. In April 1988, during an operation to evacuate the wounded from the BIRI Atlacatl in the Las Vueltas area, a UH-1H pilot was killed by guerrilla fire and only the dexterity of the co-pilot prevented the helicopter from creashing. This situation allowed Commander Ramon Torres to declare to the press in July 1989: 'All our troops are now trained in anti-aircraft combat and the phase of the war when we were afraid of gunships is over. Now we can fight by day as well as by night'.[12]

Snipers became prime targets for BIRIs and PRALs and were therefore, protected by a support squad. The FMLN also continued to manufacture home-made weapons by modifying grenade launchers or rocket launchers. These tactics were effective since in 1988, 47 aircraft were affected and 96 from January to August 1989.[13]

Another tactic used by the FMLN to weaken the FAS, was the assassination of the pilots, a mission that fell to the urban commandos and the FES. According to Herard von Santos, at least three pilots were thus victims of an attack. It was probably within the framework of these actions, that on 3 May 1985, an urban commando tried to kill the commander of the paratroopers, Major Turcios Chévez. More ambitious was the preparation for the attack on the Presidente Hotel to kill the American officers who served as instructors for the FAS pilots. But the various modalities of action against the Americans were finally abandoned.[14]

From 1984, the FMLN leaders asked Cuba and Nicaragua to supply them with MANPADS but Managua and Havana refused, fearing negative reactions from Washington.[15] The same request was made by representatives of the PCS and the ERP in Moscow in 1984. Again, the Soviets refused. Nevertheless, Cuba agreed to provide on its territory training in the handling of the Soviet-made 9K32 Strela-2 (NATO reporting name SA-7 Grail).

It was not until the November 1989 Offensive that Nicaragua finally agreed to send SA-7 anti-aircraft missile systems to El Salvador as part of Operation Mariposa, which received support from Cuba. The missile systems, versions of the model 9K32M Strela-2M (SA-7b) were supplied by North Korea after a negotiation led by Schafik Handal. About 20 ERP fighters were also sent to Cuba to receive a 3-month training to learn how they work.

Operation Mariposa was planned by the EPS in collaboration with the FMLN leaders. The CG entrusted the mission of transporting the missiles to the FAPL and the ERP. For this, they had two twin-engines, a Cessna 130 and an Aerocomander-520 piloted by Salvadorans who took off from Montelimar in Nicaragua on the night of 24 November. Cessna 130 crashed while landing on a small airstrip near El Transito in Usulutan Department with 24 SA-7 and 9K34 Strela 3 (SA-14) missile systems and one FIM-43 Redeye missile system. In Santa Cruz Porrillo, near Zacatecoluca, the second plane was about to run out of fuel after circling several times because it was unable to identify the landing area. Around 10:30 a.m. it saw torches on the ground and landed with 25 MANPADS near a marshy area where a FPL column had secured the place. GOE forces were then responsible for intercepting the rebels who had recovered the weapons, but without succeeding. The FPL column managed to escape and reach the Chinchontepec volcano. A third shipment by air arrived between 26 and 28 November. At this time the FMLN had 50 SA-7 with 75 missiles and some Redeye.

On 29 November, the DIMFA forces confronted in violent combat, the guerrillas in the Zacatecoluca valley. To support the military, two A-37Bs and a Cessna O-2A took part in the fighting. The guerrillas fired their first anti-aircraft missile against them without hitting the target, the North Korean-made MANPADS not working properly. On 1st December, the FAPL forces were still fighting those of the DIMFA which received reinforcement from a BIRI Atonal company. The

FAS helicopters, like this UH-1H armed with a US-made Mk.82 bomb calibre 250kg, were particularly feared by the guerrillas (Albert Grandolini Collection)

Cessna O-2s were prime targets for guerrilla MANPADS. One of them was shot down by a surface-to-air missile. (Albert Grandolini Collection)

FAS also sent two Cessna 0-2As which were the target of missile fire which they managed to dodge. To destroy the positions from which the MANPADS were fired, two A-37Bs were sent to drop 500-pound bombs. They were also the target of anti-aircraft missile fire. It took the dispatch of two other A-37Bs with eight bombs of 750 pounds to finally break the guerrillas resistance.

While the FAPL continued to exert pressure north of Zacatecoluca, on 4 December the DIMFA requested air support. The FAS sent two Cessna O-2As which were the target of a MANPADS which they managed to avoid. In response, the FAS sent six A-37Bs and five O-2As to bombard the area with 500 and 750 pound bombs and rockets. It was one of the most impressive bombardments of the war. If the first MANPADS shots did not hit their target, the FMLN nevertheless managed to destroy a Cessna O-2A in the Ozatlan area in the Usulutan department when a sniper killed the pilot whose plane crashed.[16]

The arrival of MANPADS on the Salvadoran battlefield marked a new stage in the conflict. The almost absolute mastery of the sky that had hitherto belonged to the FAS weakened considerably. The latter found itself forced to reduce the number of its sorties and limit its air support to ground troops, two elements which were essential to regaining the initiative from the guerrillas from 1984. The CIA clearly perceived these changes, fearing that the anti-aircraft weapons could 'degrade the government's counter-insurgency effort' and 'give the guerrillas freer control over larger areas of the country'.[17] These fears seemed to be justified since the FAES were abandoning their aggressive posture.

The FMLN arsenal then included SA-7, SA-14 and, from October 1990, it was enriched with more effective MANPADS, the 9K310 Igla-1, called SA-16 Gimlet in the NATO designation. Nevertheless, the guerrillas possessed relatively few MANPADS, so they were used carefully. At first, they served defensive purposes, for the protection of command posts and the disruption of helicopter landings. Then, as the guerrillas gained experience, they used them to shoot down any aircraft that flew over the conflict zones. One of the most common tactics was to deliberately maim and injure, not kill, enemy soldiers and then use them as bait to shoot down evacuation helicopters.

Another technique was to attack isolated armed forces or security force positions for them to call in air support in the form of AC-47s, A-37 attack aircraft and O-2A reconnaissance aircraft. Ambush sites were set up on commanding heights around the position to shoot down aircraft when busy providing air support. Four planes, a UH-1, an AC-47, an O-2 and an A-37 Dragonfly, were shot down using these tactics.

Faced with the use of MANPADS, the FAS was developing various methods to overcome this new threat. In order to reduce ambushes against helicopters in charge of medical evacuations, more doctors, able to stabilise the wounded, accompanied the troops on the ground until they could be evacuated at night. Most air operations began to be carried out in the dark, because the SA-7s possessed by the guerrillas did not have night sights. The AC-47s, A-37s and O-2s also stopped using their lights at night and were forced to act as a group, watching over each other while waiting to take advantage of a guerrilla weakness.[18]

Tactics were also used to spot and destroy MANPADS users. Hughes 500 reconnaissance helicopters skimmed the ground to locate them. Behind them, at different altitudes, were UH-1Ms, AC-47s and A-37s. Once the MANPADS operator was located, the Hughes 500s immediately attacked him to keep him occupied and called in reinforcements. As soon as the other planes were close, the Hughes 500 took off, allowing the UH-1M and the AC-47 to fire in turn. Finally, the A-37s dropped 500-pound bombs, one after the other, on the spot where the MANPADS fire was coming from.

The appearance of anti-aircraft weapons in the FMLN's arsenal also prompted the USAF to provide the FAS with Electronic Countermeasure/Infrared Countermeasure (ECM/IRCM) systems whose function was to circumvent the MANPADS infrared guidance systems in the form of electronic equipment ALQ-144

FAS helicopter gunner during a rescue mission for wounded ground troops, in area of Guazapa volcano. (Albert Grandolini Collection)

to protect helicopters and ALQ-123 for planes. The FAS also used the ALE-40 system consisting of flares.[19]

Even if these different tactics were useful to the FAS to reduce the impact of anti-aircraft attacks and if the FMLN MANPADS arsenal was still modest, the appearance of these weapons marked a turning point in the war. They shattered the last hopes of the Americans and the FAES of defeating the guerrillas militarily, while the FMLN was now able to carry out larger-scale offensives and thus to weigh more heavily in the peace negotiations.

The November 1990 offensive

Reinforced by the arrival of MANPADS, which according to the US Embassy, practically neutralised the FAS tactical advantage, affected the morale of the ground forces and reduced the aggressiveness of ground operations,[20] the guerrillas hit the military harder.

In March 1990, the BIRI Belloso returned from a 30-day operation in the Volcancillo-La Laguna region in the Chalatenango department. A company advanced slowly before colliding with a minefield, which slowed down the entire BIRI, which had to spend an additional night in the combat zone. The guerrillas took advantage of this to attack the returning company, already exhausted by the mines. The soldiers asked for help and an AC-47 intervened, strafing the guerrillas with these .50 calibre guns and managing to stop their progress. The arrival of a UH1-M firing rockets and the support of a DM-1 artillery battery placed on Cerro Sierpe, finally forced the guerrillas to withdraw. The BIRI Belloso company nevertheless lost seven killed and 12 wounded.[21]

The weakening of the FAS always remained a priority objective for the guerrillas and the Ilopango Base one of these privileged targets. In August 1990, FAPL and FAL units approached it from the north of San Salvador but were pushed back by paratroopers. In September, the guerrillas continued to carry out reconnaissance operations of the base. Finally, on 17 October, urban commandos, under the orders of Ramon Suarez and FAL forces, launched, from the neighbourhoods of Santa Lucia and Las Palmas, explosive charges fired with home-made mortars. At the same time, three RPG-7s fired on the base from the Santa Eduviges district while two FES platoons attacked the PH post in Soyapango and the electrical station in Agua Caliente. In reaction, two UH-1M attacked the guerrilla positions in Santa Eduviges. The FAL action lasted 45 minutes before they withdrew towards Tonacatepeque. They managed to damage 17 helicopters and six planes which were nevertheless, quickly repaired.[22]

The biggest offensive of the FMLN in 1990 took place in November. At that time, facing the FAES 45,000 soldiers, the guerrillas had between 6,000 and 7,000 combatants.[23] The offensive called Castigo a la Fuerza Armada antidemocratica (Punishment to the undemocratic armed force) aimed to strike the FAES manoeuver units and more specifically, the FAS. For this, the FMLN asked the Sandinista officers to provide it with new MANPADS more efficient than those of North Korean manufacture.

In October 1990, the latter sold him a batch of 28 SA-7 and SA-14 and 10 Redeye. The strategic objective of the offensive was to influence ongoing negotiations with the government, which still demanded the FMLN surrender as a condition of a peace agreement. The CG set up its command post near the Salvadoran border from a mountainous area and directed the military operations which mainly targeted San Salvador, the Guazapa, Chalatenango and Usulutan regions and was accompanied by a nationwide electricity sabotage campaign.

On 20 November, two FAL urban commando trucks, each equipped with four catapults launching gas cylinders called *tepezcuintles* and 800-pounds of explosives, moved into the Santa Lucia district of San Salvador. One of the trucks was captured by the PH, which succeeded in infiltrating the FAL urban commandos, without being able to fire whilst the other launched five explosive charges on the Ilopango Base, causing light damage. Another FAL team was firing on the base with 60mm mortars and RPG-18s. There were only light injuries among the soldiers while an O-2A was destroyed and two others damaged.

In Apopa, north of San Salvador, the FES routed the Civil Defence forces supported by 1st Infantry Brigade units while the ERP blocked the road leading from Nejapa to Quezaltepeque. The FAES sent two BIRI Belloso companies with 1st Infantry Brigade forces into this sector. An AC-47 also intervened but the FAL fired an anti-aircraft missile on it which narrowly missed it and forced it to withdraw.

On the ground, the BIRI Belloso forced the guerrillas to retreat north, around San José Guayabal. This was where they confronted a GOE unit and resisted using RPK machine guns and TNT charges. An AC-47 was sent to support the GOE and also became the target of the FAL missiles which failed to hit it. Finally, the guerrillas continued their retreat towards the Guazapa volcano.[24] In total, on 20 November, the FMLN attacked more than a dozen FAES positions in the capital, actions that were repeated for about a week.

Thus, on 27 November, the guerrillas attacked the Mariona penitentiary in San Salvador with mortar and rifle fire, killing

During the November 1990 offensive, the guerrillas again attacked the cities, forcing the FAES to reconnect with the practices of urban warfare, such as patrols in armoured vehicles (Albert Grandolini Collection)

Members of the Salvadoran Army's First Brigade saluting on Soldiers Day, 6 May 1990, in Flor Blanca Stadium, San Salvador. (Albert Grandolini Collection)

two soldiers. The next day, a car bomb exploded near the Presidential Palace without causing any casualties, while three electricity pylons were sabotaged in the capital.

The main operation was in Usulutan where the ERP forces, commanded by Raul Mijango, were tasked with carrying out an incursion into the outskirts of the city to provoke the 6th Infantry Brigade and lure it into the area of Nisperal, northwest of Santa Elena. There it would be destroyed while in Piedra de Agua, there was a force organising an anti-aircraft ambush. On 20 November, a guerrilla force of 500 fighters approached Usulutan but the 6th Brigade command decided to remain in the defensive positions occupied by the soldiers around the town.

It was not until the 22nd that 6th Brigade units engaged in combat in the Santa Elena area, provoking the intervention of the FAS. A UH-1H and two Cessna O-2A arrived on site. The guerrillas then fired an SA-14 missile to the O-2As without succeeding in reaching them. Shortly after, an A-37B appeared above the combat zone. After firing its rockets at the guerrilla positions, it was hit by SA-14 fire and crashed. After this success, the ERP command decided to withdraw its forces to prevent them from being the victims of the FAS reprisal actions.[25] Fighting also took place in San Francisco Gotera in the Morazan department and also against military detachments in Santa Elena, Puerto Parada and Concepcion Batres, in the Usulutan department.

The November 1990 offensive caused numerous victims, 233 dead, including 25 civilians and 510 injured according to the Salvadoran ambassador to the UN,[26] while many FAS aircraft were destroyed or damaged. This military campaign showed the FMLN strength, its intact and growing operational capacity.

In order to ward off any threat to Usulutan, a few weeks later, the FAES organised a new operation north of the town. There, the

These ERP fighters certainly participated in the November 1990 offensive which once again showed the military power of the FMLN. (Albert Grandolini Collection)

BIRI Atonal was to be driven by truck to the northern border of the department and then advance towards the south while the 6th Infantry Brigade had to advance from Usulutan to the north. The BIRI Atonal took position on Cerro Mono then progressed south.

The fighting began in El Nisperal, engaged by the 6th Brigade troops. A Hugues-500 helicopter screened the guerrilla positions whose fighters dispersed. It was then up to BIRI Atonal to confront the guerrillas who had succeeded in encircling their command post. The guerrillas mercilessly pounded the military with RPGs, homemade mortars and machine gun fire. It needed the intervention of the 1st company to save the command post and scare away the guerrillas. In the evening, the FMLN bombarded the buildings of the BIRI Atonal and the 6th Brigade in Usulutan with mortars.[27]

In the north of the Chalatenango department, the FAPL forces confronted the 4th Infantry Brigade units which found themselves in difficulty and requested the FAS assistance to provide air support. On 4 December, the latter sent an AC-47 to support the Gayaguanca

Battalion in the vicinity of La Laguna. About 350 to 400 FAPL fighters, led by German Serrano, coming from Cerro Cuatro Pinos, aimed to destroy this battalion and organised an anti-aircraft ambush if the FAS intervened. When an AC-47 appeared in the sky, an SA-7 shot hit it and the plane crashed.[28]

The guerrillas then entered La Laguna, approaching closer and closer to the military command post. It needed the arrival of reinforcements from the 4th Brigade, transported by 10 HH-1H helicopters, for the guerrillas to finally withdraw. The next day, the 80 men of the 3rd Airborne Squadron, transported by 10 UH-1Hs, arrived near San José to find the remains of the AC-47 crew destroyed the day before. They disembarked under heavy guerrilla fire but nevertheless managed to find a survivor of the crew and the bodies of those killed. They then joined the surroundings of La Laguna to be evacuated by helicopters, still under fire from the guerrillas who had launched their pursuit.[29]

The use of MANPADS by the FMLN prevented the evacuation of the wounded directly from the battlefield, which caused a drop in the morale of the soldiers. These two were lucky to be evacuated on time. (Albert Grandolini Collection)

A few days later, BIRI Bracamonte units were in the Cerro de Talzate in the Chalatenango department where they were under intense attack by the FAPL.[30] On 10 December, the FAS decided to organise an airborne operation to evacuate wounded BIRI soldiers who were fighting north-west of Nueva Trinidad while the FAPL installed an anti-aircraft device with two Redeye systems south-east of Las Vueltas.

On the 11th, two UH-1H escorted by a UH-1M approached the area. When they landed, they were the target of numerous light machine gun fire and the crews realised that they had been ambushed. They nevertheless managed to reach a secure base in the sector. Seven helicopters succeeded to land near the Yurique canton to evacuate the wounded. They were again the target of guerrilla attacks, but the escort of four armed helicopters opened fire and allowed the evacuation.

During the night, A-37s attacked the guerrilla positions in order to prevent the BIRI Bracamonte positions from being overwhelmed. On the 12th, the resistance of the soldiers in the Coyolar hills was broken by a new assault by 200 FAPL combatants. They were forced to cross the border with Honduras. Finally, the arrival of the BIRI Atlacatl allowed the situation to be restored after violent fighting against the FAPL.[31]

The FMLN military operations in 1990 clearly demonstrated that demanding the guerrillas disarm unconditionally and without any guarantees, was unrealistic. Awareness of this reality pushed the Americans to put pressure on the FMLN allies. On 14 December, the American ambassador in Managua, Harry Schlaudeman, informed the Nicaraguan government that the FMLN had SA-7s, SA-14s and Redeyes and accused the EPS of being responsible for these arms deliveries. The United States also challenged the Soviet government and demanded that it applied the terms of the protocol signed with Nicaragua when the USSR delivered these missiles in 1989 and which stipulated that the weapons could not be transferred.

USSR Ambassador to Nicaragua, Valery Nikolayenko, informed Bernard Aronson, State Department Assistant Secretary for Latin America, that the EPS head, General Humberto Ortega, assured him that Nicaragua never delivered any weapons to the FMLN. However, State Department Secretary James Baker gave USSR Foreign Minister Edward Shevernadze the serial numbers of the SA-14s found in the plane that crashed in Usulutan department a year earlier and which corresponded to some delivered by the USSR to the EPS in February 1986.

The United States then gave Nicaragua a note giving the reference of the Redeyes that they had delivered to the Nicaraguan Contra. In particular, this report revealed that of the 13 MANPADS captured by the EPS, at least two were found in the plane that crashed near Usulutan. Thus Washington pressured President Violeta Chamorro to demand that Humberto Ortega provide a similar list concerning missiles of Soviet origin. A few days later, General Ortega informed his government that a batch of missiles, specifically SA-7 and SA-14, had been stolen from the EPS warehouses by two captains and a major. These revelations did not fail to provoke tension between the EPS headquarters and the CG FMLN.

Finally, on 1st January 1991, the EPS publicly announced that four former officers had stolen MANPADS to deliver them to the FMLN. They were arrested along with 11 Salvadoran citizens residing in Nicaragua. The Nicaraguan government was also sending a minister to El Salvador to explain to the Cristiani government that this was an unintentional violation of the Esquipulas Accords since neither the EPS nor the government were aware of the MANPADS transfer. For its part, the USSR Ministry of Foreign Affairs denounced the handing over of any type of Soviet weapons to third parties and announced the dispatch of a mission to Nicaragua to investigate the situation of Soviet weapons.

The American efforts to dry up the MANPADS supply to the FMLN could not hide that the year 1990 was difficult for the FAES who lost 2,000 men, including 996 killed in combat. The FMLN also demonstrated its ability to use sophisticated anti-aircraft weapons, forcing the FAS to greatly reduce its operations, which considerably hampered the FAES' counter-insurgency strategy. Nevertheless, as a CIA report noted, guerrillas now favour ranged attacks that did not threaten cities. For the Americans, this FMLN moderation aimed not to jeopardise the peace negotiations, nor the relations with the UN mediators.[32] This position seemed relevant since, despite international and national condemnation of its military actions, negotiations continued.

The latest military operations

On 2nd January 1991, the guerrillas, using M-16 and AK-47 fire, shot down a US Army UH-1H helicopter at Lolotique in the San Miguel department. The helicopter, which took off from the Ilopango Base was heading for Soto Cano in Honduras, carrying, in addition to the pilot, Daniel F. Scott, Lieutenant-Colonel David H. Pickett commander of the 22nd Air Regiment 4th Battalion and Corporal Earnest G. Dawson. The pilot was killed while the other two American soldiers were injured. They were discovered by an ERP patrol and executed.[33] It was not until 22 January that the FMLN acknowledged that one of its patrols had executed the two Americans. It then took care to point out that those responsible had been captured and handed over to the judicial authorities under humanitarian protection.

On 10 January, a FAS Hugues-500E was shot down near Suchitoto. These actions, but also the rumour that the FMLN now possessed SA-16s, prompted the US government to release $43 million in military aid to El Salvador.[34] This aid enabled the FAS to procure three A-37Bs and six UH-1M helicopters. Nevertheless, on 12 March, a UH-1M was shot down by MANPADS in Alto Miro canton, San Miguel department. These FAS losses against the guerrillas' anti-aircraft weapons, forced it to carry out its attacks at night, reducing their effectiveness. Meanwhile, the loss of air support struck a blow to the morale of the soldiers engaged in more violent and direct combat. On 12 March, the FMLN launched a new attack against the 3rd Infantry Brigade garrison with mortar fire while bombs exploded against bank branches in the city.[35]

If the military operations were for the FMLN a means of strengthening its positions in the negotiations, they were used by part of the FAES to lead to their failure when the possibility of reaching an agreement became clearer. Between 7 to 18 March 1991, the FAES launched operations on the main fronts, probably to seek to support, militarily for the hardening of the government's positions. Nevertheless, they suffered heavy losses in these battles due to the minefields but above all, to the reduction in air support.

On 4 April, as a new round of negotiations resumed in Mexico City, the FAES undertook several territorial reconquest operations, particularly in areas of strong guerrilla influence, in order to demonstrate that there were no zones or 'liberated' regions. They thus succeeded in occupying the town of Perquin in the Morazan department which was one of the ERP sanctuaries.

On 11 April, near Rio Sumpul in the Chalatenango department, the detonation of several grenades was heard, followed by numerous gunshots. It was an ambush organised by about 20 GOE soldiers, which targeted the vehicle in which Antonio Cardenal Cardona, alias Jesús Rojas, one of the FMLN officials involved in negotiations with the government and 13 other FMLN militants, including political leaders, were travelling.[36] This attack was one of the hardest blows to the guerrillas in Chalatenango since Commander Miguel Lopez and a health worker were the only survivors of the operation.

For the FMLN, this ambush was:

> coldly planned by the High Command of the Armed Forces in its attempts to hinder efforts to reach a quick negotiated political solution to the conflict ... Our comrades were wounded and then coldly killed by a bullet in the headed by commandos from the Atlacatl Battalion, the same battalion that assassinated the Jesuit Fathers.[37]

These FAES operations, which risked preventing the conclusion of an agreement, led the US authorities to carry out several high-level missions in El Salvador, including that of General Colin Powell, then Chief of Staff, on 8 April, and Bernard Aronson, Under-Secretary of State for American Affairs, on the 12th, in order to neutralise the FAES toughest elements and the Right.

At the same time, Secretary of State Baker authorised Aronson to enter into direct contact with FMLN representatives. One of the first encounters occurred when Ambassador Walker visited Guazapa volcano, an area dominated by guerrillas. During a second meeting, Walker and his entourage engaged with FMLN commanders in Salvadoran refugee communities in Honduras in cordial and productive talks.[38] These meetings were important for the FMLN since American officials now treated the rebels as legitimate interlocutors, thus favouring those who advocated for peace.

The FAES launched, on 25 May, a new major offensive against all the main guerrilla territories, affecting eight of the country's

The destruction of a US Air Force UH-1H helicopter by the FMLN on 2 January 1991 and the execution of the surviving crew, did not diminish the American resolve to end the conflict in El Salvador. (Albert Grandolini Collection)

Leaning upon entire brigades trained in the USA – or by US advisers in El Salvador – the top brass of the FAES were opposed to negotiations with the FMLN and still wanted to end the war with a military victory. (Albert Grandolini Collection)

14 departments with approximately 30,000 soldiers and the entire FAS. This was the last time that the FAES High Command would use all of its operational forces in a single military campaign. The guerrillas responded with heavy blows to moving military units while landmines and ambushes caused hundreds of casualties. This strategy of attrition led to significant wear and tear on the FAES who no longer had the strength to pursue such a large-scale operation.

On 17 June, the FMLN in turn, launched another successful and spectacular military operation known as 'Operation Fair'. A column of more than a hundred guerrillas, including FES units, mobile troops and an urban unit, released all the political prisoners who were in Mariona prison, located in the vicinity of San Salvador. For this, the guerrillas carried out a complex military manoeuver where they combined actions of diversion and surprise against the military units that were in the outskirts of Mariona. It also managed to prevent the arrival of FAES reinforcements, which they pinned down and immobilised to allow an orderly retreat in buses along the Troncal del Norte Highway, carrying the 36 guerrillas who were prisoners and about 150 ordinary prisoners who had decided to accompany them.

After this new demonstration of the FMLN's operational capabilities, on 12 August, four SA-16 missile systems were discovered in Cerro Guazapa, confirming that the guerrillas had this MANPADS type and readjusted the balance of power to their advantage.[39]

Despite international pressure, military operations continued until the end of the year. On 16 October 1991, the FAPL attacked DM-1 troops defending the small town of San Miguel de Mercedes in the south of the Chalatenango department. The guerrillas managed to defeat reinforcements who fell into an ambush and had to retreat. The FAS then organised an airborne operation to recapture the lost positions. The 2nd Airborne Squadron with its 80 men was divided into two groups, each transported by five helicopters under the protection of three UH-1M and a Hughes-500E. The landing zone was bombarded beforehand by two A-37s, but at the time of the landing, the guerrilla fire was particularly intense.

The situation became even more difficult when the FMLN fired an anti-aircraft missile without hitting the target. Nevertheless, the paratroopers managed to land. They advanced north and breaking through guerrilla resistance, reached San Miguel de Mercedes where they were greeted by RPG-7 fire. After 45 minutes of fighting, the guerrillas withdrew and left the city to the paratroopers who were soon relieved by DM-1 troops.[40]

The FMLN, throughout 1991, maintained constant operations throughout the national territory, but without large-scale military campaigns, unlike the FAES which launched, from the first days of November, a final offensive when negotiations toughened after the signing of the New York Accords. On 15 November, the FMLN, in a calculated way, decreed the unilateral end of all its offensive operations on the whole of El Salvador which, of course, included the cessation of urban operations and sabotage of the economy.

On the contrary, the FAES were increasing the scale of their attacks, seriously jeopardising the possibility of quickly concluding a peace agreement. It was not counting on the US government and international community which let President Cristiani and the FAES High Command know their deep concern at the unacceptable conduct of the military.

Finally, on 21 November, after a complicated negotiation with the FAES leadership, President Cristiani announced the 'de-escalation' of the FAS and artillery military operations. The president did not mention the infantry which constituted the FAES main combat force. A part of the FAES High Command, called 'La Tandona', which brought together Colonel Ponce, Rubio, Zepeda, Montano and Carrillo, remained hostile to negotiations with the FMLN when the end of the war was practically assured. The last FAS action during the war, took place on 11 November 1991 south of Victoria in Cabañas department when two A-37Bs bombarded FMLN positions with 500-pound bombs.

During 1991, the FAES lost 870 men. In total, from 1980 to 1991, they had 11,581 deaths. On the guerrillas' side, during the same period the losses were 23,480 men.[41]

The end of the war

Following the November 1989 Offensive, the government and the FMLN returned to the negotiating table and decided to include a new actor in their discussions, the United Nations, which was to play the mediator role. This solution received the support of the United States and the agreement of the UN in December 1989. At the end of that year, President Bush informed General Woerner, then commander of Southcom, that Washington was henceforth favourable to democratic governments in Central America and that the military had to 'return to the barracks'.[42]

In early 1990, under the leadership of Alvaro de Soto, the UN team quickly assumed its role as mediator, urging both sides to clarify their positions. It also made proposals to resolve delicate issues and push for partial agreements to keep the process alive. On 16 May 1990, negotiations began in Caracas between Cristiani's government and the FMLN in the presence of UN mediators.[43] The most important negotiations were discussed by two commissions which brought together for the government, Oscar Santamaria the Prime Minister, David Escobar Galindo rector of the University and personal adviser to Cristiani, General Mauricio Vargas FAES deputy Chief of Staff and for the FMLN, Schafik Handal, Salvador Samayoa and Ana Maria Guadalupe close to Villalobos.[44]

On 4 April, in Geneva, in the presence of the UN Secretary General, representatives of the government and the FMLN signed an agreement establishing the guiding rules for the peace negotiations, from which the parties had promised not to withdraw. In addition to ending the armed conflict by political means, the process had to include the democratisation of the country, the unrestricted respect for human rights and the reunification of Salvadoran society. From that moment, as the fighting continued, a complex and dynamic mechanism of meetings and consultations began in different capitals and important cities on the American continent.

These negotiations were supported by the 'Secretary General Friends Group', composed of the governments of Colombia, Mexico, Venezuela and Spain and also the European Union and the Bush Administration. The latter had not hesitated to dispatch its State Under-Secretary, Bernard Aronson, at several key moments to 'encourage flexibility' among Salvadoran government and military leaders. UN Secretary General Javier Pérez de Cuellar was also personally intervening in the talks.

The first substantial agreement was signed on 26 July 1990 in San José, Costa Rica. It established a mutual commitment to respect human rights on each side even as the war continued. It entrusted the task of monitoring its application to a UN commission, the United Nations Observer Group in El Salvador or ONUSAL. From then on, the UN Secretary General played a key role in the negotiations, including proposing changes to the agenda negotiated in Caracas. The latter proposed to first discuss the role of the FAES, which represented one of the biggest obstacles to reaching an agreement.

So far, the FMLN had insisted on the FAES disappearance, the dissolution of the BIRI and intelligence agencies, as well as the prosecution of officers responsible for serious human rights violations, proposals rejected by both the military then the government. Therefore, the UN managed the talks so the first subject discussed around the table was that of respect for human rights and the most controversial issues were discussed later, once a climate of confidence had been established.

Despite this initial success, negotiations reached an impasse in January 1991, after the FMLN shot down a helicopter gunship carrying a group of American military advisers who were captured and later executed. They nevertheless resumed in Mexico in April on questions of the FAES future, constitutional reforms and the conditions for a ceasefire.

On 27 April, an agreement was finally signed in Mexico City, which marked further progress on the road to peace. It provided for FAES reform, the FMLN renouncing to demand their dissolution but obtaining the creation of a Policia Nacional Civil (National Civil Police or PCN), independent of the military. Another series of reforms affected the electoral system, the judicial system and human rights with the creation of a Truth Commission which had to investigate the most serious violations committed during the

Until the end of the conflict, the FAES tried to chase the guerrillas out of their strongholds, like here in La Palma in the department of Chalatenango. (Albert Grandolini Collection)

war.[45] The government also demonstrated its desire for conciliation by accepting a reform of the Constitution, while the FMLN accepted its validity for the first time.

However, the Mexico agreement did not put an end to the conflict, since no measure had yet been decided on the terms of the demilitarisation of the country and on a possible ceasefire. The following discussions stumbled on the most sensitive point concerning these questions, the simultaneous FAES and FMLN demobilisation.

If contacts were regularly maintained, the meetings in Caracas from 24 May to 3 June, in Queretaro from 16 to 22 June and in Mexico City on 9 July, did not manage to reach real agreements. Nevertheless, on 26 July 1991, the first ONUSAL elements were deployed in El Salvador. UN pressure was again needed to unblock the negotiations, as neither side wanted to make further concessions without the implementation of a ceasefire. The negotiations crisis led to urgent international interventions.

At the Moscow summit at the end of July between George Bush and Mikhail Gorbachev, the two powers evoked the resolution of the conflict in Central America. In a joint letter of 1st August to the UN Secretary General, James Baker, US Secretary of State and Aleksandr Bessmertnykh, Soviet Foreign Minister, they welcomed the progress made, but expressed their concern about the blockage of the negotiations and asked them to take personal initiatives to reach an agreement.

In September 1991, President Cristiani at the head of the government delegation and the five members of the FMLN CG, went to New York, invited by the UN Secretary General, with the aim of unblocking the talks. Until then, the two parties sought to gain positions in the negotiations by military operations but the international pressure, as well as the hopes of the Salvadoran people, became too strong. Under pressure from Washington, an agreement was signed on 25 September. Cristiani agreed to halve the FAES manpower, to create an independent civilian commission to investigate human rights violations and to disband the security forces, the PH, the PN and the GN.

For its part, the FMLN received a percentage of 20 percent men in the ranks of the newly created PCN. In exchange, it withdrew his request that its units be integrated directly into the FAES. At the end of September, all major disagreements between the two parties were resolved. Under the aegis of the UN, the Comision Nacional para la Consolidacion de la Paz (National Commission for the Consolidation of Peace or COPAZ) was formed, bringing together two representatives of the Salvadorian government, one from the FAES, two from the FMLN and one for each political party represented in the Assembly. COPAZ's mission was to monitor and

FMLN Commander Schafik Handal shook hands with the Salvadorean government representatives after the signing of the peace agreement. (Author Collection)

control the application of the agreements, in particular the FAES and security forces reorganisation.[46] With FMLN concerns over FAES demilitarisation and impunity satisfied, it announced a unilateral ceasefire as a new round of negotiations took place in New York.

The negotiator teams then moved to the UN headquarters from 16 December for the final stretch of the discussions, their conclusion being scheduled for 31 December at midnight, with the end of the Javier Pérez de Cuéllar mandate. The negotiations related to certain sensitive issues, such as the FAES reduction, the transfer of land properties to former FMLN combatants, as well as the guarantees that the guerrilla members would have to be able to reintegrate into civilian life. Following several marathon negotiations and with the intervention of experts, delegated by both the UN and the US Department of State, a text was finally signed within the time allowed, a few minutes after midnight on the last day of 1991.

After these last discussions on the modalities of its implementation, the Peace Accords, sealing the end of the conflict in El Salvador, were formally signed at the Chapultepec castle, in Mexico City, on 16 January 1992. The total ceasefire began 1st February. It would be respected by both parties.[47]

The Peace Accords devoted a chapter to the FAES which were henceforth subject to the civil power and ceased to be considered as the guarantors of the institutions. They had to demobilise all the battalions trained for the fight against insurrection, halve its manpower, which had to drop from 80,000 to 40,000 men, dissolve the security forces which depended on it, as well as its intelligence service. Its senior officers would be held accountable for human rights crimes committed during the conflict through the mechanisms provided by the Truth Commission. The police functions were devolved to the PCN which would no longer be a military body and which would have to be composed mainly of people who had not fought on either side.[48]

However, the Legislative Assembly, controlled by ARENA, approved a general amnesty law for all those involved in political crimes, which, in practice, prevented anyone found guilty from being punished for human rights violations. For its part, the FMLN was demobilising its forces, which represented approximately 8,500 combatants.[49]

The judicial system was reformed to guarantee its independence while political party status was granted to the FMLN. The agreements relating to economic and social aspects provided for the creation of reintegration programmes for ex-combatants on both sides, in

During the war, the FAES completely transformed, becoming efficient, professional and modern. (Author Collection)

particular with the transfer of land and the implementation of a national plan for the reconstruction of areas affected by the conflict. Despite these shortcomings, when came the announcement of the signing of peace in Mexico, 200,000 Salvadorans invaded the Plaza Civico in San Salvador, waving red flags and singing *Sombrero Azul* (The Blue Hat), a song that had become the FMLN official anthem.

A new El Salvador?

The signing of the Peace Accords brought about a fundamental change in the life of the country. The armed clashes, which had been considerably reduced in the weeks preceding 16 January 1992, especially after the unilateral truce proclaimed by the FMLN, came to an end. This situation was formalised on 1st February 1992 with the start of the ceasefire. That same day, the five members of the FMLN CG and most of its leaders, returned freely to the country and participated, alongside their former adversaries, in the COPAZ inaugural ceremony.

The euphoria blowing all over El Salvador reflected the popular conviction that the peace process was irreversible, despite the pitfalls it was encountering. The time seemed to have come for the birth of a new Salvador, at least the end of the violent country that it had been until a few months ago. Previously, the Legislative Assembly unanimously approved a national reconciliation law that allowed the reintegration of FMLN representatives into national life.

ONUSAL, made up of officers from various countries, settled in the country to intervene between the former enemy forces and verify compliance with the peace agreements. FAES members returned to their barracks and began a transformation process to become peacetime armed forces again. The FMLN, for its part, gradually withdrew from the regions it previously occupied to concentrate in 15 previously defined areas, and deposited its equipment and weapons, except individual ones, in closed containers under the joint control of the ONUSAL and the local FMLN commander. Both the FAES and the guerrillas had to also request authorisation from ONUSAL to carry out certain movements of their troops. A Police Division, made up of police officers from different countries, accompanied the PN, now separated from the Ministry of Defence and the only body responsible for public security, until the full establishment of the PNC.

FMLN forces proceeding to a meeting point to be disarmed by ONUSAL after the signing of the peace treaty in January 1992. (Albert Grandolini Collection)

delay. The Supreme Electoral Tribunal did not register it definitively until 14 December 1992, after it was considered disarmed.

Towards the end of May 1992, the delays recorded began to cause concern, leading the FMLN to suspend the demobilisation of its former combatants and the handing over of their weapons. UN Secretary General Boutros Ghali believed that a definitive readjustment of the dates was inevitable due to the accumulation of delays. On 23 October, he proposed to each party, a timetable providing for an extension until 15 December 1992, for the final dismantling of the FMLN military structure. Despite an initially reluctant reaction from the government, the proposal was finally accepted.

On 15 December 1992, El Salvador finally celebrated the definitive end of the armed conflict. To date, the FMLN had demobilised 12,362 combatants, some of whom were receiving land, credits and training courses in agricultural techniques to be able to exploit them. Medical assistance programmes for war-wounded were set up as well as training and credit for small business entrepreneurship.

However, new challenges and the remnants of years of war showed that peace remained fragile. Thus, political polarisation resurfaced around the dismissal of various FAES officers and compliance with the Truth Commission recommendations. Above all, the discovery of a FMLN clandestine arsenal in Managua, prompting new investigations that led to the discovery of more than 120 arms depots in El Salvador, Honduras and Nicaragua and cast doubt on the solidity of the peace process.

Another weakness of the Peace Agreement lay in its essentially military character. It left intact the economic structure, which was nevertheless one of the main factors in the outbreak of the war. This weakness was overcome when the FMLN recognised the market economy and no longer spoke of a transition to socialism. It adopted a discourse which looked like that of the European social democratic parties. In this way, the chapter of armed conflict was closed. The FMLN became a political party to fit into the democratic system and the FAES prepared for a new stage in their history. After having reduced its manpower, they reinforced its peaceful image by directing its actions towards non-military activities such as the repair of infrastructures, the distribution of medicines and literacy projects.[50]

The initial euphoria with which the country welcomed the signing of Chapultepec, gradually gave way to a certain caution and some criticism when it appeared that progress in the peace process was slower than expected in the ambitious timetable agreed between the parts. The concentration of FMLN forces took longer than expected while the same resistance was observed to achieve the effective suppression of the GN and the PH, which were only completed months late. Nevertheless, in February 1993, the first group of new police officers was graduated and the following month they were deployed to the Chalatenango department. Finally, the process of legalising the FMLN as a political party was also starting with some

The year 1992 saw the disarmament of the guerrillas, which in spite of delays, took place without major incidents. (Albert Grandolini Collection)

The end of the civil war did not prevent El Salvador from continuing to be one of the most violent societies in the Americas, the result of a combination of historical, cultural and political factors. If young Salvadorans had not experienced the war, those from urban areas with high population density, marginal and poor, integrated massively into gangs, called *Maras*, which were born in the context of the 1980s conflict. During these years, many Salvadorans left their country to settle in the United States, particularly in California where some formed gangs to confront the already existing gangs. The most important was the *Mara*

The phenomenon of gangs, called *Mara*, was a legacy of the war that plagued Salvadoran society, especially among young people lacking prospects. (Albert Grandolini Collection)

Salvatrucha which was born in Los Angeles and San Francisco. When peace returned to El Salvador, the American authorities sent back to their country many members of the *Mara Salvatrucha* who found there a fertile ground for their criminal activities.

In 2001, there would be four large gangs in El Salvador bringing together 30,000 people, half of whom belong to the *Mara Salvatrucha*. They reigned over juvenile delinquency, which was expressed by public disorders, clashes between rival gangs, attacks on persons and private property, as well as homicides. They were also linked to the sale of drugs. Alongside this delinquency, organised crime was developing, which posed a greater threat to Salvadoran society by practising drug trafficking, theft, kidnapping, extortion, murder and smuggling.

The organised crime actions reached various spheres of society, as shown by the cases of corruption of certain members of the police institution, the judicial system and politicians. Faced with these problems, in 2003 the President Francisco Flores government created Plan Mano Dura, which involved using the PNC and FAES to fight crime and dismantle gangs. Nevertheless, between January and July 2005, 2,109 murders were committed nationwide, a considerable increase from the 1,501 that occurred during the same months of 2004. The figures were more alarming in 2006, with 3,888 homicides and another 3,424 in 2007.

It was in this context of rising criminal violence that the Salvadoran Right managed to hold on to executive power for four presidential terms, imposing its hegemony within society. From 1994, the FMLN conquered spaces at the legislative and municipal levels but did not manage to obtain a sufficient share of power to complete the peace agreements in their socio-economic aspect. The Right hegemony encouraged the establishment of a liberal agenda anchored in economic globalisation and the giving up of the agricultural sector. This suggested that the clear winner of the peace agreements was business, the elite formed by the Salvadoran wealthiest, whose prosperity had steadily increased. Nevertheless, in terms of political democratisation, progress had been undeniable since 1992.

For its part, following the Peace Accords, the FMLN transformed itself into a legitimate political party, growing slowly but steadily until it became the main political force in the country. This route was not without difficulties. The end of the war and above all the crisis of socialist ideology, gave rise to ideological differences and struggles for power within it, undermining its cohesion. In the 1994 elections, it won only 21 of the 84 legislative seats. Faced with this failure, the RN and the ERP, led by Villalobos, proposed to abandon Marxism-Leninism and to transform the FMLN into a social democratic party, which provoked numerous oppositions. The conflict ended when the RN and the ERP left the FMLN at the beginning of 1995 to create a new political party which would not be successful.[51]

In 1995, the three remaining organisations (PCS, FPL and PRTC) chose to dissolve and then re-found the FMLN as a unified organisation. From this moment, it was divided into different factions opposed by ideological differences and the definition of the political strategy. The result of these conflicts was the expulsion of the minority factions leaders or those who had less weight in the organisation. For this reason, Facundo Guardado, former FPL commander, was expelled in October 2001 and Francisco Jovel, former PRTC secretary general of the PRTC, in 2002.

Under the leadership of Schafik Handal, the FMLN still defined itself as Marxist-Leninist and adopted a strategy of transition towards socialism and the deepening of democracy. To achieve this, he advocated creating a series of broad political alliances with sectors that were considered democratic but not Left-wing – a strategy similar to that advocated by the PCS in the 1970s.

Nevertheless, there were clear qualitative differences as to the meaning of the concept of socialism with that provided by the FMLN in the 1980s. From now on, the latter no longer rejected the existence of private property, even if it reduced its role in the economy and subordinated it to the social interest. Nor did it oppose representative democracy on principle, although it intended to give it a more radical character through what it called 'popular control'.

This strategy of openness allowed the FMLN to forge alliances and achieve success. If since 1994 it had accumulated a significant electoral flow, sufficient to have significant weight in the Legislative Assembly and to control a large number of town halls, in particular San Salvador, it was not so to win presidential elections. This trend was gradually reversed during the 2000s when the democratic transition showed signs of non-consolidation due to the emergence of growing social violence and the non-existence of political alternation while the economic model in place did not meet the basic needs of the majority of the population. If ARENA and the Right failed in their management of the country, the FMLN did not seem ready, in the eyes of large sectors of the population, to assume its leadership.

From 1980 to 1991, the FAES suffered a loss of 11,581 killed in action and dozens of thousands wounded (many of them severely). (Albert Grandolini Collection)

Finally, in 2009, Mauricio Funes, the FMLN candidate won the presidential elections and then the legislative elections. The Right hegemony was finally defeated. The possibility of significant changes in the country at the socio-economic level raised great expectations which were nonetheless disappointed, despite the election in 2014 of a former guerrilla commander, Salvador Sanchez Cerén, as the new President of the Republic. The disappointments caused successively by the Right and the Left led to the election, in 2019, of a candidate who was neither a member of the FMLN nor ARENA – Nayib Bukelele.

The new president made it his mission to fight gangs and by 2020, the homicide rate was down 60 percent. This was still insufficient and in March 2022, the government declared a state of emergency and arrested nearly 53,000 suspected gang members. On an economic level, Bukelele gave Bitcoins legal tender in 2021 despite the International Monetary Fund opposition. When this currency lost half of its value in 2022, El Salvador found itself threatened with a sovereign default, leaving an uncertain future hanging over this little-known country.

CONCLUSION

The peace agreements signed at the beginning of 1992 put an end to a singular conflict. At the start of the war, the FMLN had many assets to win, significant and quality armament, areas they controlled, a command that knew how to demonstrate strategic flexibility, the support of Cuba and Nicaragua. They allowed it to quickly take the strategic initiative after his defeat during the January 1981 offensive. However, contrary to what happened in Cuba in 1959 and in Nicaragua in 1979, it did not manage to defeat the FAES.

A number of factors explain why the Salvadorans were not able to achieve the kind of total victory that the Sandinistas had managed. From the end of 1983 to 1986, the FAES – thanks to the influx of American funds (the total amount of this aid during the 10 years of war amounting to 4.4 billion dollars[1]) – equipped themselves with modern military equipment, received training and tactical support enabling them to regain the initiative.

The FAS modernisation, the use of intelligence, small elite units and counter-insurgency tactics, temporarily turned the war in their favour. The massive support from Washington was thus a stabilising factor, guaranteed that the FAES would not be defeated militarily. On a political level, it was also under the impetus of the United States that the 1984 presidential elections took place, which marked another success of their counter-insurgency strategy, demonstrating that the democratic process could be achieved in El Salvador.

The Basic Intensity War doctrine implemented by the United States and its ally, the Salvadoran state, had some success, preventing the seizure of power by guerrilla forces and achieving structural changes in the economy and society to enable it to establish a democratic system. For Professor Crandall, this strategy deployed in El Salvador became a politico-military model which he called 'the Salvadoran option' and which played a key role in American foreign policy in the following decades. This was studied as a successful example of counter-insurgency and nation building influencing American strategy in other parts of the world, notably in Iraq or Afghanistan at the beginning of the twenty-first century. This doctrine nevertheless, failed to destroy the FMLN, which remained both a military and political force capable of challenging the Salvadoran state.

In response to the FAES success, the FMLN indeed modified its tactics. It fully embraced the concept of protracted people's war, including the massive use of landmines that had devastating consequences on the military and their psyches. It was also intensifying its sabotage campaigns against the country's infrastructure, causing considerable damage to an already fragile Salvadoran economy. The massive FAES counter-insurgency operations and the urban commandos or FES raids maintained a very tense situation for the civilian population, the war continuing without foreseeable conclusion. From 1987 until the FMLN final offensive in November 1989, it was indeed difficult to clearly identify which side would win the war.

The FMLN sought to regain the initiative with the November 1989 Offensive. The latter, from a military point of view, was not considered a success for the guerrillas because of the strong FAES resistance which still benefited substantial assistance from the United States. This new failure also demonstrated, as in 1981, the lack of massive popular support to the FMLN. The 1989 offensive nevertheless served as a propaganda stunt for the guerrillas and events such as the massacre of Jesuit priests, influenced the decision of the US Congress to halve military aid to El Salvador. Above all, it demonstrated the FAES inability to defeat the FMLN, whose capabilities were underestimated.

The strategic impasse in which the Salvadoran conflict found itself was only resolved in the political events taking place outside the country. By the time of the 1989 offensive, the Cold War was coming to an end and the East–West interests in which El Salvador had played an important role, were diminishing. In 1990, the Sandinistas, leading FMLN allies, lost the elections and the political momentum that the FMLN was building at the time faded. For its part, the US government, now led by Bush, no longer considered American interests in El Salvador as essential as its predecessor, President Reagan. This dynamic was so powerful that in barely two years, the war found its conclusion without a clear winner or loser. Instead of clashing, former enemies had to settle their differences peacefully and took it upon themselves to rebuild and govern the country.

For about 12 years, Salvadorans engaged in horrific violence. Various sources estimate the loss of life to have exceeded 75,000, mostly civilians (about 60,000). If we take into account that in the 1980s the population of El Salvador was around 4.5 million, this means that almost two percent of the population perished in the conflict. The latter was also responsible for the disappearance of 8,000 people, no less than 12,000 maimed for life, mainly because of landmines, around 12,000 political prisoners and more than a million displaced people.[2] Added to these already dramatic consequences were the traumas resulting from the numerous human rights violations that occurred during these years.

According to the Truth Commission, between 85 and 90 percent of these human rights violations were perpetrated by the FAES, security forces and Death Squads, between five and 10 percent by the guerrillas and five percent unidentified responsiblity.[3] No society can emerge unscathed from such a long and violent conflict, the traces of which are still visible today in the polarisation and resentment that persist and which, as certain studies indicate, would have a share of the responsibility in the rise in crime and the emergence of youth and adult gangs.

The peace agreements have indeed, left many important issues unresolved. The economic structure has remained intact, which is why El Salvador remains one of the countries with the highest income inequality. On the other hand, the transition to peace was accompanied by the implementation of liberal economic policies. The reduction in public spending in the context of an economy seriously damaged by the war, and the blocking of any hint of a redistributive economic policy, have prevented an improvement in the economic situation for the majority of Salvadorans, while the economy has not been able to create enough jobs for the thousands of young people entering the labour market. This is, at least, one of the additional reasons explaining the high levels of violence and the symbol of the FMLN failure whose initial project was precisely aimed at reducing the social inequalities which led to the conflict of the 1980s.

SELECTED BIBLIOGRAPHY

Alvarez, Alberto Martin, 'From Revolutionary War to Democratic Revolution. The Farabundo Marti National Liberation Front (FMLN)' in *El Salvador*, Berghof Conflict Research, 2010

Alvarez, Alberto Martin, 'De la guerra revolucionaria a la revolucion democratica. El FMLN en El Salvador', *Revista Realidad*, 132, 2012

Amnesty International, *El Salvador. 'Death Squads'- A Government Strategy*, October 1988

Argumedo Najarro, Marco Antonio, 'La Fuerza aerea y los ataques a la 3a Brígada de infanteria en San Miguel', *Guerreros*, Año 6, Cuarto Trimestre 2019

Barrera, Roman Alfonso, 'Remenbranzas de guerra', *Guerreros*, Año 7, Segundo Trimestre 2020

Benitez Manaut, Raul Guillermo, *La teoria militar y la guerra civil en El Salvador*, Universidad Nacional Autonoma de Mexico, 1986

Bermudez Torres, Lilia Margarita, *La estrégia militar de la administracion Reagan en Centroamerica : de la opcion invasion a la guerra de baja intensidad*, Universidad Nacional Autonoma de Mexico, 1985

Briscoe, Charles H., 'San Miguel : The Attack on El Bosque', *Veritas*, Vol. 3, n°3, 2007

Cale, Paul P., 'The United States Military Advisory Group in El Salvador', *Small Wars Journal*, 1996

CIA, 'El Salvador : A Net Assessment of the War', February 1986

Consalvi, Carlos Enriquez *Broadcasting the Civil War in El Salvador*, University of Texas Press, 2010

Contreras Rodriguez, Marta Elma, *El processo revolucionario en El Salvador*, Universidad Nacional Autonoma de Mexico, 1988

Corum, James S., 'The Air War in El Salvador', *Airpower Journal*, Summer 1998

Crandall, Russell, *The Salvador Option. The United States in El Salvador*, Cambridge University Press, 2016

D'Haeseleer, Brian, *The Salvadorian Crucible: American Counter-insurgency in El Salvador, 1979-1992*, American University, 2015

Dye, Dale, 'Showdown at Cerron Grande. Blooding the Airborne Bataillon', *Soldiers of Fortune*, November 1984

Escalona Terron, Maria Teresa, *La radio como instrumento de lucha politica : Experiencia de Radio Farabundo Marti, 1982-1992*, Universidad de El Salvador, 2002

Garibay, David *Des armes aux urnes. Processus de paix et réinsertion politique des anciennes guérillas en Colombie et au Salvador*, Institut d'étude politique de Paris-Science Po, 2003

Garcia Fernandez, Anibal, *La presencia militar argentina en El Salvador: el caso del Batallon de Inteligencia 601, (1976-1983)*, Universidad Nacional Autonoma de Mexico, 2017

Giampetri, Sergio M., & Stone Sr, John H., *A Counter-Insurgency Study: an Analysis of Local Defenses*, Naval Postgraduate School, 2004

Haggerty, Richard A, (Ed.), *El Salvador, a country study*, Library of Congress. Federal Research Division, 1990

Heigh, Suzanne M., *Counter-insurgency strategies for effective conflict termination: US Strategies in El Salvador*, Naval Postgraduate School, 1990

Hernandez Arias, Miguel, *Fenix, Cenizas de un operacion estadounidense que no renacio*, Centro de Documentacion de los Movimientos Armados, 2006

Hernandez Diaz, Nelson E., 'El poder aéreo en el conflicto salvadoreño', *Guerreros*, Año 1, Diciembre 2014

Hernandez Maldonaldo, Diego Andrés, *Reconstruccion historica de la guerra civil salvadoreña a través de excombatientes del FMLN: caso Guazapa, 1981-1982*, Universidad de El Salvador, 2018

Hone, Matthew James, 'El impacto tactico de la intervencion de EE. UU. en la guerra de El Salvador', *Revista de Humanidades y Ciencias Sociales*, n°5, July-December 2013

Hone, Matthew James, *La participacion directas de las fuerzas estadounidenses en Centro America durante la guerra fria: el caso de El Salvador*, Universidad Nacional Autonoma de Mexico, 2015

Informe de la Comision de la verdad para El Salvador, *De la locura a la esperanza. La guerra de 12 años en El Salvador*, 1993

Jackson Martinez, Maria Teresa, El processo de pacificacion en El Salvador (1984-1992), Universidad Nacional Autonoma de Mexico, 1994

Kolakis, Peter G., 'Combloc Connection', *Soldiers of Fortune*, July 1990

Kruijt, Dirk, *Guerrillas. War & Peace in Central America*, Zed Books, 2008

Ladwig III, Walter C., 'Influencing Clients in Counter-insurgency. US Involvment in El Salvador Civil War, 1979–92', *International Security*, Vol. 41, N°1, Summer 2016

Martinez Peñate, Oscar, *El Salvador, el soldado y la guerrillera*, Nuevo Enfoque, 2008

Martinez Peñate, Oscar, *El Salvador del conflicto armado a la negociacion, 1979-1989*, Nuevo Enfoque, 2013

Mauro Araujo, Americo, *Un tiempecito después de terminada la guerra*, Manuscript, 2011

Ministerio de Educacion, *Historia 2, El Salvador*, MINED, 2009

Moroni Bracamonte, José Angel & Spencer, David E, *Strategy and Tactics of the Salvadoran FMLN Guerillas*, Greenwood Publishing Group, 1995

Nott, David, 'Embers of a Brush Fire War', *Soldiers of Fortune*, December 1989

Paszyn, Danuta, 'The Soviet Attitude to Political and Social change in Central America, Case Studies: Nicaragua, El Salvador and Guatemala', *School of Slavonic and East European Studies*, 1996

Paz Fiumara, Maria, *Exitos y fracasos : las Fuerzas Armadas y de Seguridad en En Salvador y Haiti*, CLACSO, 2004

Pinkstone, Bobby Ray, *The Military Instrument of Power in Small Wars: The Case of El Salvador*, US Army Command and General Staff College, 1996

Salisbury, Steven, 'The Taking of El Tablon. A Victory for Morazan Voters', *Soldiers of Fortune*, November 1984

Steve Salisbury, 'Death from the Deep. Close-combat Naval Commandos in Salvador', Soldiers of Fortune, October 1985

Sanchez Ramos, Irene, *Tiempo politico y movimientos armados. El FMLN en El Salvador, 1970-1992*, Universidad Autonoma de Mexico, 1997

Schwartz, Benjamin C., *American Counter-insurgency Doctrine and El Salvador. The Frustrations of Reform and the Illusions of Nation Building*, Rand, 1991

Silva, Luciano S., The War in El Salvador : A Retrospective, US Army War College, 1996

Spencer, David E., 'Custom-Built Cavalry. Salvo Ingenuity Turns Trucks into Warhorses', *Soldier of Fortune*, June 1988

Spencer, David E., *From Vietnam to El Salvador. The Saga of the FMLN Sappers and Other Guerilla Special Forces in Latin America*, Praeger, 1996

Sprenkels, Ralph, 'Las relaciones urbano-rurales en la insurgencia salvadoreña', in Jorge Juarez Avila (Coord.), *Historia y debates sobre el conflicto armado salvadoreño y sus secuelas*, Institutos de Estudios Historicos, Antropologicos y Arqueologicos, 2014

Tumiatti, Marco, *Reagan's foreign policy and the War Powers Resolution. El Salvador and Nicaragua as test cases of the limits on presidential powers*, Universita Ca'Foscari Venezia, 2019

US General Accounting Office, *El Salvador. Military Assistance Has Helped Counter but not Overcome the Insurgency*, April 1991

Vallenilla, Marianao, *Evolución de la Fuerza Armada de El Salvador en el marco de la ayuda militar brindada por los Estados Unidos de América bajo la presidencia de Ronald Reagan (1981-1989)*, Universidad Catolica Andrés Bello, February 2022

Von Santos, Herard, 'Cazadores de Guerillas', *Guerreros*, Año 4, Marzo 2017

Von Santos, Herard, *La muerte desde el cielo. La Historia de los Paracaidistas Salvadoreños, 1962–2012*, Tomo 2, 2019

Walker, Greg, 'Blue Badges of Honor', *Soldiers of Fortune*, February 1992

Much of the information can be consulted on various websites and online archives. Many FMLN documents can be consulted on the cedema.org website as well as on marxist.org. Concerning the political and military situation in El Salvador and American policy, hundreds of documents are online on the US Department of State website, foia.state.gov, as well as on the CIA website, cia.gov.

NOTES

Chapter 1

1. Sergio M. Giampetri and John H. Stone Sr, *A Counter-Insurgency Study : an Analysis of Local Defenses*, Naval Postgraduate School, 2004, p.24.
2. Matthew James Hone, *La participacion directas de las fuerzas estadounidenses en Centro America durante la guerra fria: el caso de El Salvador*, Universidad Nacional Autonoma de Mexico, 2015, pp.78–79.
3. The National Campaign Plan was a civic action programme designed at the request of the Americans and implemented in 1983 in the department of San Vicente.
4. Brian D'Haeseleer, *The Salvadorian Crucible : American Counter-insurgency in El Salvador, 1979-1992*, American University, 2015, p.232.
5. Brian D'Haeseleer, p.232.
6. Marco Tumiatti, *Reagan's foreign policy and the War Powers Resolution. El Salvador and Nicaragua as test cases of the limits on presidential powers*, Universita Ca'Foscari Venezia, 2019, p.118.
7. Raul Guillermo Benitez Manaut, *La teoria militar y la guerra civil en El Salvador*, UNAM, 1986, p.362.
8. Matthew James Hone, *La participacion directas*, pp.18-19.
9. Suzanne M. Heigh, *Counter-insurgency strategies for effective conflict termination : US Strategies in El Salvador*, Naval Postgraduate School, 1990, p.145.
10. Marianao Valenilla, *Evolucion de la Fuerza Armada de El Salvador en el marco de la ayuda militar brindado por los Estados Unidos de America bajo la presidencia de Ronald Reagan (1981-1989)*, Universidad Catolica Andrés Bello, February 2022, p.91.
11. Luciano S. Silva, *The War in El Salvador : A Retrospective*, US Army War College, 1996, p.13.
12. Bobby Ray Pinkstone, *The Military Instrument of Power in Small Wars : The Case of El Salvador*, US Army Command and General Staff College, 1996, p.14.
13. Bobby Ray Pinkstone, p.3.
14. Paul P. Cale, 'The United States Military Advisory Group in El Salvador', *Small Wars Journal*, 1996, pp.14-15.
15. Valenilla, p.92.
16. Matthew James Hone, *La participacion directas*, pp.175-179.
17. Greg Walker, 'Blue Badges of Honor', *Soldiers of Fortune*, February 1992. pp.32–34
18. Matthew James Hone, *La participacion directas* p.197.
19. James S. Corum, 'The Air War in El Salvador', *Airpower Journal*, Summer 1998, p.36.
20. Matthew James Hone, 'El impacto tactico de la intervencion de EE. UU. en la guerra de El Salvador', *Revista de Humanidades y Ciencias Sociales*, n°5, July–December 2013, p.145.
21. Matthew James Hone, *La participacion directas*, pp.196–201.
22. Matthew James Hone, 'El impacto tactico de la intervencion de EE. UU. en la guerra de El Salvador', p.140.
23. Matthew James Hone, 'El impacto tactico de la intervencion de EE. UU. en la guerra de El Salvador', p.147.
24. Anibal Garcia Fernandez, *La presencia militar argentina en El Salvador : el caso del Batallon de Inteligencia 601, (1976-1983)*, Universidad Nacional Autonoma de Mexico, 2017.
25. Oscar Martinez Peñate, *El Salvador, el soldado y la guerrillera*, 2008, pp.137-138.
26. Herard von Santos, 'Cazadores de Guerillas', *Guerreros*, Año 4, Marzo 2017, pp.9-13.
27. Richard A. Haggerty (Ed.), *El Salvador, a country study*, Library of Congress. Federal Research Division, 1990, p.248.
28. Brian D'Haeseleer, p.241.
29. Matthew James Hone, *La participacion directas*, p.80.
30. James S. Corum, p.35.
31. Paul P. Cale, p.25.
32. Lilia Margarita Bermudez Torres, *La estratégia militar de la administracion Reagan en Centroamerica : de la opcion invasion a la guerra de baja intensidad*, Universidad Nacional Autonoma de Mexico, 1985, p.185.
33. Matthew James Hone, *La participacion directas*, p.85.
34. Herard von Santos, *La muerte desde el cielo. La Historia de los Paracaidistas Salvadoreños, 1962–2012*, Tomo II, 2016, pp.110-111.
35. Valenilla, p.94.
36. Herard von Santos, *La muerte desde el cielo*, pp.244–245.
37. Brian D'Haeseleer, p.245.
38. Matthew James Hone, *La participacion directas*, p.88.
39. Herard von Santos, *La muerte desde el cielo*, p.266.
40. Oscar Martinez Peñate, *El Salvador, el soldado y la guerrillera*, 2008, p.126.
41. Matthew James Hone, *La participacion directas*, p.123.
42. Valenilla, p.94.
43. CIA, 'El Salvador : A Net Assessment of the War', February 1986, p.6.
44. James S. Corum, p.27.
45. Nelson E. Hernandez Diaz, 'El poder aéreo en el conflicto salvadoreño', *Guerreros*, Año 1, Diciembre 2014, p.41.
46. Brian D'Haeseleer, p.237.
47. Herard von Santos, *La muerte desde el cielo*, pp.256–257.
48. Valenilla, p.118.
49. James S. Corum, p.34.
50. Herard von Santos, *La muerte desde el cielo*, pp.257–259.
51. Valenilla, p.93.
52. James S. Corum, p.35.
53. Herard von Santos, *La muerte desde el cielo*, pp.113-116.
54. Brian D'Haeseleer, p.238–239.
55. Richard A. Haggerty (Ed.), p.267.

Chapter 2

1. David E. Spencer, *From Vietnam to El Salvador : The Saga of the FMLN Sappers and Other Guerrilla Special Forces in Latin America*, Praeger Press, 1996, p.57.
2. Herard von Santos, *La muerte desde el cielo*, pp.117-138.
3. Carlos Enriquez Consalvi, *Broadcasting the Civil War in El Salvador*, University of Texas Press, 2010, p.172.
4. Herard von Santos, *La muerte desde el cielo*, pp.143-156.
5. Steve Salisbury, 'The Taking of El Tablon. A Victory for Morazan Voters', *Soldiers of Fortune*, November 1984, pp.77-79.
6. *El Pais*, 19 March 1984.
7. David E. Spencer, *From Vietnam to El Salvador*, pp.87-88.
8. Charles H. Briscoe, 'San Miguel : The Attack on El Bosque', *Veritas*, Vol. 3, n°3, 2007, p.11.
9. Charles H. Briscoe, pp.15-18.
10. Herard von Santos, *La muerte desde el cielo*, pp.167-179.
11. Brian D'Haeseleer, p.259.
12. Valenilla, p.121.
13. Brian D'Haeseleer, p.199.
14. Americo Mauro Araujo, *Un tiempecito después de terminada la guerra*, 2012, p.25.
15. Matthew James Hone, *La participacion directas*, p.152.
16. Valenilla, p.122.
17. David E. Spencer, *From Vietnam to El Salvador*, p.59.
18. Dale Dye, 'Showdown at Cerron Grande. Blooding the Airborne Bataillon', *Soldiers of Fortune*, November 1984, p.59.
19. Herard von Santos, *La muerte desde el cielo*, pp.180–205.
20. Valenilla, p.123.
21. David E. Spencer, *From Vietnam to El Salvador*, p.60.
22. Herard von Santos, *La muerte desde el cielo*, pp.213–220.
23. Herard von Santos, *La muerte desde el cielo*, p.221.
24. Oscar Martinez Peñate, *El Salvador del conflicto armado a la negociacion, 1979-1989*, Nuevo Enfoque, 2013, p.145.
25. Carlos Enriquez Consalvi, p.198.
26. Herard von Santos, *La muerte desde el cielo*, pp.222–223.
27. Carlos Enriquez Consalvi, p.209.
28. Americo Mauro Araujo, p.26.
29. James S. Corum, p.34.
30. Herard von Santos, *La muerte desde el cielo*, pp.224–244.
31. Carlos Enriquez Consalvi, p.XXXIII.
32. Herard von Santos, *La muerte desde el cielo*, pp.101-106.
33. José Angel Moroni Bracamonte and David E. Spencer, *Strategy and Tactics of the Salvadoran FMLN Guerillas*, Greenwood Publishing Group, 1995, p.184.
34. José Angel Moroni Bracamonte and David E. Spencer, *Strategy and Tactics*, pp.23–24.
35. Carlos Enriquez Consalvi, p.214.
36. José Angel Moroni Bracamonte and David E. Spencer, *Strategy and Tactics*, p.23.

Chapter 3

1. Matthew James Hone, 'El impacto tactico de la intervencion de EE. UU. en la guerra de El Salvador', p.136.
2. Americo Mauro Araujo, p.28.
3. José Angel Moroni Bracamonte and David E. Spencer, *Strategy and Tactics*, p.28.
4. Brian D'Haeseleer, p.257.
5. Informe de la Comision de la verdad para El Salvador, *De la locura a la esperanza. La guerra de 12 años en El Salvador*, 1993, p.31.
6. Brian D'Haeseleer, p.253.
7. Suzanne M. Heigh, p.172.
8. Brian D'Haeseleer, p.254.
9. Brian D'Haeseleer, p.248–249.
10. Walter C. Ladwig III, 'Influencing Clients in Counter-insurgency. US Involvment in El Salvador Civil War, 1979–92', *International Security*, Vol. 41, N°1, Summer 2016, p.132.
11. David Garibay, *Des armes aux urnes. Processus de paix et réinsertion politique des anciennes guérillas en Colombie et au Salvador*, Institut d'étude politique de Paris-Science Po, 2003, p.327.
12. Brian D'Haeseleer, p.251.
13. Richard A. Haggerty (Ed.), p.177.
14. Ralph Sprenkels, 'Las relaciones urbano-rurales en la insurgencia salvadoreña', in Jorge Juarez Avila (Coord.), *Historia y debates sobre el conflicto armado salvadoreño y sus secuelas*, Institutos de Estudios Historicos, Antropologicos y Arqueologicos, 2014, p.36.
15. Matthew James Hone, *La participacion directas*, p.206.
16. Americo Mauro Araujo, p.29.
17. Brian D'Haeseleer, p.258.
18. Ministerio de Educacion, *Historia 2, El Salvador*, MINED, 2009, p.211.
19. Brian D'Haeseleer, pp.264–265.
20. Oscar Martinez Peñate, *El Salvador del conflicto armado a la negociacion*, p.171.
21. Richard A. Haggerty (Ed.), p.205.
22. Oscar Martinez Peñate, *El Salvador del conflicto armado a la negociacion*, p.172.
23. Brian D'Haeseleer, pp.267–268.
24. David E. Spencer, *From Vietnam to El Salvador*, pp.113-115.
25. Herard von Santos, *La muerte desde el cielo*, pp.294–297.
26. Herard von Santos, *La muerte desde el cielo*, p.107.
27. Herard von Santos, *La muerte desde el cielo*, p.248.
28. Matthew James Hone, *La participacion directas*, p.119.
29. Herard von Santos, *La muerte desde el cielo*, pp.248–253.
30. Matthew James Hone, *La participacion directas*, p.114.
31. Herard von Santos, *La muerte desde el cielo*, p.281.
32. Herard von Santos, *La muerte desde el cielo*, pp.282–286. The capture of Nidia Diaz was a blow for the FMLN since it intervened while in the same month, the GN arrested Napoleon Romero García (Miguel Castellanos), leader of the FPL Metropolitan Front. Castellanos began working as an intelligence agent for the GN. These two captures of senior FMLN commanders were proof for the FAES and the government that the FMLN was being defeated. On 24 October 1985, Nidia Diaz was one of the FMLN leaders released in exchange for that of President Duarte's daughter.
33. Herard von Santos, *La muerte desde el cielo*, pp.287–293.
34. Americo Mauro Araujo, p.33.
35. Valenilla, p.125.
36. Nelson E. Hernandez Diaz, p.43.
37. José Angel Moroni Bracamonte and David E. Spencer, *Strategy and Tactics*, pp.59-66.
38. Brian D'Haeseleer, p.259.
39. David E. Spencer, *From Vietnam to El Salvador*, pp.90–95.
40. Steve Salisbury, 'Death from the Deep. Close-combat Naval Commandos in Salvador', *Soldiers of Fortune*, October 1985. p.47.
41. José Angel Moroni Bracamonte and David E. Spencer, *Strategy and Tactics*, p.143.
42. David E. Spencer, *From Vietnam to El Salvador*, pp.63-63.
43. José Angel Moroni Bracamonte and David E. Spencer, *Strategy and Tactics*, pp.87–91.
44. Herard von Santos, *La muerte desde el cielo*, p.246.
45. Brian D'Haeseleer, p.271.
46. CIA, 'El Salvador : A Net Assessment of the War', February 1986, p.17.
47. Miguel Hernandez Arias, *Fenix, Cenizas de un operacion estadounidense que no renacio*, Centro de Documentacion de los Movimientos Armados, 2006, p.5.
48. Diego Andrés Hernandez Maldonaldo, *Reconstruccion historica de la guerra civil salvadoreña a través de excombatientes del FMLN : caso Guazapa, 1981-1982*, Universidad de El Salvador, 2018, p.28.
49. Miguel Hernandez Arias, p.23.
50. Miguel Hernandez Arias, p.10.
51. Americo Mauro Araujo, pp.34-36.
52. Miguel Hernandez Arias, p.18.
53. David E. Spencer, *From Vietnam to El Salvador*, pp.115-117.
54. Miguel Hernandez Arias, p.37.
55. Miguel Hernandez Arias, p.44.
56. Miguel Hernandez Arias, p.65.
57. Miguel Hernandez Arias, p.49.
58. Miguel Hernandez Arias, p.100.
59. Miguel Hernandez Arias, p.108.
60. David E. Spencer, *From Vietnam to El Salvador*, pp.101-106.
61. Marco Antonio Argumedo Najarro, 'La Fuerza aerea y los ataques a la 3a Brígada de infanteria en San Miguel', *Guerreros*, Año 6, Cuarto Trimestre 2019, pp.64–65.

Chapter 4

1. CIA, 'El Salvador : A Net Assessment of the War', February 1986, p.9.
2. David Nott, 'Embers of a Brush Fire War', *Soldiers of Fortune*, December 1989. p.70.
3. Irene Sanchez Ramos, *Tiempo politico y movimientos armados. El FMLN en El Salvador, 1970-1992*, Universidad Autonoma de Mexico, 1997, pp.129-130.
4. Matthew James Hone, *La participacion directas*, pp.203-204.

5 David E. Spencer, *From Vietnam to El Salvador*, pp 70–75.
6 David E. Spencer, 'Custom-Built Cavalry. Salvo Ingenuity Turns Trucks into Warhorses', *Soldiers of Fortune*, June 1988. p.88.
7 José Angel Moroni Bracamonte and David E. Spencer, *Strategy and Tactics*, pp.107-108.
8 The J-28 were units of the ABFPM Battalions trained at the end of 1984 by the FES to carry out attacks and ambushes.
9 Herard von Santos, *La muerte desde el cielo*, pp.298–308.
10 José Angel Moroni Bracamonte and David E. Spencer, *Strategy and Tactics* pp.143-145.
11 Herard von Santos, *La muerte desde el cielo*, pp.309–312.
12 Herard von Santos, *La muerte desde el cielo*, p.316.
13 José Angel Moroni Bracamonte and David E. Spencer, *Strategy and Tactics*, pp.161-164.
14 Herard von Santos, *La muerte desde el cielo*, pp.312–315.
15 Benjamin C Schwartz, 'American Counter-insurgency Doctrine and El Salvador. The Frustrations of Reform and the Illusions of Nation Building', *Rand*, 1991, p.30.
16 Herard von Santos, *La muerte desde el cielo*, pp.317–319.
17 Oscar Martinez Peñate, *El Salvador del conflicto armado a la negociacion* pp.71–72.
18 Americo Mauro Araujo, p.16.
19 Oscar Martinez Peñate, *El Salvador del conflicto armado a la negociacion*, pp.74–78.
20 Americo Mauro Araujo, p.17.
21 Martha Elma Contreras Rodriguez, *El processo revolucionario en El Salvador*, Universidad nacional autonoma de Mexico, 1988, p.230.
22 Edoardo Sancho Castañeda, pp.217–218.
23 Americo Mauro Araujo, p.18.
24 Martha Elma Contreras Rodriguez, pp.188-195.
25 Oscar Martinez Peñate, *El Salvador del conflicto armado a la negociacion*, p.151.
26 Brian D'Haeseleer, p.286.
27 Maria Teresa Jackson Martinez, *El processo de pacificacion en El Salvador (1984-1992)*, Universidad Nacional Autonoma de Mexico, 1994, p.58.
28 Brian D'Haeseleer, p.288.
29 David Garibay, p.328.
30 Oscar Martinez Peñate, *El Salvador del conflicto armado a la negociacion*, p.169.
31 Alberto Martin Alvarez, 'De la guerra revolucionaria a la revolucion democratica. El FMLN en El Salvador', *Revista Realidad*, 132, 2012, p.170.
32 Brian D'Haeseleer, p.307.
33 Dirk Kruijt, p.85.
34 Danuta Paszyn, 'The Soviet Attitude to Political and Social change in Central America, Case Studies : Nicaragua, El Salvador and Guatemala', *School of Slavonic and East European Studies*, 1996, pp.150-151.
35 José Angel Moroni Bracamonte and David E. Spencer, *Strategy and Tactics*, p.180.
36 Peter G. Kolakis, 'Combloc Connection', *Soldiers of Fortune*, July 1990. pp.43–44.

Chapter 5
1 Benjamin C Schwartz, p.53.
2 Brian D'Haeseleer, pp.233–234.
3 Brian D'Haeseleer, p.312.
4 Alberto Martin Alvarez, 'De la guerra revolucionaria a la revolucion democratica. El FMLN en El Salvador', p.164.
5 Suzanne M. Heigh, p.175.
6 Brian D'Haeseleer, p.309.
7 Alberto Martin Alvarez, 'From Revolutionary War to Democratic Revolution. The Farabundo Marti National Liberation Front (FMLN) in El Salvador', *Berghof Conflict Research*, 2010, p.26.
8 Richard A. Haggerty (Ed.), p.165.
9 Brian D'Haeseleer, p.312.
10 Carlos Gregorio Lopez Bernal, *El Salvador 1960-1992 : reformas, utopia revolucionaria y guerra civil, As revoluções na America Latina Contemporanea. Entre o ciclo revolucionario e as democracias restringidas*, Pulso & Letra Editores, 2017, p.276.
11 Informe de la Comision de la verdad para El Salvador, p.35.
12 US General Accounting Office, *El Salvador. Military Assistance Has Helped Counter but not Overcome the Insurgency*, April 1991, p.14.
13 Oscar Martinez Peñate, *El Salvador del conflicto armado a la negociacion*, p.217.
14 Brian D'Haeseleer, p.313.
15 Walter C. Ladwig III, p.130.
16 Richard A. Haggerty (Ed.), p.236.
17 Amnesty International, *El Salvador. 'Death Squads'- A Government Strategy*, October 1988, p.7.
18 Suzanne M. Heigh, p.174.
19 Steve Salisbury, 'Patrolling Hot Water. SOF Sails Salvador's Troubled Seas', *Soldiers of Fortunes*, December 1984. p.62.
20 Herard von Santos, *La muerte desde el cielo*, p.54.
21 Walter C. Ladwig III, p.133.
22 Matthew James Hone, 'El impacto tactico de la intervencion de EE. UU. en la guerra de El Salvador', pp.128-129.
23 Sergio M. Giampetri and John H. Stone Sr, p.27.
24 Brian D'Haeseleer, p.317.
25 Valenilla, pp.130-131.
26 Americo Mauro Araujo, p.53.
27 Oscar Martinez Peñate, *El Salvador del conflicto armado a la negociacion*, p.175.
28 David Garibay, p.373.
29 Brian D'Haeseleer, p.321–323.
30 Oscar Martinez Peñate, *El Salvador del conflicto armado a la negociacion*, p.185.
31 Richard A. Haggerty (Ed.), p.259.
32 Maria Teresa Escalona Terron, *La radio como instrumento de lucha politica : Experiencia de Radio Farabundo Marti, 1982-1992*, Universidad de El Salvador, 2002, pp.80–82.
33 Informe de la Comision de la verdad para El Salvador, p.89.
34 David Nott, 'Embers of a Brush Fire War'. p.71.
35 Dirk Kruijt, p.141.
36 Brian D'Haeseleer, p.324.
37 Carlos Gregorio Lopez Bernal, p.277.

Chapter 6
1 Dario Salvador Hernandez Vega, '1980-1992, Guerra civil en El Salvador ?', *Guerreros*, Año 9, Segundo Trimestre 2022, p.62.
2 Brian D'Haeseleer, p.327.
3 Herard von Santos, 'La contraofensiva estrategica del FMLN y la arte operacional', *Guerreros*, Año 5, Septiembre 2018, p.8.
4 Dirk Kruijt, p.76.
5 Brian D'Haeseleer, p.327.
6 Yvon Grenier, 'Understanding the FMLN : A Glossary of Five Words', *Conflict Quarterly*, Spring 1991, p.63.
7 Herard von Santos, 'La contraofensiva estrategica del FMLN y la arte operacional', *Guerreros*, Año 5, Septiembre 2018, pp.11-13.
8 Brian D'Haeseleer, p.328.
9 Steve Salisbury, 'Battle of Five Cities', *Soldiers of Fortune*, September 1990. p.52.
10 Herard von Santos, *La muerte desde el cielo*, pp.321–335.
11 José Angel Moroni Bracamonte and David E. Spencer, *Strategy and Tactics*, pp130-131.
12 Herard von Santos, *La muerte desde el cielo*, pp.338–348.
13 Herard von Santos, 'La contraofensiva estrategica del FMLN y la arte operacional', p.19.
14 Carlos Balmore Vigil, 'El brazo acorazado en la ofensiva', *Guerreros*, Año 2, Diciembre 2015, pp.10-15.
15 Herard von Santos, 'Encontro con la muerte en Ayutuxtepeque', *Guerreros*, Año 1, Diciembre 2014.
16 Steve Salisbury, 'Battle of Five Cities'. p.70.
17 Carlos Balmore Vigil, 'El brazo acorazado en la ofensiva', pp.16-18.
18 Carlos Balmore Vigil, "Ofensiva 'Hasta el Tope' en Ciudad Delgado', *Guerreros*, Año 1, Diciembre 2014, p.10.
19 Carlos Balmore Vigil, 'El brazo acorazado en la ofensiva', p.21.
20 Oscar Martinez Peñate, *El Salvador, el soldado y la guerrillera*, 2008, p.141.
21 Brian D'Haeseleer, p.330.
22 Brian D'Haeseleer, pp.331.
23 Informe de la Comision de la verdad para El Salvador, pp.44–45.
24 Brian D'Haeseleer, p.333.
25 Suzanne M. Heigh, p.180.
26 Edward J. Bishop, 'Inside Salvador's Tet', *Soldiers of Fortune*, May 1990. p.87.
27 Herard von Santos, *La muerte desde el cielo*, 2016, pp.351–403.
28 Steve Salisbury, 'Battle of Five Cities'. p.51.
29 Marco Antonio Argumedo Najarro, pp.69–74.
30 Herard von Santos, 'La contraofensiva estrategica del FMLN y la arte operacional', p.20.
31 Herard von Santos, p.411.
32 Brian D'Haeseleer, p.329.
33 Brian D'Haeseleer, p.326.
34 Steve Salisbury, 'Battle of Five Cities'. pp.52–53.

35 José Angel Moroni Bracamonte and David E. Spencer, *Strategy and Tactics* p.137.
36 Yvon Grenier, p.75.
37 Brian D'Haeseleer, p.338.

Chapter 7
1 Brian D'Haeseleer, pp.339–340.
2 Danuta Paszyn, pp.144-145.
3 Alberto Martin Alvarez, 'From Revolutionary War to Democratic Revolution.', pp.28–29.
4 Danuta Paszyn, pp.147-149.
5 David Garibay, p.441.
6 This hypothesis seems plausible given Castro's resentment of Soviet policy in Central America, that was, the abandonment of solidarity with the revolutionary struggle in favour of Détente.
7 Suzanne M. Heigh, p.183.
8 Alberto Martin Alvarez, 'De la guerra revolucionaria a la revolucion democratica. El FMLN en El Salvador', p.178.
9 Danuta Paszyn, pp.157-159.
10 Brian D'Haeseleer, p.344.
11 Steve Salisbury, 'Battle of Five Cities'.p.53.
12 David Nott, 'Embers of a Brush Fire War'. p.71.
13 Herard von Santos, *La muerte desde el cielo*, pp.421–423.
14 Herard von Santos, *La muerte desde el cielo*, pp.426–430.
15 José Angel Moroni Bracamonte and David E. Spencer, *Strategy and Tactics*, p.145.
16 Herard von Santos, *La muerte desde el cielo*, pp.433–445.
17 Brian D'Haeseleer, p.347.
18 José Angel Moroni Bracamonte and David E. Spencer, *Strategy and Tactics* p.148.
19 Herard von Santos, *La muerte desde el cielo*, pp 464–465.
20 Brian D'Haeseleer, p.346.
21 José Angel Moroni Bracamonte and David E. Spencer, *Strategy and Tactics*, pp.108-109.
22 Herard von Santos, *La muerte desde el cielo*, pp.448–454.
23 Us General Accounting Office, *El Salvador. Military Assistance Has Helped Counter but not Overcome the Insurgency*, April 1991, p.8.
24 Herard von Santos, *La muerte desde el cielo*, pp.456–459.
25 Herard von Santos, *La muerte desde el cielo*, pp.458–461.
26 Tyroler, Deborah. "El Salvador: Update On Rebels' "limited Offensive"." (1990). https://digitalrepository.unm.edu/noticen/4767
27 Steve Salisbury, 'Another Salvo in El Salvador', *Soldiers of Fortune*, July 1991. p.47.
28 Nelson E. Hernandez Diaz, p.47.
29 Herard von Santos, *La muerte desde el cielo*, pp.467–471.
30 Oscar Martinez Peñate, *El Salvador, el soldado y la guerrillera*, pp.296–303.
31 Herard von Santos, *La muerte desde el cielo*, pp.471–474.
32 Herard von Santos, *La muerte desde el cielo*, p.474.
33 Informe de la Comision de la verdad para El Salvador, p.180.
34 Us General Accounting Office, *El Salvador. Military Assistance Has Helped Counter but not Overcome the Insurgency*, April 1991, p.5.
35 Marco Antonio Argumedo Najarro, p.66.
36 Roman Alfonso Barrera, 'Remenbranzas de guerra', *Guerreros*, Año 7, Segundo Trimestre 2020, pp.14-16.
37 Maria Teresa Escalona Terron, pp.112-113.
38 David Garibay, p.445.
39 Nelson E. Hernandez Diaz, p.48.
40 Herard von Santos, *La muerte desde el cielo*, pp.478–481.
41 Herard von Santos, *La muerte desde el cielo*, p.482–483.
42 Dirk Kruijt, p.137.
43 Suzanne M. Heigh, p.184.
44 Dirk Kruijt, p.143.
45 Carlos Gregorio Lopez Bernal, p.280.
46 Maria Teresa Jackson Martinez, pp.61–62.
47 Carlos Gregorio Lopez Bernal, p.281.
48 David Garibay, p.450.
49 Carlos Gregorio Lopez Bernal, p.283.
50 Maria Paz Fiumara, *Exitos y fracasos : las Fuerzas Armadas y de Seguridad en En Salvador y Haiti*, CLACSO, 2004, p.15-16.
51 Luciano S. Silva, p.33.

Conclusion
1 Suzanne M. Heigh, p.194.
2 Ministerio de Educacion, p.229.
3 Carlos Enriquez Consalvi, p.XX.

ACKNOWLEDGEMENTS

This book would not have been written without the support, encouragements and help of Tom Cooper and Bill Norton. I want to thank them and also for their patience and benevolence towards me. I also thank Albert Grandolini who had the kindness to share the photos of his collection.

ABOUT THE AUTHOR

David François, from France, earned his PhD in Contemporary History at the University of Burgundy and specialised in studying militant communism, its military history and relationship between politics and violence in contemporary history. In 2009, he co-authored the Guide des archives de l'Internationale communiste published by the French National Archives and the Maison des sciences de l'Homme in Dijon. He regularly contributes articles for various French military history magazines and is a regular contributor to the French history website *L'autre côté de la colline*.